Petter Gottschalk

The Convenience of Corporate Crime

Financial Motive – Organizational Opportunity –
Executive Willingness

DE GRUYTER

ISBN 978-3-11-128011-0
e-ISBN (PDF) 978-3-11-076695-0
e-ISBN (EPUB) 978-3-11-076698-1

Library of Congress Control Number: 2021946767

Bibliographic information published by the Deutsche Nationalbibliothek
The Deutsche Nationalbibliothek lists this publication in the Deutsche Nationalbibliografie;
detailed bibliographic data are available on the Internet at http://dnb.dnb.de.

© 2023 Walter de Gruyter GmbH, Berlin/Boston
This volume is text- and page-identical with the hardback published in 2022.
Cover image: franckreporter / E+ / Getty Images
Typesetting: Integra Software Services Pvt. Ltd.
Printing and binding: CPI books GmbH, Leck

www.degruyter.com

Petter Gottschalk
The Convenience of Corporate Crime

Contents

Part II: **Empirical Studies**

Introduction

Almond and Van Erp (2020: 171) phrased the question: "Why do people commit unlawful activities for the benefit of the collective entities to which they belong?" Corporate crime is organizational offending to benefit the business of the organization (Dodge, 2020; Schoultz and Flyghed, 2021). Corporate crime is resulting from wrongdoing, misconduct, and deviant behavior by one or several corporate officials (Khanna et al., 2015). Corporate actions that harm organizational actors and/or society and that are punishable by law represent corporate crime (Alcadipani and Medeiros, 2020). Corporate officials from within an organization engage in crime in pursuit of the interests of an organization (Dewan and Jensen, 2020; Naumovska et al., 2020). Organizational officials commit corporate crime in the larger interests of an organization, such as bribing potential customers, avoiding taxes by evasion, polluting the environment, and misrepresenting accounting to get unjustified government subsidies or to manipulate investors (Forti and Visconti, 2020; Haines, 2014; Van Erp et al., 2019a, 2019b).

Corporate crime, often called organizational offenses or business crime, typically results from actions of several individuals in more or less rooted cooperation (Kawasaki, 2020; Pinto et al., 2008). If a business representative commits a crime on behalf of the organization, it is corporate crime (Friedrich, 2021). Corporate crime is a deviant dysfunction potentially caused by multiple factors (Alcadipani and Medeiros, 2020). Corporate crime is illegal and harmful acts, committed by members of legitimate organizations, primarily for the benefit of these organizations (Oliveira and Silveira, 2020). People within the corporation commit crime, not the corporation itself, since the corporation is a fictious person rather than a natural person (Alalehto, 2020). Corporate crime is committed for the corporation and not against it (Schoultz and Flyghed, 2021; Tombs and Whyte, 2020). Corporate crime is the conduct of corporations acted by employees on behalf of the corporations that are organizational violations since it is committed by individuals during their normal activities as employees or representatives of the corporations and have organizational motives such as achieving organizational goals (Shichor and Heeren, 2021).

Corporate crime leads to individuals as defendants because a company cannot face prosecution and incarceration (Burns and Meitl, 2020; Cohen, 2020). Often the only relevant punishment for a public or private enterprise is a fine that potentially can ruin the organization. Collateral consequences of a conviction for certain kinds of corporate crime can ruin a company. However, the United States and other countries have designed ways to do a criminal settlement that does not trigger collateral consequences. The wrongdoer may be a publicly held firm where imposing a large-scale fine on it might not ruin it. In many countries, corporate fines are modest. The fine can represent one month's revenue or one year's profit. In addition, many

https://doi.org/10.1515/9783110766950-001

countries have laws restricting the scope of criminal liability, so it is impossible to convict companies for many kinds of crime. An example is deferred prosecution agreement (Arlen, 2020).

Arlen and Buell (2020) found that the United States model of corporate crime control combines corporate criminal liability with a practice of reducing sanctions, and often withholding conviction, for companies that assist enforcement agencies in identifying more serious criminal violations.

At this point, however, it is important to emphasize that this book is not about law and legal institutions. Rather, the book builds on perspectives from disciplines such as management, organizational behavior, sociology, criminology, and psychology.

Corporate crime represents violations of integrity as well as failure to comply with moral standards, as in the example of corruption managed by Siemens executives in Germany (Eberl et al., 2015).

Corporate crime may ultimately provide an individual with some tangible benefit, such as a promotion, bonus pay, or gifts for exceptional performance, as well as benefit individual members of the organization collectively (Kennedy, 2020: 178):

> Yet, the primary purpose of committing a corporate crime is to provide a benefit to the corporation. Accordingly, corporate crimes have a distinctly organizational focus irrespective of whether they are committed by one person or 100 persons.

As argued by Walburg (2020: 343), too little insight exists about the extent, structures, and development of white-collar crime and its multifaceted varieties, especially when it comes to corporate crime:

> (. . .) this is largely explicable by the well-known and persistent difficulties of measuring undetected acts of corporate wrongdoing (. . .)

Pontell et al. (2014: 10) argued that the lack of focus on corporate crime is "partly a function of the visibility of the offense and the ease with which it can be officially pursued".

Law-and-order policies are mainstream strategies in many countries. Yet Alvesalo-Kuusi and Barak (2020: 1) found that such policies have not been extended to corporate crime:

> On the contrary, many societies have witnessed the downsizing of both the regulation and enforcement of harms caused by the powerful. Corporate crime prevention in particular has been somewhat ignored by academics, even within critical criminological and socio-legal studies.

Bittle and Hébert (2020) made the same finding that lack of regulation and deregulation cause absence of corporate law-and-order enforcement. Downsizing of regulation, lack of regulation and deregulation, and downsizing of enforcement improve the convenience of corporate crime.

Convenience is savings in time and effort, reduced pain and strain, and other factors that make a certain path or choice attractive. Convenience is the state of being able to proceed with something with little effort or difficulty, avoiding pain and strain (Mai and Olsen, 2016). Convenience addresses the time and effort exerted before, during, and after an action or avoidance of action (Collier and Kimes, 2012). A convenient individual is not necessarily neither bad nor lazy. On the contrary, the person can be seen as smart and rational (Sundström and Radon, 2015). The theory of convenience suggests that strength of financial motive, the extent of organizational opportunity, and the personal willingness for deviant behavior determine the likelihood of corporate crime. Convenience theory builds on and extends opportunity theory and the fraud triangle as described in previous publications (Gottschalk, 2019, 2020).

In the perspective of preventing and prosecuting corporate crime, Haines and Macdonald (2021: 299) argue that addressing corporate crime and harm is not simply an issue of enforcement and compliance:

> Neither is it one of digging deeper to find the ultimate root of the problem – the reproduction of power relations is nothing new to criminology. Understanding the direction of prevailing winds that shape business activity is important though in understanding where change is possible. Grappling with injustice is just that – looking for sources of influence ultimately requires going beyond blanket classifications of law – in all its forms – as either helpful or unhelpful, and understanding which law, from which place and used in which way within a field of struggle is important.

Within the context or framing of organizational or corporate crime and the actors or perpetrators of these offenses, this book makes crime mainly an endogenous phenomenon. The book offers a holistic approach for making sense out of several case studies through the theory of convenience. Exogenous factors are included where appropriate, such as criminal market forces.

The first part of this book presents theoretical perspectives on corporate crime. Corporate crime is white-collar crime that benefits the organization rather than the individual (Chapter 1), which can be explained by convenience theory (Chapter 2). Detected and prosecuted corporate crime require corporate deviance accounts (Chapter 3) and a crime-response match (Chapter 4).

The second part of this book presents a number of case studies of corporate crime, where corporate offending reflects criminal market structures. The first case is concerned with the Swedish telecommunications company Telia that is involved in corruption to obtain mobile phone licenses in countries such as Uzbekistan (Schoultz and Flyghed, 2020a, 2020b, 2021). The Dutch telecommunications company VimpelCom has the same practice, and so does the Norwegian telecom enterprise Telenor (Deloitte, 2016). There are criminal market forces requiring corporate crime in the form of corruption (Chapter 5).

The second case is concerned with Danske Bank in Denmark that is involved in money laundering and tax evasion for Russian oligarchs and organized Russian criminals (Bruun Hjejle, 2018). Swedbank in Sweden is another bank involved in the same services for their bank clients (Clifford Chance, 2020; Milne, 2020). Other

Scandinavian banks involved in illegal services for their clients include Nordea in Sweden (Kristjánsson, 2016; Mannheimer Swartling, 2016) and DNB in Norway (Kleinfeld, 2019, 2020; Kibar, 2020a, 2020b; Seljan et al., 2019). There are criminal market forces requiring corporate crime in the form of money laundering and tax evasion when providing wealth management services (Chapter 6).

The third case is concerned with Trafigura in the United Kingdom that is involved in environmental crime by dumping toxic waste in the Ivory Coast and Norway. One corporate crime project was about getting rid of the dangerous waste after Trafigura was denied access to waste disposal at the usual site in Africa. The redirection of the Probo Emu tanker to Norway is considered the project (Gulating, 2013, 2015; Knudssøn and Bakke, 2009; Maksimentsev and Maksimentseva, 2020). There are criminal market forces requiring corporate crime in the form of environmental harm in waste disposal (Chapter 7).

The fourth case is concerned with ABB in Switzerland that is involved in cartels by agreeing with competitors such as Nokia in Finland who should serve specific markets and customers with communication and power cables, and who should stay away from the same markets and customers, without fear of punishment (Jaspers, 2020: 106):

> Leniency offers corporations the possibility to come clean about their involvement in cartel conduct in exchange for immunity or reduction of financial penalties. In Europe, nearly 60 percent of detected cartels are discovered through leniency.

Cartel activities are not limited to cable markets involving companies like ABB and Nokia. Cartels do also exist among their customers in the construction business (Brandvol, 2016; Gedde-Dahl et al., 2007; Landre, 2006; Lilleås, 2011). Cartels are associations of independent corporations in the same industry that strive to reduce competition (Chapter 8).

In the car manufacturing industry, German car producer Volkswagen was one of the manufacturers who committed emission standards violation. Their computer software enabled the vehicles to pass emission tests under laboratory conditions while emitting forty times the level of pollution allowed in the United States during normal use (Chapter 9).

The final case study in this book is about Wirecard in Germany. Wirecard was founded in 1999 to handle digital money transactions for pornography and gambling. In 2020, the financial institution went bankrupt. The Wirecard scandal is a series of accounting frauds that resulted in the insolvency of the German payment processor where € 2 billion disappeared (Chapter 10).

All case studies in this book build on publicly available information about corporate wrongdoing. Nevertheless, corporations described in this book might be tempted to contest the material and challenge judgments in the case studies. Some of the organizations mentioned here might even have attempted to block publication to prevent criticism and challenge the legitimacy of some of the text. However, this kind of corporate attitude towards criticism and transparency is just another reason for the importance of publishing this book.

In the final two chapters, the extent of crime is discussed in terms of statistics and estimates (Chapter 11), and some of the cases have in common that they involved tax havens in the corporate misconduct (Chapter 12).

Cases of corporate misconduct and crime steadily emerge in the public domain by media reports and research articles. For example, Mulinari et al. (2021) studied the Japanese pharmaceutical firm Astellas. At a meeting in Milan, Italy with over one hundred doctors from mostly European countries present, Astellas executives attempted to promote an off-label prostate cancer drug enzalutamide. An anonymous Astellas Europe employee reported the incident to the Prescription Medicines Code of Practice Authority (PMCPA) in the UK. Astellas was then suspended. Like in so many other cases presented in this book, Astellas executives initially denied wrongdoings. Later, they accepted investigation findings and punishment rulings (Mulinari et al., 2021: 71):

> The company's official explanation for wrongdoings is one of "significant cultural and compliance failings created and caused by the actions and behaviors of some of its very senior managers" in Europe. It its report, The PMCPA attributed Astellas's gross misconduct and dishonesty to "multiple organizational and cultural failings" within the company, and to a corporate culture that prioritized "the bottom line" over compliance obligations and ethical norms.

The priority of compliance suffered under the priority of the bottom line in terms of profits. When the bottom line is struggling and not meeting investor expectations, compliance is indeed potentially violated in many corporate settings as presented in this book. Furthermore, as emphasized in several case studies in this book, also Astellas applied the procedure of scapegoating (Mulinari et al., 2021: 75):

> According to Astellas Europe, "the email indicated that there was a conscious decision by one individual" (. . .), but that "as an organization" Astellas had been completely unaware of the email up until this point. Hence, the company submitted there "was no dishonesty or deliberate attempt to mislead" – except by this single rogue employee. Astellas Europe also stated that, "immediate action had been taken to address the conduct of this senior member of staff.

As illustrated in so many of the cases presented in this book, scapegoating is often combined with other measures, such as denials and excuses. The blame game by misleading attribution of guilt is an approach to improve the convenience of corporate crime as documented in the case studies this book.

A question has been raised whether any of the corporations mentioned in this book will attempt to terminate publication to prevent criticism and to challenge the text. While not very likely, such a corporate approach would in itself be a reflection on the message in this book. The book says that corporate criminal liability is often limited, and corporations can survive their own self-inflicted scandals. It would thus be contrast to lack of liability to approach the author or the publisher to make them liable for text that is extracted from public sources.

Part I: **Theoretical Perspectives**

1 Characteristics of Corporate Offenders

In the perspective of critical management studies, corporations are instruments of domination and exploitation. Corporations perform actions that inflict harm with various levels of intensity, from killing people to defrauding people. Since maximizing profits is the main goal for most corporate executives, their actions are often in conflict with societal interests (Alcadipani and Medeiros, 2020: 291):

> Since their emergence, large corporations have controlled an increasing percentage of economic activity and have displaced the social costs of their operations, the so-called externalities, to workers and communities. For example, some of the externalities that were disguised or neglected by firms were pollution, crowded cities, industrial accidents, violent business cycles leading to unemployment, and the exhaustion of easily available natural resources.

Alcadipani and Medeiro (2020) found that corporations are extremely powerful actors in society who can shape their environment, undermining the state as an agent that can regulate corporate activities. Powerful corporations can change social institutions, laws, and regulations. Corporations may promote legislation that benefits corporate activity at the expense of citizens. Corporations may privatize functions that have historically been performed by public governments, and they can enter into emerging markets where no public governments are present.

According to Oliveira and Silveira (2020: 2), corporations represent capitalism's main power over the world:

> Their power has no boundaries: they influence policies and actions in nations, regions, and local communities and establish themselves as private tyrannies (. . .) Corporations are present everywhere and in almost every aspect of our lives and work. However, corporations are dangerous to society because they commit serious corporate crimes against consumers, workers, the environment, communities, and countries. Furthermore, corporate financial crimes are committed by legitimate businesses that operate in lawful and transnational markets. Global capitalism is supported by transnational practices, which transcend the geographic boundaries of states but do not necessarily originate from state-owned agencies or players. These practices operate in the economic, political, and cultural-ideological dimensions.

Oliveira and Silveira (2020) found that crime committed by corporations – such as environmental pollution, bribing government officials, money laundering, bank fraud, slave labor, and business email compromise – are part of social structures. They argued that transnational corporations are companies globally integrated and politically organized by a transnational capitalist class. Rather than perceiving corporate crime as dysfunction in organizations, they argued that corporate crime occurs within corporation's own dynamics, in which the corporate power of political and economic influence seems to be limitless and supports a destructive version of capitalism.

https://doi.org/10.1515/9783110766950-002

The Offense-Based Perspective

Erp (2018: 1) found that corporate crime seems endemic to modern society:

> Newspapers are filled on a daily basis with examples of financial manipulation, accounting fraud, food fraud, cartels, bribery, toxic spills and environmental harms, corporate human rights violations, insider trading, privacy violations, discrimination, corporate manslaughter or violence, and, recently, software manipulation. Clearly, the problem of corporate crime transcends the micro level of the individual 'rotten apple', although corporate crimes are ultimately committed by individual members of an organization, they have more structural roots, as the enabling and justifying organizational context in which they take place plays a defining role. Accounts of corporate fraud, misrepresentations, or deception that foreground individual offender's motivations and characteristics, often fail to acknowledge that organizational decisions are more than the aggregation of individual choices and actions, and that organizational are more than simply the environment in which individual action takes place.

This quote is interesting, as it mixes both the offense-based perspective and the offender-based perspective on corporate crime. The offense-based perspective is concerned with the various forms of corporate crime, such as fraud, environmental harm, and financial manipulation. The offender-based perspective is concerned with the individuals who commit corporate crime and the organizational context in which it takes place (Van Erp, 2018: 1):

> Organization studies have therefore become increasingly preoccupied with explaining organizational dysfunctional and antisocial behavior, misconduct, and deviancy known as "the dark side of organization", and also have an important contribution to make to our understanding of corporate crime and its prevention.

Offense-based approaches to corporate crime emphasize the actions and nature of the illegal act as the defining agent (Galvin et al. 2018; Piquero, 2018). For example, corporate crime is typically a non-violent offense (Berghoff and Spiekermann, 2018). The offense-based tradition is concerned with the criminal act in itself, drawing upon legal definitions, motives, and means (Piquero and Schoepfer, 2010). For example, Edelhertz (1970: 3) defined white-collar crime as "an illegal act or series of illegal acts committed by non-physical means and by concealment or guile to obtain money or property, to avoid the payment or loss of money or property, or to obtain business or personal advantage". Because offender status is not included in the definition of offense-based approaches, and status is free to vary independently from the definition in most legislations; an offense-based approach allows measures of status to become external explanatory variables. The offense-based tradition represents a critique against using offender characteristics as part of the definition. For instance, Shapiro (1990: 347) argues that this "confuse[s] acts with actors, norms with breakers, the modus operandi with the operator".

An argument for the offense-based perspective is that everyone now can commit fraud on the Internet, an act that was impossible when Sutherland (1939) first coined the term white-collar crime eight decades ago (Geest et al., 2017: 544):

In sharp contrast to the 1940s however, when most financial crimes were out of reach for ordinary people, in modern-day society the opportunity structure for white-collar crime has dramatically changed. The growth of the credit economy, the increase of the service sector, increased urbanization, and the advent of the internet – to name but a few factors – have increasingly democratized the phenomenon of financial crimes and fraud. With the advancement of technology, crimes labeled as 'white-collar' do not require employment or specific skills and have increasingly come within range of the poor and disadvantaged who disproportionately came in contact with the criminal justice system then and now.

White-collar criminals commit financial crime where a great variety of options can be found, as illustrated in Figure 1.1. Fraud, theft, manipulation, and corruption are four main categories of financial crime with a number of subcategories. Fraud can be defined as intentional perversion of truth for the purpose of inducing another in reliance upon it to part with some valuable thing belonging to him or to surrender a

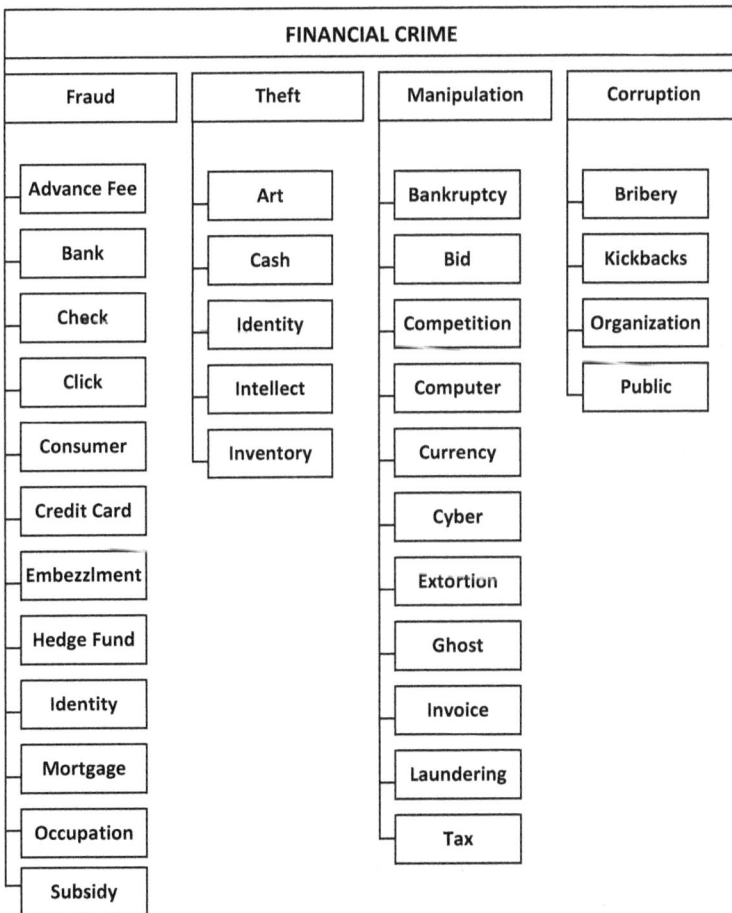

Figure 1.1: Main categories and subcategories of financial crime.

legal right. Fraud is unlawful and intentional making of a misrepresentation, which causes actual prejudice, or which is potentially prejudicial to another. Fraud refers to the intentional misrepresentation of the truth in order to manipulate or deceive a company or individual. Fraud is to create a misjudgment or maintain an existing misjudgment to induce somebody to do something that the person or organization otherwise would not do (Elisha et al., 2020). Bank fraud is a typical example. Bank fraud is a criminal offence of knowingly executing a scheme to defraud a financial institution.

Theft can be defined as the illegal taking of another person's, group's, or organization's property without the victim's consent. For example, identity theft combined with identity fraud is the unlawful use of another's personal identifying information (Piquero et al., 2021). It involves financial or other personal information stolen with the intent of establishing another person's identity as the thief's own. It occurs when someone uses personally identifying information, like name, social security number, the date of birth, government passport number or credit card number without the owners' permission, to commit financial crime.

Manipulation can be defined as a means of gaining illegal control or influence over others' activities, means and results. For example, bankruptcy crime is criminal acts committed in connection with bankruptcy or liquidation proceedings. A person filing for bankruptcy or a business that has gone into liquidation can hide assets after proceedings have been initiated, and thereby preventing creditors from collecting their claims. However, most of the criminal acts are typically committed before bankruptcy/liquidation proceedings are initiated, e.g., the debtor has failed to keep accounts or has unlawfully withdrawn money from the business.

Corruption is defined as the giving, requesting, receiving, or accepting of an improper advantage related to a position, office, or assignment (Ashforth et al., 2008). The improper advantage does not have to be connected to a specific action or to not doing this action. It will be sufficient if the advantage can be linked to a person's position, office, or assignment (Artello and Albanese, 2021). An individual or group is guilty of corruption if they accept money or money's worth for doing something that he is under a duty to do anyway, that he is under a duty not to do, or to exercise a legitimate discretion for improper reason. Corruption is to destroy or pervert the integrity or fidelity of a person in his discharge of duty, it is to induce to act dishonestly or unfaithfully, it is to make venal, and it is to bribe. Corruption involves behavior on the part of officials in the public or private sectors, in which they improperly and unlawfully enrich themselves and/or those close to them, or induce others to do so, by misusing the position in which they are placed. Corruption covers a wide range of illegal activity such as kickbacks, embezzlement, and extortion. Corruption entails "mistreatment of suppliers, customers, or competitors" (Kolthoff, 2020: 434).

The various main categories and subcategories of financial crime in Figure 1.1 imply varying sanctions and penalties around the globe. An example is corruption, where there is demand for a bribe and supply of a bribe. In the United States, the most serious offense is to offer and supply a bribe. In China, the most serious offense is to request and receive a bribe (Wang, 2020). In Norway, the law does not distinguish the extent of seriousness between bribe-giver and bribe-taker, but the courts nevertheless punish bribe-takers more harshly.

In addition to these four main categories of white-collar crime that are committed by both individuals and corporations, there are two additional categories committed by corporations. The first category is environmental crime where the typical example is pollution. The other category is crime against workers that includes cases of sexual and racial discrimination, violations of wage laws, rights to organize, breaches of privacy, workplace safety, and human rights violations (Tombs and Whyte, 2020).

The Offender-Based Perspective

The offender-based definition has its origin in the work of Sutherland (1939), who defined white-collar crime based on the social and occupational status of the offender as a crime committed by a person of respectability and high social status in the course of the offender's occupation. The offender-based definition emphasizes some combination of the actor's high social status, power, or respectability as the key features of white-collar crime (Benson et al. 2021), as well as the violation of public trust (Sohoni and Rorie, 2021).

This book applies the offender-based rather than the offense-based definition of corporate crime by white-collar offenders, which is consistent with Sutherland's (1939: 2) approach when he introduced the term:

> White-collar criminality in business is expressed most frequently in the form of misrepresentation in financial statements of corporations, manipulation in the stock exchange, commercial bribery, bribery of public officials directly or indirectly in order to secure favorable contracts and legislation, misrepresentation in advertising and salesmanship, embezzlement and misapplication of funds, short weights and measures and misgrading of commodities, tax frauds, misapplication of funds in receiverships and bankruptcies. These are what Al Capone called "the legitimate rackets". These and many others are found in abundance in the business world.

The book applies this definition by emphasizing that the white-collar offender has legitimate access to resources to commit and conceal crime in the course of occupational and professional activity. Corporate crime is committed during the course of legitimate occupational activity, by persons of high and respectable social status for organizational gain. Corporate white-collar crime benefits the organization more directly than individuals that committed the offense (Craig and Piquero, 2017).

White-collar crime is illegal acts that violate responsibility or public trust for personal or organizational gain. It is one or a series of acts committed by non-physical means and by concealment to obtain money or property, or to obtain business or personal advantage (Leasure and Zhang, 2018). The offender has legitimate access, where legitimacy is a generalized perception or assumption that the actions of an individual are desirable, proper, and appropriate within some socially constructed system of norms, roles, and values (Fitzgibbon and Lea, 2018). Legitimacy is an assessment of the appropriateness of an individual's actions (Bundy and Pfarrer, 2015). The offender has high social status, power, and enjoys respectability.

Given the offender-based perspective, the text in this book disagrees with Galvin et al. (2018) who includes all kinds of non-violent crime with financial motive. For us, identity theft or credit card abuse in a private context is no white-collar crime. Bank fraud or CEO fraud using the Internet in a private context is no white-collar crime. A distinct term like white-collar crime can lose meaning by including more and more offenders and offenses. While it is certainly true that many wear white-collar, everyone knows what the term means in criminology. It is financial crime by members of the elite in society. Those who attempt to stay above the law and feel they are too powerful to fail and too powerful to jail, those are the typical white-collar offenders (Pontell et al., 2014).

White-collar criminology makes a distinction between occupational crime and corporate crime. Self-interested individuals commit occupational crime in their profession against their employers (e.g., embezzlement or receipt of bribes) and other victims (Shepherd and Button, 2019). Organizational officials commit corporate crime in the larger interests of an organization, such as bribing potential customers, avoiding taxes by evasion, and misrepresenting accounting to get unjustified government subsidies. As argued by Alalehto (2018), an organization does not think or act by itself because it lacks ethical, philosophical, sociological, and psychological properties. Therefore, offenders of both occupational crime and corporate crime are individuals. Nevertheless, a corporation is a legal entity with its own rights and its own obligations. Rights include copyrights and other protection regulations. Obligations include tax payments, environmental protection, and other duties that rest with the organization rather than individuals in the organization.

By corporate crime, individuals such as board members and chief executives serve the benefit of the organization. Of course, individuals may benefit personally as a side effect of the corporate financial crime since the interests of the organization may coincide with the interests of individual members. While a corporation cannot feel, does not have a mind, and does not think, the corporation nevertheless acts and is the actor when executives and others attempt to improve organizational performance in illegal ways (Bundy and Pfarrer, 2015; Scott and Lyman, 1968).

The organizational connection of white-collar offenses is particularly evident when crime is committed on behalf of the business. The organizational anchoring of crime is obvious in corporate offenses as crime takes place within the business and to the benefit of the business (Bradshaw, 2015). While offenders often hide occupational crime individually to enrich himself or herself by abusing corporate resources (Hansen, 2009; Shepherd and Button, 2019), corporate crime is often hidden by a group of individuals to improve business conditions.

The offender-based white-collar perspective originates from Edwin Sutherland. Sutherland is one of the most cited criminologists in the history of the criminology research field. Sutherland's work has inspired and motivated a large number of scholars in the field associated with his work. His ideas influence, challenge, and incentivize researchers. Sutherland based his research on white-collar crime on his own differential association theory. This learning theory of deviance focuses on how individuals in organizations learn to become criminals. Differential association theory assumes that individuals learn criminal behavior in interaction with other persons. Berghoff and Spiekermann (2018: 290) are among those emphasizing the importance of Sutherland's work:

> The assessment of the offences committed in the corporate world began to change in light of the theories of sociologist and criminologist Edwin Hardin Sutherland, who not only established the criminological term 'white-collar crime' in 1939, but also made clear that crimes were not exclusively committed by lower-class offenders. Sutherland, who had among other things previously worked on juvenile delinquents in ghettos of recent immigrants, pointed to certain parallels such as the influence of cultural milieus. This concept violated existing prejudices that high-ranking persons would not or only in highly exceptionally circumstances commit crimes and that economic crimes were due to 'merely technical violations', which 'involve no moral culpability'. Sutherland, who is considered one of the most influential criminologists of the twentieth century, vehemently contradicted widespread views that criminality was caused by poverty or biological and psychological factors.

Sutherland's (1939, 1983) concept of white-collar crime has been so influential for various reasons. First, there is Sutherland's engagement with criminology's neglect of the kinds of crime of the powerful and influential members of the elite in society. Next, there is the extent of damages caused by white-collar crime. Sutherland emphasized the disproportionate extent of harm caused by the crime of the wealthy in comparison to the much researched and popular focus on crime by the poor, and the equally disproportionate level of social control responses. Third, there is the focus on organizational offenders, where crime occurs in the course of their occupations. A white-collar criminal is a person who, through the course of his or her occupation, utilizes own respectability and high social status to perpetrate an offense. Fourth, the construction of the corporation as an offender indicates that organizations might be accountable for misconduct and crime. Finally, there is the ability to theorize deviant behaviors of elite members. Sutherland's groundbreaking challenge of mainstream criminology as neglecting the crime of the upper class and the dominating focus on crime of the poor has inspired many researchers. This was a major insight that began a dramatic shift and broadening in the subject matter of criminology that continues today.

While Sutherland's concept of white-collar crime has enlightened sociologists, criminologists and management researchers, the concept may have confused attorneys, judges, and lawmakers. In most jurisdictions, there is no offense labelled white-collar crime. There are offenses such as corruption, embezzlement, tax evasion, fraud, and insider trading, but no white-collar crime offense. Sutherland's contribution to the challenge of concepts such as law and crime, researchers consider one of the strengths of his work as he showed that laws and legal distinctions that the elite produces politically and socially in very specific ways. For lawmakers, there is nothing intrinsic to the character of white-collar offenses, which makes them somehow different from other types of offenses.

One reason for this confusion is that white-collar crime in Sutherland's research is both a crime committed by a specific type of person, and it is a specific type of crime. Later research has indicated, as applied in this book, that corporate crime is no specific type of crime, it is only a crime committed by a specific type of individual in a corporate setting. However, white-collar crime may indeed sometime in the future emerge as a kind of crime suitable for law enforcement as Sutherland envisaged it in his offender-based approach to crime, focusing on characteristics of the individual offender to determine the categorization of the type of crime.

While white-collar criminal as a term was introduced by Sutherland in 1939, other terms such as robber baron had been introduced several decades earlier. Robber barons are the powerful and wealthy in the upper class of society who defines what is right and what is wrong, and who change the laws when they themselves are in danger of breaking the laws (Petrocelli et al., 2003). The rich and mighty people can behave like robber barons because they make the laws and because they control law enforcement. Spiekermann (2018: 363) presents the case of the Spreckels family as an example of robber barons:

> Claus Spreckels (1828–1908) was surely one of the notorious 'robber barons' of the time . . . When in 1876 the Kingdom of Hawaii and the United States arranged a first reciprocity treaty, which included a bounty for cane sugar imports to the United States, Spreckels took his chance and erected, after corrupting the king and the government, large-scale sugar plantations. Within a few years, Claus Spreckels established a vertically integrated sugar empire, which not only included plantation and refining but also financing, transport and wholesale trade. Although harshly criticized for exploiting coolie work and corrupting the Sandwich Islands, his political influence in California and Washington, DC generated continuous political support for his business interests.

Sutherland's broader engagement with criminological and sociological theory in general, such as his theory of differential association and social learning, has been and is influential. One aspect of the theory of differential association – social disorganization – has had a significant influence on later researchers. Sutherland's work is the foundation in all teaching, research, and policing of white-collar corporate crime today.

Corporate Crime Seriousness

Alcadipani and Medieros (2020) found that corporate crime tends to be perceived as and treated as corporate irresponsibility and not as misconduct, wrongdoing, offending, and law violation. People who do not profit from corporate activity and are victims of displacement, unemployment, and misery are the result of irresponsibility and not crime. Debates around companies' social irresponsibility emerged from a dissatisfaction with corporate initiatives that claimed to be socially responsible. While the management literature had been dominated by CSR (corporate social responsibility), the management practice has been dominated by CSIR (corporate social irresponsibility), where corporate harmful actions are considered mere irresponsibility. Social irresponsibility is the choice of an action that is inferior to an alternative action when the effects upon all stakeholders are considered. The action may involve a gain by one party at the expense of the total system. Davies (2020) found that relatively few harmful actions by corporations are criminalized or subject to prosecution.

Examples of CSIR are environmental disasters, corruption scandals, and corporate actions that harm customers and employees. While receiving the less serious label of irresponsibility, most examples should receive the label of crime. Neither companies nor executives are prosecuted. CSIR can harm companies in the form of reputation loss that can cause difficulties in attracting customers, investors, and employees (Alcadipani and Medeiros, 2020: 288):

> CSIR can also produce moral anger on the part of important stakeholders, and media coverage of CSIR increases the financial risk for companies involved in "acts of irresponsibility".

Nevertheless, the main characteristics of the CSIR perspective are that corporate environmental crime can be excused as irresponsible environmental degradation and pollution that are inevitable, that corporate financial crime can be excused by criminal market forces, and that labor law violations can be excused by legitimate exploitation of employees as resources.

Similarly, to Alcadipani and Medieros (2020), Oliveira and Silveira (2020: 1) used the lenses of the Global South in Brazil when discussing corporate crime by the Global North in their essay:

> The basic premise of the essay is that corporate crimes occur in a corporate dynamic, the main force of contemporary capitalism over the world. We use the post-colonial thinking, more specifically the concepts of necrocapitalism, a version of contemporary capitalism characterized by imperialism, which refers to contemporary forms of accumulation, which involve the subjugation of life to the power of death.

Oliveira and Silveira (2020) found that in many countries, the idea that corporations do not commit crime still prevails. Also, the role of law is ambiguous concerning corporate damage. There is an impossibility of charging corporations with crime.

Corporations are considered entities, while criminal laws derive from individual principles, and the laws and punishments imputed to individuals cannot be imputed to corporations. The legal systems of different countries react to corporate offenses in various ways, where the most common characteristic of reactions seem to be a combination of helplessness by local authorities and varying perceptions of seriousness and responsibility.

Corporate crime seriousness can be influenced by the perception of corporations. As argued by Alalehto (2018), an organization does not think or act by itself because it lacks ethical, philosophical, sociological, and psychological properties. Therefore, offenders of both occupational crime and corporate crime are individuals as natural persons. Two years later, Alalehto (2020: 112) claimed that the concept of corporate crime is a logical contradiction as long as the corporation was defined as the offender who implicitly can think and act:

> Thus, the corporation was assumed to have a consciousness and ability to act morally and ethically given the principles of the social contract in the same way as a physical individual. So, if the corporation did something illegal it could be accused of being an offender acting immorally in relation to the law of the contextual society. But this basic philosophical assumption led to one fundamental theoretical problem for the research of corporate crime, i.e., the impossible task of finding the cause of crimes committed by fictious persons.

Therefore, people within corporations commit crime, not the corporation itself. Even if it is difficult to identify the person or persons who committed the crime, it is still people who commit crime. The advantage for corporate offenders is that they can hide behind the gates of the corporation, thereby making it even more challenging to attribute blame to them. Large corporations typically have gatekeepers such as public relations departments, media spokespersons, and internal and external lawyers who assist in secrecy and confidentiality. The corporation can initially be blamed for a scandal, yet corporate accounts and the secrecy of offenders can make corporate crime seem less serious (Dewan and Jensen, 2020; Schoultz and Flyghed, 2020a, 2020b, 2021).

Structural conditions influence individual decision-making in organizations. A facilitative culture can neutralize offender responsibility for deviant behavior. However, a crime-facilitative culture cannot cause criminality in itself. It is still individuals who decide to take criminal action (Alalehto, 2020).

The seriousness of corporate crime might depend on who is the victim (Levi and Jones, 1985). Research results have indicated that crime is considered more serious if the victim is an individual rather than an organization. The difference may reveal an underlying attitude that organizations, given their presumed levels of collective resources, can better survive victimization (Cullen et al., 1982). Generally, crime seriousness seems dependent on the perceived consequences of the perceived wrongfulness.

When Sutherland (1939) introduced the term white-collar crime, he wanted to draw attention to the fact that anyone, regardless of social class, can commit criminal acts (Piquero, 2018). He emphasized privileged individuals in positions that they could abuse to commit and conceal crime, and he emphasized corporations involved in corruption and fraud. He emphasized elite offenses that the public and the criminal justice system should take more serious.

Eighty years later, Piquero (2018) argued that white-collar crime is a growing problem in terms of both the numbers of people affected as well as the amount of harm caused to victims. Nevertheless, people do not necessarily consider white-collar crime very serious. Michel (2016) found that white-collar offenders are still significantly more likely to avoid criminal indictment, prosecution, conviction, and incarceration compared with street offenders.

White-collar crime is hard to detect, and detection is obviously a precondition for any indictment and prosecution (Friedrich, 2021). It is usually obvious when a street crime has occurred, while financial crime by the elite usually is less apparent (Cullen et al., 2006: 346):

> The difference in visibility is tied directly to the nature of the crimes involved in each offense category. Missing property, a mugging, or an assault are forced upon a victim's attention. By contrast, the very structure of most corporate acts insulates workers or citizens from knowledge of their victimization. Typically, corporate offenders are not present physically at the scene of the crime, and the effects of their victimization are diffused over time.

Logan et al. (2019) argued that public support for the indictment, prosecution, conviction, and imprisonment of white-collar offenders is on the rise. However, some studies show an association between political ideology and punitive philosophies, where conservatives favor greater control and punishment of traditional street crime as compared to liberals. Features of each political perspective suggest that the association is a reversal when it comes to white-collar crime. Reducing and punishing white-collar offenders may seem more important to liberals than to conservatives (Unnever et al., 2009). This reversion of attitudes is in line with the switch hypothesis (Zimring and Hawkins, 1978).

Logan et al. (2019: 225) further argued that the number of people incarcerated for white-collar offenses in the United States has been steadily rising for the past two decades:

> There are now more white-collar offenders in jail or prison than ever before, and public support for the prosecution and imprisonment of white-collar offenders is on the rise. The United States Sentencing Commission reports an increase in the rate of white-collar offenders sentenced to federal prison. For example, between 1997 and 2009, the incarceration rate for fraud rose from 64.8 to 74.9 and has remained stable through 2015.

White-collar offenders are individuals who had high occupational status. The sentencing outcome can reflect the seriousness of their crime. Some research finds that high occupational status decreases punishment, showing that auto thieves receive a harsher punishment compared to physicians involved in medical fraud (Tillman and Pontel, 1992). Other research finds that occupational status increases punishment, with higher occupational status health care professionals given more severe sentences than lower-level health care professionals do (Payne et al., 2011). Still other research finds no effect at all from occupational status on length of prison sentence for white-collar offenders.

Perceptions of crime seriousness in the population still distinguish between offenses resulting in physical harm and the ones not resulting in such harm. Public opinion thus considers white-collar offenses not resulting in physical damages as not very serious. In a study by Isenring (2008), white-collar offenses are severely condemned, even when there is no physical harm involved in the crime. The study seems to show a greater sensitivity with respect to white-collar offenses, especially towards white-collar crime perpetrated by corporations, such as a corporation bribing a public official. On the other hand, the study showed a difference between street crime and white-collar crime with regard to punishment. Respondents preferred a more severe sentence passed on street criminals rather than on white-collar offenders.

When perceptions of crime seriousness distinguish between offenses resulting in physical harm and no such harm, it is interesting to notice the perceptions of rising seriousness of environmental crime by corporate offenders. Environmental harm and crime have received increased attention in recent years (Böhm, 2020; Gibbs and Boratto, 2017; Huisman and Van Erp, 2013; Lynch, 2020). Physical harm often results from environmental crime by corporate offenders (Van Erp, 2020).

Goossen et al. (2016) studied relationships between basic human values and white-collar crime. They tested seven value constructs in relation to three types of white-collar crime: tax evasion, insurance fraud, and bribery. They found that the relationships between values and white-collar offenses are particularly evident for values of universalism, power, and stimulation. Universalism is a value concerned with understanding, appreciation, tolerance, and protection of the welfare of all people and of nature. Power is a value concerned with social status and prestige, control or dominance over people and resources. Stimulation is a value concerned with excitement, novelty, and challenge in life. While universalism and stimulation were positively associated with the condemnation of white-collar crime, power had a negative association as a value construct.

The seriousness of white-collar elite crime was emphasized by Hausman (2018: 392) who found that offenders present "a long-term danger to the U.S. business climate". Honest businesspersons – who must have access to capital to succeed – suffer because financial investors, public authorities, and the general public lose faith in business enterprises.

Corporate crime seriousness is linked to corporate criminal liability. Lack of liability is a concept that features across regulatory offenses, financial crime, and environmental crime that disable the attribution of liability to corporations in criminal courts (Whyte, 2014). Hamdani and Klement (2008: 271) found that the doctrine of corporate liability is notoriously controversial:

> For decades, scholars have argued that imposing criminal liability on business entities is both ineffective and inconsistent with the fundamental principles of individual culpability and moral condemnation underlying criminal law. It is therefore not surprising that the federal government's post-Enron campaign against corporate crime has reignited debate over the proper use of criminal law to target business enterprises.

Not only is the doctrine of corporate liability controversial. The doctrine also discourages disclosure of wrongdoing (Patterson, 2021: 423):

> Under the doctrine of respondeat superior, U.S. corporations have long been held criminally liable for the conduct of employees acting within the scope of their employment. Standing alone, this de jure system of enforcement provides perverse incentives to corporations dealing with internal malfeasance; the threat of vicarious liability discourages corporations from seeking to discover, disclose, and investigate because such efforts will only assist enforcement authorities in imposing higher corporate sanctions. The Department of Justice has, in a series of revisions to the Justice Manual, attempted to counteract this dynamic by emphasizing individual, rather than corporate-level, liability in prosecuting business organizations, developing a de facto regime for sanctioning and controlling corporate crime.

The government in the United States made both the energy company Enron and the consulting firm Arthur Andersen collapse because of accounting fraud and destruction of evidence. At Arthur Andersen, 28,000 employees lost their jobs. Corporate fines in the United States can be of such a magnitude that the fined company goes bankrupt. This is very different from government fines in other countries that are mainly symbolic rather than harmful. For example, when construction companies are fined in Norway for their cartel activity as described later in this book, the modest money amounts do not really harm their businesses. Those in favor of harsh corporate penalties posit that only the threat of going out of business can effectively deter organizational misconduct (Hamdani and Klement, 2008).

A general perspective is that entities do not commit crime; individuals do. Corporations cannot be imprisoned; only individuals can (Fischel and Sykes, 1996: 320):

> Corporations are legal fictions, and legal fictions cannot commit criminal acts. Nor can they possess mens rea, a guilty state of mind. Only people can act and only people can have a guilty state of mind.

A competing perspective is that employees and executives are agents for their corporations. Then the corporations can and should be criminally prosecuted for criminal acts of their agents. In the terminology of principal-agent theory, the corporation might be defined as the principal, while executives are agents. The principal-agent theory suggests that the organization is a nexus of contracts. A corporation is a web of contractual relationships consisting of individuals who band together for their mutual economic benefit (Fischel and Sykes, 1996). The theory argues that a principal is often unable to control an agent who does work for the principal, while at the same time being responsible for the agent's behavior (Bosse and Phillips, 2016; Chrisman et al., 2007; Pillay and Kluvers, 2014).

Corporate Offender Profiling

Ever since Sutherland (1939) coined the term white-collar crime, there has been extensive research and debate what to include and what to exclude from this offense category (e.g., Benson and Simpson, 2015; Logan et al., 2019; Pontell et al., 2014; Schoepfer and Piquero, 2006; Stadler et al., 2013). In accordance with Sutherland's original work, convenience theory emphasizes the position and trust enjoyed by the offender in an occupational setting. Therefore, the organizational dimension is the core of convenience theory where the offender has access to resources to commit and conceal financial crime.

The typical profile of a white-collar criminal includes the following attributes (e.g., Benson and Simpson, 2018; Logan et al., 2019; Pontell et al., 2014; Schoepfer and Piquero, 2006; Stadler et al., 2013):

- The person has high social status and considerable influence, enjoying respect and trust, and belongs to the elite in society.
- The elite have generally more knowledge, money, and prestige and occupy higher positions than other individuals in the population occupy.
- Privileges and authority by the elite are often not visible or transparent but known to everybody.
- Elite members are active in business, public administration, politics, congregations, and many other sectors in society.
- The elite are a minority that behaves as an authority towards others in the majority.
- The person is often wealthy and has a strong preference for narcissistic success.
- The person is typically well educated and connects to important networks of partners and friends.
- The person exploits his or her position to commit corporate crime.
- The person does not look at himself or herself as a criminal, but rather as a community builder who applies personal rules for own behavior.
- The person may be in a position that makes the police reluctant to initiate a crime investigation.
- The person can hide behind the walls of the corporation where others communicate accounts of what is going on.
- The person has access to resources that enable involvement of top defense attorneys and can behave in court in a manner that creates sympathy among the public, partly because the defendant belongs to the upper class similar to the judge, the prosecutor, and the attorney.

However, one of the theoretical challenges facing scholars in this growing field of research is to develop an accepted definition of white-collar crime. While the main characteristics are the foundation, such as economic crime committed by a person of respectability and high social status in the course of an occupation, other aspects lack precision (Kang and Thosuwanchot, 2017).

White-collar crime is a unique area of criminology due to its atypical association with societal influence compared to other types of criminal offenses. White-collar crime conceptualization occurs in its relationship to status, opportunity, and access in a corporate setting. This is the offender-based perspective. In contrast, offense-based approaches to white-collar crime emphasize the actions and nature of the illegal act as the defining agent. In their comparison of the two approaches, Benson and Simpson (2018) discuss how offender-based definitions emphasize societal characteristics such as high social status, power, and respectability of the actor. Because status is not included in the definition of offense-based approaches and status is free to vary independently from the definition in most legislation, an offense-based approach allows measures of status to become external explanatory variables.

Benson and Simpson (2018) approach white-collar crime utilizing the opportunity perspective. They stress the idea that individuals with more opportunities to offend, with access to resources to offend, and that hold organizational positions of power are more likely to commit white-collar crime. Opportunities for crime depend on the nature of economic and productive activities of various business and government sectors within society.

Benson and Simpson (2018) do not limit their opportunity perspective to activities in organizations. However, they emphasize that opportunities are normally greater in an organizational context. Convenience theory, however, assumes that crime is committed in an organizational context to make the term white-collar crime relevant. This is in line with Sutherland's (1939, 1983) original work, where he emphasized profession and position as key characteristics of offenders.

The white-collar offender is a person of respectability and high social status who commits financial crime in the course of his or her occupation (Leasure and Zhang, 2018). In the offender-based perspective, white-collar criminals tend to possess many characteristics that are consistent to expectations of high status in society. There is both attained status and ascribed status among white-collar offenders. Attained status refers to status that individuals accrue over time and with some degree of effort, such as education and income. Ascribed status refers to status that does not require any specific action or merit, but rather requires physically observable characteristics, such as race, age, and gender.

The main offender characteristics remain privilege and upper class. Early perception studies suggest that the public think that white-collar crime is not as serious as other forms of crime. Most people think that street criminals should receive harsher punishments. One explanation for this view is self-interest (Dearden, 2017: 311):

Closely tied to rational choice, self-interest suggests that people have views that selfishly affect themselves. Significant scholarly research has been devoted to self-interest-based views. In laboratory conditions, people often favor redistribution taxes when they would benefit from such a tax. This self-interest extends into non-experimental settings as well. For example, smokers often view increasing smoking taxes less favorably than non-smokers do.

In this line of thinking, people may be more concerned about burglary and physical violence that may hurt them. They may be less concerned about white-collar crime that does not affect them directly. Maybe those who are financially concerned with their own economic well-being will be more concerned with white-collar crime (Dearden, 2017).

White-collar perpetrators have social power associated with different occupational activities across the society. Power and authority at the hands of individuals enable white-collar crime. The power essentially comes from the positions individuals legitimately occupy. Businesses and their executives tend to be recidivists who get away with light punishment (Haines and Macdonald, 2021; Sutherland, 1983).

State-Corporate Crime

The long-lasting influence of Sutherland upon criminological, sociological, and more recently also on management thinking is observable across the globe, but in particular in the United States and Europe. Sutherland exposed crime by individuals who people thought of as almost superior, and people who apparently did not need to offend as a means of survival. Businesspersons and professionals frequently commit serious wrongdoing and harm with little fear of facing criminal justice scrutiny. It can be true that poverty and powerlessness is a cause of one kind of crime while excessive power can be a cause of another kind of crime.

Sutherland exemplified the corporation as an offender in the case of war crime where corporations profit heavily by abusing the state of national emergency during times of war. Corporate form and characteristics as a profit-maximizing entity are shaping war profiteering. War profiteering is organizational crime by powerful organizations that may commit environmental crime, state-corporate crime, and human rights violations. Corporations break the law, and they get away with it, according to Sutherland (Müller, 2018).

Interdependent interests and incentives connect state affairs with corporate affairs (Ken and León, 2021: 4):

By "the state", we refer to a bureaucratic, fragmented, and crowded ensemble of institutions and actors that organize social, economic, and political relations of power, despite competing priorities.

Ken and León (2021) studied state-corporate harm in the U.S. pork packing industry during the Covid-19 pandemic. In 2020, when over 67,000 meatpacking and processing workers were infected with the virus, the state allowed and encouraged this industry to harm worker health and lives to continue to slaughter pigs.

The powerful in the upper class of society define their own identity in terms of what is right and what is wrong for them, sometimes in a state-corporate alignment (Tombs and Whyte, 2020; Zysman-Quirós, 2020). If they themselves break their own laws, then there is a need to change the laws rather than punish law violators (Petrocelli et al., 2003).

Denial of responsibility for crime depends on the situation. For example, in a state-corporate alignment, the corporation can attempt to blame the state (Bernat and Whyte, 2020; Rothe, 2020; Rothe and Medley, 2020; Tombs and Whyte, 2020; Zysman-Quirós, 2020). In the case of profit-driven environmental crime, the corporation can claim that multiple factors cause pollution and other kinds of harm (Böhm, 2020; Budo, 2021; Lynch, 2020; Wingerde and Lord, 2020). Furthermore, the corporation can blame a too complex regulatory environment (Braithwaite, 2020; Lehman et al., 2020).

Whyte (2014: 237) argues that the perspective of state-corporate crime brings the important role of the state into the study of social harm caused by corporations:

> The state-corporate crime framework allows us to place at the centre of our analysis an understanding of how the state, in various ways, produces corporate crime, or at the very least, assists in the production of corporate crime – corporate crime is not something that simply happens when states are not vigilant enough, nor is it simply the unintended consequence of normally benign functions of administration.

Laws and regulations have conventionalized and normalized several types of corporate crime, ensuring that the capital, in the form of the corporation, continues to prosper regardless of its damaging effects on the capacity for society to develop and reproduce (Oliveira and Silveira, 2020: 12):

> Historically, corporations have obtained political power and favoring regulatory laws, have monopolized or mapped markets, and have transformed themselves into powerful institutions through special privileges granted to them. Therefore, the strictly legal definition of corporate crime conceals the destructive character of capitalism. Likewise, the concept of 'state-corporate crime' developed in the literature conceals this issue; it reinforces the neoliberal discourse by stating that it is a crime initiated or facilitated by the state.

The concept of state-corporate crime takes as its starting point the mutually reinforcing relationships between state institutions and private corporations (Bernat and Whyte, 2020). The powerful and wealthy in the upper class of society define their own identity in terms of what is right and what is wrong for them, sometimes in a state-corporate alignment (Rothe, 2020; Rothe and Medley, 2020).

As described later in this book, convenience dynamics in white-collar crime can take place at different levels such as the individual, the organizational, and the national level. Dynamics also take place between these levels. For example, dynamics of state-corporate crime occurs between the national and organizational levels (Bernat and Whyte, 2020: 127):

> This growing body of literature on state-corporate crimes takes as its starting points the mutually reinforcing relationships between state institutions and corporations.

In system dynamics terms as describe later (Randers, 2019; Sterman, 2018), a mutually reinforcing relationship is a positive feedback loop, where increased state involvement in corporate crime will cause increased corporate involvement in state crime. Over time, a positive feedback loop can cause exponential growth in state-corporate crime. The opposite of a positive feedback loop is a negative feedback loop, where for example increased corporate crime causes a reaction in terms of reduced state crime that in turn reduces corporate crime.

Osoria (2021) studied state-corporate crime caused by the Covid-19 pandemic in Purerto Rico. He applied the framework of the regime of permission to describe the dynamics of state-corporate crime in capitalist societies as a lens to analyze the intertwined relationship between exceptionality, corruption, and state-corporate crime. The regime of permission suggests that the state neither controls nor intervenes against corporate crime as long as corporate activity is considered beneficial to the state (Whyte, 2014: 244):

> Corporate power in this sense is wholly reliant upon a series of regimes of permission, including the permission to trade as a separate entity, investment regimes which permit limited liability, the application of the separate entity in criminal law, the permission for corporations to act as holders of "rights" and so on. Crucially, within those regimes of permission we also find the co-ordinates of impunity – a corporate veil which shields owners from civil liability and a de facto corporate veil which shields both owners and managers from criminal liability.

The framework of the regime of permissions suggests that corporations are permitted by the state to commit crime for which they are not considered liable. Lack of liability is a concept that features across regulatory offenses, financial crime, and environmental crime that disable the attribution of liability to corporations in criminal courts. Rather than controlling order in the market economy, regulatory agencies attempt to mitigate problems that are the product of state regimes of permission.

Haines and Macdonald (2021: 298) found that regimes of permission to enable business activity, and regulation to control it, can be intertwined in the case of licenses granted to enterprises:

> This in turn shapes which forms of business activity are supported, and which resisted. In this context, licensing emerges as a key aspect of regimes of permission that needs more attention. Just as corporate law creates personhood out of a legal fiction, licenses pertaining to land use create a fiction of the visceral connection between the fate of humanity and the fate of the planet we inhabit.

Osoria (2021) found that the regime of permission during the Covid-19 pandemic in Puerto Rico led to permission for corporate corruption, tax fraud, and human rights violations. Since Puerto Rico has a number of manufacturing facilities for Covid-19 vaccines, pharmaceutical corporations were permitted by the state to extract large profits from the production without the corporations exercising any sort of social responsibility. The state's only concern was for the corporations to produce as many vaccines as possible by leaving transnational corporations such as Abbott and Roche completely unregulated and not liable for any wrongdoing.

As argued by Tombs and Whyte (2020: 17), corporations can have no meaningful existence without the state:

> They can have no legal basis for their function as the primary institution through which capital is reproduced and can have no infrastructure or indeed political allies or representatives in government.

Whyte (2014) distinguished between state-initiated crime and state-facilitated crime. State-initiated crime is the active involvement of state agencies in the production of particular criminal processes and events. It can also mean the failure of state agencies to control corporate crime. Corporate crime occurs at the direction of, or with the explicit or tacit approval of, the government. State-initiated corporate crime thus represents a criminal conspiracy. State-facilitated crime implies the failure of state agencies to control corporate crime. There is no attempt to restrain deviant business activities, and the state is unwilling to pursue any effective regulation due to shared state-corporate goals.

2 Theory of Offending Convenience

Convenience in our context of corporate crime is bad. Convenience is an attribute of financial motive for illegitimate gain, an attribute of organizational opportunity to commit and conceal crime, as well as an attribute of personal willingness for deviant behavior. Convenience considerations are present within all three dimensions. More generally, convenience can be both good and bad. Practically every action we take involves some calculation of convenience, to us or others. For example, convenient technologies can be smart and help us in various situations. Then convenience is good.

Convenience is a concept that was theoretically mainly associated with efficiency in time savings. Today, convenience is associated with a number of other characteristics, such as reduced effort and reduced pain. Convenience is linked to terms such as fast, easy, and safe. Convenience says something about attractiveness and accessibility. A convenient individual is not necessarily neither bad nor lazy. On the contrary, the person can be seen as smart and rational (Sundström and Radon, 2015).

In the marketing literature, convenience store is a term used to define three phases in retailing. First, retailers identified a business opportunity in offering a new retail format based on the self-service idea. Self-service replaced over-the-counter service. Next, retailers identified customers' willingness to pay a little more if the store was always open and situated in the neighborhood or co-located with a gas station. Finally, e-commerce represents another kind of convenience, where the ordering process can take place from home (Sundström and Radon, 2015). In all three instances, there are costs associated with convenience (Locke and Blomquist, 2016). In the case of self-service, customers have to find and physically handle items by themselves. In the case of online shopping, customers have to find and electronically handle items by themselves. Just like convenience is a driver for consumers when shopping, convenience is a driver for executives and other members in the elite when struggling to reach personal and organizational goals.

In the marketing literature, distinctions are made between decision convenience, access convenience, benefit convenience, transaction convenience, and post benefit convenience (Seiders et al., 2007). In the current convenience theory for white-collar crime, we make distinctions between economical convenience, organizational convenience, and behavioral convenience.

Crime Convenience Orientation

Convenience orientation is conceptualized as the value that individuals and organizations place on actions with inherent characteristics of saving time and effort as well as avoiding strain and pain. Convenience orientation can be considered a

https://doi.org/10.1515/9783110766950-003

value-like construct that influences behavior and decision-making. Mai and Olsen (2016) measured convenience orientation in terms of a desire to spend as little time as possible on the task, in terms of an attitude that the less effort needed the better, as well as in terms of a consideration that it is a waste of time to spend long hours on the task. Convenience orientation toward illegal actions increases as negative attitudes towards legal actions increase. The basic elements in convenience orientation are the individual attitudes toward the saving of time, effort and discomfort in the planning, action and achievement of goals. Generally, convenience orientation is the degree to which an individual or a group of individuals are inclined to save time and effort to reach goals.

Convenience orientation refers to a person's or persons' general preference for convenient maneuvers. A convenience-oriented person is one who seeks to accomplish a task in the shortest time with the least expenditure of human energy (Berry et al., 2002; Farquhar and Rowley, 2009).

In the marketing literature, convenience orientation is for example measured in terms of stage in a person's life cycle, family size, economic status, social status, and education (Sundström and Radon, 2015). Similar characteristics of convenience orientation might be developed for individuals in the elite regarding white-collar crime.

Convenience in the decision-making process is not only concerned with one alternative being more convenient than another alternative. Convenience is also concerned with the extent to which an individual collects information about more alternatives and collects more information about each alternative. Market research indicates that consumers tend to make buying decisions based on little information about few alternatives (Sundström and Radon, 2015). A similar process can be explored for white-collar crime where the individual avoids the effort of collecting more information about more alternatives that might have led to a non-criminal rather than a criminal solution to a challenge or problem.

It is not the actual convenience that is important in convenience theory. Rather it is the perceived, expected and assumed convenience that influences choice of action. Berry et al. (2002) make this distinction explicit by conceptualizing convenience as individuals time and effort perceptions related to an action. White-collar criminals probably vary in their perceived convenience of their actions. Low expected convenience can be one of the reasons why not more members of the elite commit white-collar offenses.

Convenience is of value because time and effort are associated with value. Time is a limited and scarce resource. Saving time means reallocating time across activities to achieve greater efficiency. Similarly, effort can be reallocated to create value elsewhere. The more effort is exerted, the more outcomes can be expected in return (Berry et al., 2002).

Convenience in white-collar crime relates to savings in time and effort by privileged and trusted individuals to reach a goal. Convenience is here an attribute of an illegal action. Convenience comes at a potential cost to the offender in terms of the likelihood of detection and future punishment. In other words, reducing time and effort now entails a greater potential for future cost. 'Paying for convenience' is a way of phrasing this proposition (Farquhar and Rowley, 2009).

Convenience is the perceived savings in time and effort required to find and to facilitate the use of a solution to a problem or to exploit favorable circumstances. Convenience directly relates to the amount of time and effort that is required to accomplish a task. Convenience addresses the time and effort exerted before, during, and after an activity. Convenience represents a time and effort component related to the complete illegal transaction process or processes (Collier and Kimes, 2012).

What privileged individuals in the elite think and feel about time and effort varies. Chen and Nadkarni (2017: 34) found that many CEOs can be characterized by time urgency where they have the feeling of being chronically hurried:

> Time urgency is a relatively stable trait. Time-urgent people are acutely aware of the passage of time and feel chronically hurried. They often create aggressive internal deadlines and use them as markers of the timely completion of team tasks. They regularly check work progress, increase others' awareness of the remaining time, and motivate others to accomplish commitments within the allotted time.

People differ in their temporal orientation, including perceived time scarcity, the degree to which they value time, and their sensitivity to time-related issues. Facing strain, greed or other situations, an illegal activity can represent a convenient solution to a problem that the individual or the organization otherwise find difficult or even impossible to solve. The desire for convenience thus varies among people (Berry et al., 2002; Farquhar and Rowley, 2009).

Convenience motivates the choice of action. An important element in convenience is saving time in terms of efficiency in task completion, and another element is avoiding more problematic, stressful and challenging situations. Convenience can be both an absolute construct and a relative construct. As an absolute construct, it is attractive to commit crime as such. As a relative construct, it is more convenient to commit crime than to carry out alternative actions to solve a problem or gain benefits from a possibility. Convenience is an advantage in favor of a specific action to the detriment of alternative actions. In white-collar crime, it seems that convenience is mainly a relative construct. Decision making implies a choice between alternatives, where one alternative might be relatively more convenient. Convenience is a matter of perception in advance of possible criminal actions. Convenience must be viewed as a significant variable whose understanding involves complexity in multiple meanings (Sundström and Radon, 2015).

For example, the flexibility to choose the exact moment for making a deal or another kind of action can also be perceived as a matter of convenience. Convenience might mean selecting a proper occasion, which, in turn, is about timing. There may be more reluctance to do something at a certain point in time than willingness to save or spend time. Thus, when something is convenient, it could mean saving time as well as spending time and doing it at the right moment (Sundström and Radon, 2015).

In addition to time convenience and timing convenience, there may be place convenience, where a potential offender finds the spatial circumstances convenient for crime (Sundström and Radon, 2015). In white-collar crime, the organizational setting is typically characterized by spatial convenience.

Three main dimensions to explain white-collar crime have emerged. All of them link to convenience. The first dimension is concerned with economic aspects, where convenience implies that the illegal financial gain is a convenient option for the decision-maker to cover needs. The second dimension is concerned with organizational aspects, where convenience implies that the offender has convenient access to premises and convenient ability to hide illegal transactions among legal transactions. The third dimension is concerned with behavioral aspects, where convenience implies that the offender finds convenient justification.

Convenience orientation is introduced in this book as an explanation for white-collar crime among CEOs and other privileged individuals in politics, public administration, and private businesses. This book thus makes a case for a specific way of explaining elite member behavior.

A question worth addressing is what other explanatory hypotheses should be considered. There is a need to place the convenience perspective in a broader setting of proposed or rival explanations. The question is what other approaches exist to explaining the relevant behavior, and whether the convenience approach applies in other contexts as well. Future research might focus on a discussion of what counts as a satisfactory explanation.

To address this question, it is relevant to go back to Sutherland (1983) who coined the term white-collar crime. He emphasized attitudes in society where white-collar crime is considered less serious than traditional street crime. While convenience theory emphasizes factors at the individual and organizational level, Sutherland (1983) emphasized hypotheses at the community level. Convenience theory is including explicit representations of society level factors such as criminal market structures such as cartels, national corruption magnitude, and law enforcement mechanisms.

Berghoff and Spiekermann (2018: 290) are among those emphasizing the importance of Sutherland's work:

> The assessment of the offences committed in the corporate world began to change in light of the theories of sociologist and criminologist Edwin Hardin Sutherland, who not only established the criminological term 'white-collar crime' in 1939, but also made clear that crimes were not exclusively committed by lower-class offenders. Sutherland, who had among other things previously worked on juvenile delinquents in ghettos of recent immigrants, pointed to certain parallels such as the influence of cultural milieus. This concept violated existing prejudices that high-ranking persons would not or only in highly exceptionally circumstances commit crimes and that economic crimes were due to 'merely technical violations', which 'involve

no moral culpability'. Sutherland, who is considered one of the most influential criminologists of the twentieth century, vehemently contradicted widespread views that criminality was caused by poverty or biological and psychological factors.

As Agnew (2014: 2) formulates it: "crime is often the most expedient way to get what you want" and "fraud is often easier, simpler, faster, more exciting, and more certain than other means of securing one's ends".

The notion of convenience may seem rather obvious and not especially illuminating. When convenience orientation is simply defined as the degree to which a trusted individual is inclined to save time, effort and pain to reach a goal, then it might sound more like an aspect of prudence rather than deviant criminal behavior. However, as pointed out in this book, some CEOs will employ illegal or objectionable means in striving to reach goals. This type of behavior is not necessarily different from the behavior of others in positions of power and authority (e.g., politicians, officers of universities, church officials, heads of major philanthropies, etc.), but the degrees of freedom enjoyed by many CEOs make the CEO position nevertheless very special in terms of convenience.

Different Concepts of Convenience

Convenience is the state of being able to proceed with something with little effort or difficulty, avoiding pain and strain (Mai and Olsen, 2016). The extent to which individuals in privileged positions choose to violate the law in difficult situations or tempting situations is dependent on their convenience orientation. Convenience comes at a potential cost to the offender in terms of the likelihood of detection and future punishment. In other worlds, reducing time and effort now entails a greater potential for future cost. Paying for convenience is a way of phrasing this proposition (Farquhar and Rowley, 2009).

Orientation is a function of the mind involving awareness of the situation. This book conceptualizes convenience orientation as the value that individuals and organizations in a given situation place on actions with inherent characteristics of saving time and effort. Convenience orientation is a value-like construct that influences behavior and decision-making. Mai and Olsen (2016) measured convenience orientation in terms of a desire to spend as little time as possible on the task, in terms of an attitude that the less effort needed the better, as well as in terms of a consideration that it is a waste of time to spend a long time on the task.

Convenience is a phenomenon that we observe in many aspects of human life. For example, convenience stores and convenience shopping is associated with easy access to goods and services. A theory of convenience finds application in a number of areas where people prefer alternatives that are associated with savings in time and effort, and with avoidance of pain and problems. For example, a convenience theory of cheating suggests that cheating is a preferred alternative in certain situations.

Convenience is similar to comfort that focuses on relief and ease (Carrington and Catasus, 2007).

This book focuses on theory of convenience as convenience relates to white-collar misconduct and crime. Misconduct can be understood as the violation of rules and norms (Dewan and Jensen, 2020), while crime can be understood as the violation of laws that are sanctioned by punishment. Convenience theory attempts to integrate various theoretical explanations for the occurrence of white-collar misconduct and crime. Convenience theory suggests that organizational opportunity to commit and conceal financial crime is at the core of deviant behavior convenience to avoid threats and exploit possibilities (Vasiu and Podgor, 2019).

This book is mainly concerned with offenders rather than offenses. To offend is to cause displeasure, anger, resentment, or wounded feelings. It is to be displeasing or disagreeable. It can also be to violate a moral, a guideline, a rule or a law. The offender-based perspective emphasizes characteristics of actors such as social and occupational status, respectability and power (Benson, 2020; Dodge, 2009; Friedrichs et al., 2018; Piquero and Schoepfer, 2010; Pontell et al., 2014; Stadler et al., 2013; Sutherland, 1983).

The purpose of convenience theory is to integrate a number of theoretical approaches to explain and understand white-collar crime that Sutherland (1983) first defined. Convenience theory applies the concept of convenience in terms of savings in time and effort (Farquhar and Rowley, 2009), as well as avoidance of pain and obstacles. Convenience is a relative concept concerned with the efficiency in time and effort as well as reduction in pain and solution to problems (Engdahl, 2015). A convenient individual is not necessarily neither bad nor lazy. On the contrary, the person can be seen as smart and rational (Sundström and Radon, 2015).

From a resource-matching perspective, convenience directly relates to the amount of time and effort (resources) that a task requires for its accomplishment. However, convenience is a more comprehensive construct than simply examining ease of use perceptions that also addresses the amount of effort in an interaction. Ease of use is the degree to which an alternative action is free of effort. Convenience addresses the time and effort exerted before, during, and after an action or avoidance of action (Collier and Kimes, 2012).

Blickle et al. (2006) found that if the rationally expected utility of an action by a white-collar offender clearly outweighs the expected disadvantages resulting from the action, thereby leaving some net material advantage, then the offender would commit the offense in question.

As a relative construct, convenience theory is line with the crime-as-choice perspective. This perspective by Shover et al. (2012) suggests that it is a conscious choice among alternatives that leads to law violation. Convenience motivates the choice of action. Convenience is a matter of perception in advance of possible criminal actions. Convenience is a significant variable whose understanding involves complexity in multiple meanings (Sundström and Radon, 2015).

Convenience is a term found in studies of consumer behavior. Convenience theory adds something important to our understanding of white-collar offenders because it:

A. Disaggregates the dimensions of a white-collar offender's decisions about deviant behavior before, under, and after an illegal act.
B. Explains why illegitimate actions find preference at the detriment of legitimate actions.
C. Provides a way to think about why organizations might do nothing despite being an arena for crime.

Elite members with a strong convenience orientation favor actions and behaviors with inherent characteristics of saving time and effort. They have a desire to spend as little time as possible on challenging issues and situations that may occur. They have an attitude that the less effort needed the better, and they think that it will be a waste of time to spend a long time on a problem. They prefer to avoid the problem rather than handle it. They want to avoid discomfort and pain. They want to survive and prosper in the upper echelon of society in the best possible way. Convenience motivates the choice of action and behavior. An important element is avoiding more problematic, stressful and challenging situations.

Corporate Crime Convenience Themes

A combination of motive, opportunity and willingness determine the extent of white-collar crime convenience as illustrated in the structural model in Figure 2.1.

In the financial motive dimension, profit might be a goal in itself or an enabler to exploit possibilities and to avoid threats. Possibilities and threats exist both for individual members of the organization as well as for the organization as a whole. It is convenient to exploit possibilities and to avoid threats by financial means.

In the organizational opportunity dimension, convenience can exist both to commit white-collar crime and to conceal white-collar crime. Offenders have high social status in privileged positions, and they have legitimate access to crime resources. Disorganized institutional deterioration causes decay, lack of oversight and guardianship cause chaos, while criminal market structures cause collapse.

The personal willingness for deviant behavior focuses on offender choice and perceived innocence. The choice of crime can be caused by deviant identity, rational consideration, or learning from others. Justification and neutralization cause the perceived innocence at crime. Identity, rationality, learning, justification, and neutralization all contribute to making white-collar crime action a convenient behavior for offenders.

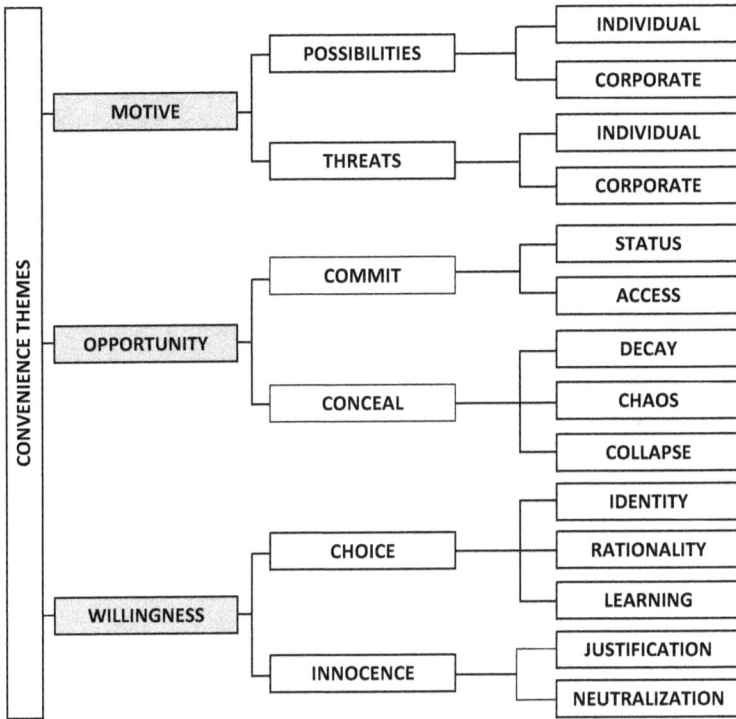

Figure 2.1: Structural model of convenience theory.

Convenience of Financial Motive

The economical dimension of convenience theory focuses on financial motives that the offender has to exploit and explore possibilities, and to reduce and avoid threats. Possibilities and threats are motives both for individuals and for the organization, as illustrated in Figure 2.1. Corporate possibilities and threats are discussed here.

Possibilities for the corporation include reaching business objectives by ignoring whether or not means are legitimate or illegitimate (Campbell and Göritz, 2014; Jonnergård et al., 2010; Kang and Thosuwanchot, 2017). Ends simply justify means that might represent crime. It may be so important to have a bottom line in accounting that satisfies investors and others that crime emerges as potentially acceptable. Dodge (2009: 15) suggests that tough rivalry among executives make them commit crime to attain goals: "The competitive environment generates pressures on the organization to violate the law in order to attain goals".

Goalsetting is often perceived in a positive light, meaning that ambitious goals increase performance (Locke and Latham, 2013). However, there is also evidence suggesting that high performance goals can lead to unethical behavior (Simmons,

2018). Welsh et al. (2020) argue that this is not only because of rewards associated with goal attainment, but also because of changing morale reasoning processes related to the goal. As such, high goal commitment facilitates unethical behavior by increasing not only the motivation to achieve the goal but also the motivation to justify doing so by any means necessary (Locatelli et al., 2017). This is known as state morale disagreement, a process through which individuals justify unethical behavior (Moore, 2015). It is part of the dark side of ambitious goals. Escalation of commitment to ambitious goals increases the likelihood of misconduct and crime (Sleesman et al., 2012, 2018). Escalation of commitment is defined as "decision-making in the face of negative feedback about prior resource allocations, uncertainty surrounding the likelihood of goal attainment, and choice about whether to continue" (Keil et al., 2000: 392).

Corporate greed implies that the organization is never satisfied, as it always wants more profit (Goldstraw-White, 2012). Greed reflects needs and desires that are socially constructed, and the needs and desires can never be completely covered or contended. There is a strong preference to maximize wealth for the corporation, possibly at the expense of violating the laws, rules, and guidelines. Economic greed is a strong motive for financial crime (Bucy et al., 2008; Hamilton and Micklethwait, 2006).

Corporations enter into exchange relationships with suppliers, customers, banks, consultants, and others. Exchanges can be thought of as discrete events nested within continuous relationships that are developing and changing over the course of time. Reciprocity such as kickbacks might be natural according to expectations in an exchange relationship to secure future business possibilities (Huang and Knight, 2017).

Finally, in the motive of possibilities for corporations, making as much profits as possible might be the ultimate goal (Naylor, 2003). Rather than viewing profits as an enabler to invest and expand, profits as such might be the final goal in itself. Financial crime can be an attractive strategic decision (Lopez-Rodriguez, 2009; Menon and Siew, 2012).

Moving down in Figure 2.1 to threats, the threat of corporate collapse and bankruptcy might cause exploration and exploitation of illegal avenues to survive, where moral panic can occur (Kang and Thosuwanchot, 2017). The survival of the corporation can become so important that no means come across as unacceptable in the current situation. Sometimes, fraud and corruption are considered temporary measures to recover from a crisis (Geest et al., 2017), where the measures will be terminated when the crisis is over. A crisis is a fundamental threat to the organization, which is often characterized by ambiguity of cause, effect, and means of resolution (König et al., 2020).

Financial balance is a strong motive for corporate economic crime (Brightman, 2009). In some markets, the only way to survive is to implement financial practices similar to the ones applied by competitors. If corruption is the name of the game, every participant on the market has to provide bribes to stay in business (Berghoff,

2018; Bradshaw, 2015). Furthermore, threats from monopolies are a strong motive for financial crime (Chang et al., 2005). Similarly, if a cartel is the name of the game, the only way to survive might be to join the cartel, where cartel members divide markets among themselves (Freiberg, 2020; Goncharov and Peter, 2019).

Threats are often noticed very late, both by individuals and by organizations. Handling threats thus becomes a matter of urgency. Individuals and firms "fail to detect threats and prevent calamities not because of an absence of signals or insufficient knowledge (or faulty awareness), but because attention bandwidth and information-processing fidelity are inherently limited" (Downing et al., 2019: 1890).

Convenience of Organizational Opportunity

High social status in privileged positions creates power inequality compared to those without any status in their positions. The perspective of power inequality suggests that, for example, family members in family firms wield significant influence in their firms (Patel and Cooper, 2014). Family members often have legitimate access to firm resources that nonfamily executives in the firm cannot question.

Individuals with high social status in privileged positions can cooperate to create a business climate of "organized irresponsibility" (Berghoff, 2018: 425):

> The term implies that management had conspired to prevent efficient controls and therefore facilitated and promoted corruption.

Leaders reinforce a culture of financial crime by ignoring criminal actions and otherwise facilitate unethical behavior. At the same time, they try to distance themselves from criminal actions (Pontell et al., 2021: 9):

> High status corporate criminals often go to great lengths to distance themselves from the crimes committed by their subordinates and to hide any incriminating evidence of their role in the decisions that authorized those criminal acts.

Dewan and Jensen (2020) studied high social status individuals in times of scandals that can change the role of status from being an asset to being a liability. They defined scandal as the disruptive publicity of misconduct, that is, a situation after detection and disclosure to the public. While the importance of status in convenience theory is related to prevention of blame before disclosure, Dewan and Jensen's (2020: 1657) research was concerned with status after disclosure:

> Because scandal diminishes the effectiveness of factors that make status an asset, status offers less protection during a scandal. At the same time that scandal decreases the protective benefits of status, the factors that make status a liability remain or are augmented.

Status can thus be a liability in the context of blaming, shaming, and labeling of misconduct and crime. High status creates high expectations that are seriously violated in a scandal. The disappointment causes an expectation of consequence for the person responsible for the disappointment.

For many white-collar offenders, there is not much challenge in committing financial crime. They typically have high status and access to relevant resources. The main challenge is often to conceal committed crime, where relevant issues are decay, chaos, and collapse as illustrated in Figure 2.1. Decay in the form of institutional deterioration improves conditions of convenience for crime concealment (Barton, 2004; Donk and Molloy, 2008). Institutional deterioration can occur conveniently, resulting from external legitimacy where deviance is the norm (Kostova et al., 2008; Pinto et al., 2008; Rodriguez et al., 2005). An offender's actions have a superficial appearance of legitimacy also internally, since both legal and illegal actions in the company occur in a manner characterized by disorganization (Benson and Simpson, 2018). Conventional mechanisms of social control are weak and unable to regulate the behavior within the organization (Pratt and Cullen, 2005). Concealment of crime occurs conveniently by simply disappearing among other seemingly legitimate transactions.

Social disorganization is the inability of an organization to realize common values of its members and maintain effective social control. Social disorganization implies that the ability of social bonds to reduce delinquent behavior is absent (Forti and Visconti, 2020; Hoffmann, 2002; Onna and Denkers, 2019). Differential reinforcement of crime convenience develops over time as individuals become vulnerable to various associations and definitions conducive to delinquency.

Social disorganization occurs because the human nature is selfish, and people are unwilling to share a common culture. In the perspective of life-courses with age-graded determinants of crime, it is interesting to notice that white-collar crime represents adult-onset offending. White-collar offenders are people who live more or less conventional law-abiding lives until they are adults and who then commit crime. Moving into the elite as an adult reduces social controls through social bonds (Benson and Chio, 2020).

Misconduct and crime can be hard to detect because signals of deviant behavior drown or disappear in noise (Gomulya and Mishina, 2017). Karim and Siegel (1998) define four possible outcomes in the decision matrix of an observer. First, the observer notices a noise signal when it is a crime signal (called a miss). Second, the observer notices a crime signal when it is a crime signal (called a hit). Third, the observer notices a noise signal when it is a noise signal (called a correct identification). Finally, the observer notices a crime signal when it is a noise signal (called a false alarm). The more frequent false alarms and misses occur, the greater the opportunity is successfully to conceal white-collar crime. Szalma and Hancock (2013) found that control functions typically have low signal alertness, and that such functions lack the ability to recognize and interpret patterns in signals. One reason might be that control functions have dysfunctional cognitive style and achievement motivation (Martinsen et al., 2016).

Misreporting in accounting is often a convenient way of concealing illegal transactions (Qiu and Slezak, 2019). Lack of transparency makes concealment in accounting convenient (Davidson et al., 2019; Goncharov and Peter, 2019). Managers can withhold bad news by accounting misrepresentation (Bao et al., 2019), since financial statements are a substantive component of a firm's communications with its stakeholders (Gupta et al., 2020). Balakrishnan et al. (2019) found that reduced corporate transparency in accounting is associated with increased corporate tax aggressiveness. Accounting fraud in terms of account manipulation is lacking transparency (Toolami et al., 2019).

Since accounting is no machine that can provide correct answers regarding the financial health of a company, since accounting information has limited representational properties, and since accounting cannot fully inform decision-makers (O'Leary and Smith, 2020), determination of final accounting figures are often left to the discretion of financial managers.

Concealing illegal transactions may result from the failure of auditors to do their job. Alon et al. (2019) argue that accounting and auditing functions have undergone a legitimacy crisis in recent years. Auditors are supposed to serve as gatekeepers to protect shareholders and other stakeholders, but deviant corporate management tend to hire and control auditors instead of letting auditors report to the board of directors or the supervisory board (Hurley et al., 2019). Skeptical auditors tend to be replaced by less skeptical auditors. Reporting fraud to public authorities will also harm auditors (Mohliver, 2019: 316):

> As organizations, audit firms are often severely penalized for client malfeasance. Yet the individual auditors working for these firms are susceptible to "motivated blindness" stemming from conflicts of interest that bias their moral judgment toward choices that help their clients.

Shadnam and Lawrence (2011) found that morale collapse increases the tendency to financial crime. In fact, repetition of criminal actions might institutionalize such actions (Hatch, 1997). Dion (2008) found that the larger the corporation, the less deterrence effect from laws on financial crime, which may have to do with increased convenience in concealing crime.

Lack of oversight and guardianship causes chaos. The agency perspective suggests that a principal is often unable to control an agent who does work for the principal. The agency perspective assumes narrow self-interest among both principals and agents. The interests of principal and agent tend to diverge, they may have different risk willingness or risk aversion, there is knowledge asymmetry between the two parties, and the principal has imperfect information about the agent's contribution (Bosse and Phillips, 2016; Chrisman et al., 2007; Pillay and Kluvers, 2014; Williams, 2008). According to principal-agent analysis, exchanges can encourage illegal gain for both principal and agent.

Concealing crime is convenient also because others than the offender is incapable of making sense of actions that have occurred (Weick, 1995). People tend to trust what an elite member does, based on the authority position occupied by the offender. Sense making links to crime signal detection by the challenge of perceiving and understanding a crime signal versus a noise signal, as discussed above. People without experience are unable to make sense of weak signals from white-collar offenders. They are not able to frame or categorize through words what the signal is about (Holt and Cornelissen, 2014). Even when crime signals are reported to the criminal justice system, police detectives are often unable to successfully investigate financial crime (Gilmour, 2020).

Convenience of Deviance Willingness

As illustrated in Figure 2.1, the willingness for deviant behavior derives from choice and innocence in convenience theory. White-collar crime can be the result of a choice based on identity, rationality, and learning, and white-collar crime can be the result of innocence based on justification and neutralization. Personal willingness for deviant behavior implies a positive attitude towards violating social norms, including formally enacted laws, rules, and regulations (Aguilera et al., 2018).

The personality trait of narcissism expects preferential treatment. A pervasive pattern of grandiosity, a need for admiration, and an empathy deficit characterize narcissism. Narcissistic identification is a special type of narcissism, where the offender sees little or no difference between self and the corporation. The company money is personal money that can be spent whatever way the narcissist prefers (Galvin et al., 2015). While grandiosity and admiration belong to the motivational dimension of convenience theory, empathy deficit belongs to the willingness dimension of convenience theory where the offender possesses a sense of entitlement (Nichol, 2019). The offender shows unreasonable expectations to receive and obtain preferential treatments (Zvi and Elaad, 2018).

The choice of crime might derive from sensation seeking. Craig and Piquero (2017) suggest that the willingness to commit financial crime by some white-collar offenders has to do with their inclination for adventure and excitement. Offenders are not only seeking new, intense, and complicated experiences and sensations, as well as exciting adventures, they are also accepting the legal, physical, financial, and social risks associated with these adventures.

Learning from others by differential association was introduced by Sutherland (1983), who coined the term white-collar crime several decades earlier. The differential association perspective suggests that offenders associate with those who agree with them, and distance themselves from those who disagree. The choice of crime is thus caused by social learning from others with whom offenders associate (Akers, 1985).

Innocent justification can occur as the offender feels entitled to financial crime after negative life events (Engdahl, 2015). The perspective of negative life events suggests that events such as divorce, accident, lack of promotion, and cash problems can cause potential offenders to consider white-collar crime a convenient solution.

By application of neutralization techniques (Sykes and Matza, 1957), they deny responsibility, injury, and victim. They condemn the condemners. They claim appeal to higher loyalties and normality of action. They claim entitlement, and they argue the case of legal mistake. They find their own mistakes acceptable. They argue a dilemma arose, whereby they made a reasonable tradeoff before committing the act (Jordanoska, 2018; Kaptein and Helvoort, 2019; Siponen and Vance, 2010). Such claims enable offenders to find crime convenient, since they do not consider it crime, and they do not feel guilty of wrongdoing. These are the most frequently cited neutralization techniques in the research literature for white-collar offenders:

1. *Disclaim responsibility for crime: Not responsible for what happened.* The offender here claims that one or more of the conditions of responsible agency did not occur. The person committing a deviant act defines himself or herself as lacking responsibility for his or her actions. In this technique, the person rationalizes that the action in question is beyond his or her control. The offender views himself as a billiard ball, helplessly propelled through different situations. He denies responsibility for the event or sequence of events.

2. *Refuse damage from crime: There is no visible harm from the action.* The offender seeks to minimize or deny the harm done. Denial of injury involves justifying an action by minimizing the harm it causes. The misbehavior is not very serious because no party suffers directly or visibly because of it.

3. *Refuse victim from crime: There is nobody suffering from the action.* The offender may acknowledge the injury but deny any existence of victims or claims that the victim(s) are unworthy of concern. Any blame for illegal actions are unjustified because the violated party deserves whatever injury they receive.

4. *Condemn those who criticize: Outsiders do not understand relevant behavior.* The offender tries to accuse his or her critics of questionable motives for criticizing him or her. According to this technique of condemning the condemners, one neutralizes own actions by blaming those who were the target of the misconduct. The offender deflects moral condemnation onto those ridiculing the misbehavior by pointing out that they engage in similar disapproved behavior. In addition, the offender condemns procedures of the criminal justice system, especially police investigation with interrogation, as well as media coverage of the case.

5. *Justify crime by higher loyalties: It was according to expectations.* The offender denies the act was motivated by self-interest, claiming that it was instead done out of obedience to some moral obligation. The offender appeals to higher loyalties. Those who feel they are in a dilemma employ this technique to indicate that the dilemma must be resolved at the cost of violating a law or policy. In the context of an organization, an employee may appeal to organizational

values or hierarchies. For example, an executive could argue that he or she has to violate a policy in order to get things done and achieve strategic objectives for the enterprise.

6. *Claim blunder quota: It was a necessary shortcut to get things done.* The offender argues that what he or she did is acceptable given the situation and given his or her position. The person feels that after having done so much good for so many for so long time, others should excuse him or her for more wrongdoings than other people deserve forgiveness. Others should understand that the alleged crime was an acceptable mistake. This is in line with the metaphor of the ledger, which uses the idea of compensating bad acts by good acts. That is, the individual believes that he or she has previously performed a number of good acts and has accrued a surplus of good will, and, because of this, can afford to commit some bad actions. Executives in corporate environments neutralize their actions through the metaphor of the ledger by rationalizing that their overall past good behavior justifies occasional rule breaking.

7. *Claim legal mistake: This should never pop up as illegal in the first place.* The offender argues that the law is wrong, and what the person did should indeed not pop up as illegal. One may therefore break the law since the law is unreasonable, unfair, and unjustified. The offender may argue that lawmakers sometimes criminalize behaviors and sometimes decriminalize more or less randomly over time. For example, money involved in bribing people were treated as legal expenses in accounting some decades ago, while corruption today is considered a misconduct and therefore criminalized.

8. *Claim normality of action: Everyone else does and would do the same.* The offender argues that it is so common to commit the offense, so that it one can hardly define it as an offense at all. The offense is no deviant behavior since most people do it or would do it in the same situation. The offender might even suggest that what may constitute deviant behavior is when people in the same situation obey the law.

9. *Claim entitlement to action: It is sometimes a required behavior in this position.* The offender claims to be in his right to do what he did, perhaps because of a very stressful situation or because of some misdeed perpetrated by the victim. This is defense of necessity, which is a kind of justification that if the rule breaking seems necessary in the mind of the offender, one should feel no guilt when carrying out the action.

10. *Claim solution to dilemma: The benefits of action outweigh costs.* The offender argues a dilemma arose whereby he or she made a reasonable tradeoff before committing the act. Tradeoff between many interests therefore resulted in the offense. A dilemma represents a state of mind in which it is not obvious for an offender what is right and what is wrong to do. For example, the criminal carries out the offense to prevent what seems to be a more serious offense from happening.

11. *Justify necessity of crime: It was necessary to carry out the offense.* The offender claims that the offense belongs into a larger picture in a comprehensive context, where the crime is an illegal element among many legal elements to ensure an important result. The offense was a required and necessary means to achieve an important goal. For example, a bribe represents nothing in dollar value compared to the potential income from a large contract abroad. Alternatively, a temporary misrepresentation of accounts could help save the company and thousands of jobs.

12. *Claim role in society: It is a natural maneuver among elite members.* The offender argues that being a minister in the government or a chief executive officer in a global company is so time-consuming that little time is available for issues that seem trivial. Shortcuts are part of the game. Some shortcuts may be illegal, but they are nevertheless necessary for the elite member to ensure progress. If someone is to blame, then subordinates are supposed to provide advice and control what the elite member is doing.

13. *Perceive being victim of incident: Others have ruined my life.* The incident leads to police investigation, prosecution, and possible jail sentence. Media is printing pictures of the offender on the front page, and gains from crime disappear as public authorities conduct asset recovery without considering the harm caused to the offender. Previous colleagues and friends have left, and so has the family. The offender perceives being a loser and made victim of those who reacted to his crime after disclosure.

14. *Gather support: Nobody thinks it is wrong.* Most colleagues, friends, and others in the upper echelon of society think what the offender did, is quite acceptable. The supporters communicate to the public, the media, and others that it is ridiculous that the offender becomes subject to police investigation and eventually subject to prosecution and conviction. The supporters argue that it is completely misleading to portrait the white-collar offender as a criminal. The supporters may suggest that the offender was unlucky and made an unintentional mistake. They may argue that in the eyes of the public, the offense can emerge as misconduct, but certainly not crime. The offender potentially made a shortcut for very good reasons, which is tolerable and not objectionable. Given such massive support from those who condemn the criminal justice system, the offender gathers support that cause a fundamental reduction in his or her potentially guilty mind. The guilty mind may further deteriorate as the offender hires top defense attorneys who tell the offender that it is the state or someone else who, without any acceptable or plausible reason, is out there to catch him or her for an act that certainly was no crime.

15. *Claim rule complexity*: It is impossible to understand what is right and what is wrong. Some laws, rules and regulations are so complex that compliance is random. The regulatory legal environment is supposed to define the boundaries of appropriate organizational conduct. However, legal complexity is often so

extreme that even specialist compliance officers struggle to understand what to recommend to business executives in the organization.

Lehman et al. (2019: 6) define rule complexity in terms of components and connections:

> First, a rule is more complex to the extent that it comprises more components that together describe the actions and outcomes necessary for compliance. A rule with a high number of components contains more detail and requires more actions to constitute compliance. Second, a rule is more complex to the extent that it has more connections to or functional dependencies upon other rules in the same system. A rule with a high number of connections refers to actions or outcomes that may be affected by activities pertaining to another rule or set of rules.

Neutralizations are not merely after-the-fact rationalizations where offenders can live with and accept what they have done. Neutralizations imply a deterministic or causal relationship available before the offense takes place. The use of neutralization techniques function as a means of making it possible to commit violations while at the same time reducing a guilt feeling (Cohen, 2001). When potential offenders apply neutralization techniques in advance of potential criminal actions, then their willingness for criminal behaviors might increase. A simple example is speeding on the highway, where the offender can drive to fast because of neutralizations such as everyone else does it, there is something wrong with the speed limit, or nobody will get hurt anyway. Neutralizations ahead of a criminal act protect the offender from harm to his or her self-image.

Dynamics of White-Collar Convenience

Figure 2.2 presents the dynamic model of convenience theory. The model has the same elements as the structural model of convenience theory in Figure 2.1. Just like in Figure 2.1, Figure 2.2 breaks down financial motive into individual and corporate possibilities as well as individual and corporate threats. The model breaks down organizational opportunity into committing crime and concealing crime, where the convenience to commit crime is dependent on privileged status and access to resources, while the convenience to conceal crime is dependent on functional decay, oversight chaos and external collapse. The model breaks down personal willingness into crime choice and crime innocence, where crime choice is dependent on deviant identity, rational decision, and deviant learning, while crime innocence is dependent on justification and neutralization.

Figure 2.2 illustrates causal relationships in the dynamic model. An arrow represents a cause-and-effect relationship. For example, a stronger financial motive can cause initiatives for organizational opportunity expansion. On the other hand, a greater organizational opportunity for white-collar crime can make the financial motive stronger. Similarly, when the personal willingness for deviant behavior is higher, then organizational opportunity expansion might occur. On the other hand, a greater organizational opportunity can cause a higher personal willingness. Motive might be stronger or weaker; opportunity might be greater or smaller, while willingness might be higher or lower.

All causal relationships in Figure 2.2 are positive in the system dynamics sense of the word, which means that one increase causes another increase, while one decrease causes another decrease (Randers, 2019; Sterman, 2018). It is thus a change in the same direction from the cause to the effect in the relationship. For example, as stated above, an increase in financial motive can cause an increase in organizational opportunity, while a decrease in financial motive can cause a decrease in organizational opportunity. Similarly, an increase in personal willingness can cause an increase in organizational opportunity, while a decrease in personal willingness can cause a decrease in organizational opportunity.

In the system dynamics terminology (Randers, 2019; Sterman, 2018), financial motive, organizational opportunity, and personal willingness are endogenous variables, as they influence and are influenced by other variables in the dynamic model. In addition, to commit crime and to conceal crime represents endogenous variables in the model, as the convenience to commit crime might increase the convenience to conceal crime, and vice versa. Similarly, crime choice and crime innocence are endogenous variables in the model, as a stronger willingness to choose crime can influence the ability to justify crime, while the ability to justify crime can influence crime as a choice. All other themes in the model in Figure 2.2 are endogenous variables, as they only influence other variables without other variables influencing them.

It is possible to follow causal paths in Figure 2.2. For example, a change in the privileged status of potential offenders causes change in the convenience to commit crime, which in turn represents a change in organizational opportunity, which in turn causes a change in personal willingness, and so forth. If the privileged position of a potential offender increases, for example by enjoying sole and exclusive access to all financial transactions, then the organizational opportunity to commit crime increases, which in turn might strengthen the personal willingness to become an offender.

The dynamic model of convenience theory in Figure 2.2 has several causal loops. Either a causal loop can be reinforcing as a positive feedback loop, or it can be stabilizing as a negative feedback loop. All loops in the figure are positive loops. For example, when the financial motive becomes stronger, then the organizational opportunity increases, which causes the motive to become even stronger. Another example is the loop including all three dimensions: The financial motive strengthens, the organizational opportunity increases, the personal willingness becomes higher, and the financial motive becomes even stronger. Furthermore, in Figure 2.2 there is a positive loop involving committing crime and concealing crime, as well as

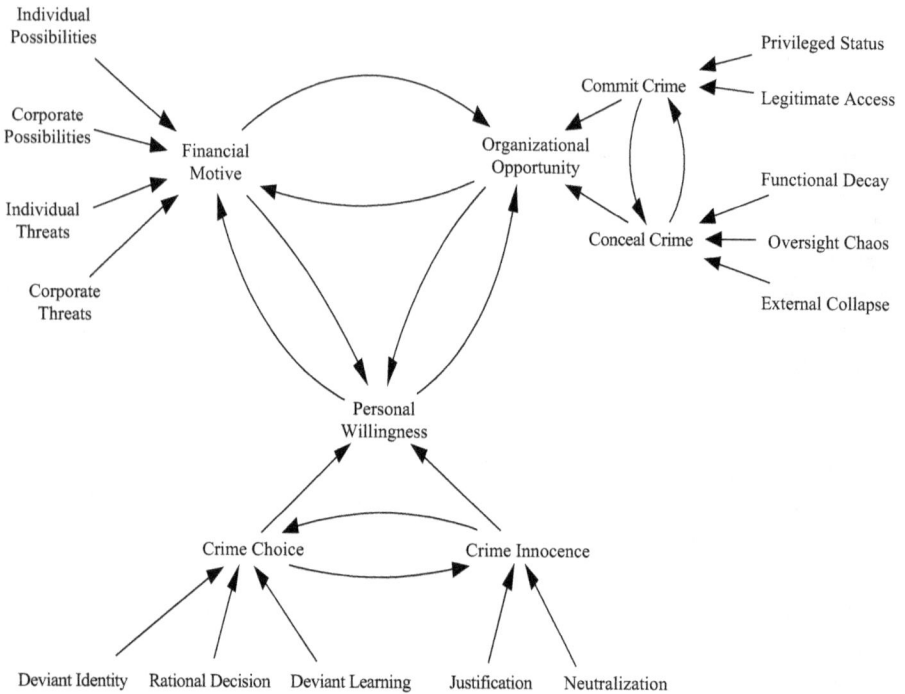

Figure 2.2: Dynamic model of convenience theory.

a positive loop between crime choice and crime convenience. The assumption is that increased convenience in committing crime will link to an increased convenience in concealing crime, while an increased willingness to choose crime will link to an increased ability to feel innocent.

In the model in Figure 2.2, several factors are modeled as exogeneous variables, while they might in themselves represent dynamics if modeled as endogenous variables. An example is oversight chaos created by social disorganization. The social disorganization perspective argues that crime is a function of people dynamics in the organization and between organizations, especially weak social controls, and not necessarily a function of each individual within such organizations (Forti and Visconti, 2020; Hoffmann, 2002; Pratt and Cullen, 2005),

In a detection perspective, financial motives, organizational opportunities, as well as personal willingness make observation and monitoring more or less impossible. However, over time the extent of trust versus controls of executives and others in privileged positions might change. Reduction in trust implies that vulnerability receives minor acceptance based on positive expectations of the motives and actions of another (Dearden, 2016, 2017, 2019). Abuses of trust are easier to detect when the level of trust decreases and the level of suspicion increases.

Social Conflict Perspectives

Violations of laws regarding corruption, cartels, money laundering, environmental pollution, worker safety, and other offenses by corporations can be characterized by convenience for the offending organizations. There are convenient financial gains to be made, there are convenient organizational opportunities to commit and conceal crime, and there is convenient willingness for deviant behavior by executives in corporations. In many jurisdictions, the criminal justice system is reluctant to prosecute and convict corporations as they are not held liable for harm and damage. Sometimes, individual executives are held liable and have to leave the corporation so that the organizations can continue in the same line of doing business. The reluctance becomes particularly evident when there is state-corporate crime, where the state either initiates or facilitates corporate wrongdoing.

In capitalistic societies with a market economy, the role of the state is both to stimulate and to regulate activities of business enterprises. Corporations provide goods and services to people, and they provide jobs and thus income to people. Attractive business opportunities have to be in place to stimulate investors and entrepreneurs to create and develop enterprises that operate on the markets. The problem of crime arises when people think that what corporations do is wrong and should be punished. When corporations are punished financially, they try to compensate by defrauding customers. For example, when corrupt telecom corporations are caught and punished for corruption, then they might attempt to compensate by raising their mobile phone charges to customers. When cartel members are caught and punished for illegal market manipulation, then they might attempt to compensate by firing subordinates to become more efficient.

The phenomenon of state ambivalence and reluctance towards corporate crime can be understood in the perspective of social conflicts. This perspective suggests that the powerful in society define what is right and what is wrong. The mighty people and corporations can behave like robber barons because they make the laws and because they control law enforcement. The ruling class does not consider white-collar offenses as regular crime, and certainly not similar to street crime. Nevertheless, individuals in the elite and small businesses committing crime tend to be prosecuted if crime is detected and evidence of wrongdoing is present, as long as they are not too powerful and do not have too excellent defense attorneys.

Social conflict theory views financial crime as a function of the conflict that exists in society. The theory suggests that class conflict causes crime in any society, and that those in power create laws to protect their rights and interests. For example, embezzlement by employees is as a violation of law to protect the interests of the employer. However, it might be argued that an employer must and should protect own assets. Bank fraud is a crime to protect the powerful banking sector. However, in the perspective of conflict theory one might argue that a bank should have systems making bank fraud impossible. If an employee has no opportunity to commit embezzlement, and if a fraudster has no opportunity to commit bank fraud, then these kinds of financial crime would not occur, and there would be no need to have laws against such offenses. Law enforcement protects powerful companies against counterfeit products, although they should be able to protect themselves by reducing opportunities for the production of counterfeit products.

Social conflict theory holds that laws and law enforcement are used by dominant groups in society to minimize threats to their interests posed by those whom they perceive as dangerous and greedy. Crime is defined by legal codes and sanctioned by institutions of criminal justice to secure order in society. The ruling class secures order in the ruled class by means of laws and law enforcement. Conflicts and clashes between interest groups are restrained and stabilized by law enforcement.

According to social conflict theory, the justice system is biased and designed to protect the wealthy and powerful. The wealthy and powerful can take substantial assets out of their own companies at their own discretion whenever they like, although employed workers in the companies were the ones who created the values. The superrich can exploit their own wealth that they created as owners of corporations as long as they do not hurt other shareholders. Employees have no right to object. It is no crime to take out values from own enterprises and build private mansions for the money. This is no crime by the owners. Even when the owners just inherited the wealth created by earlier generations, they can dispose freely of it for private consumption. Similarly, top executives who are on each other's corporate boards grant each other salaries that are ten or twenty times higher than regular employee salaries. As Haines (2014: 21) puts it, "financial practices that threaten corporate interests, such as embezzlement, are clearly identified as criminal even as obscenely high salaries remain relatively untouched by regulatory controls". Furthermore, sharp practices such as insider trading that threaten confidence in equities markets have enjoyed vigorous prosecution, since the powerful see them as opaque transactions that give an unfair advantage to those who are not members of the market institutions.

Karl Marx, who analyzed capitalism and suggested the transition to socialism and ultimately to communism, created the basis for social conflict theorizing. Capitalism is an economic system in which persons privately own trade, industries, firms, shops, and means of production and operate these enterprises or profit. Socialism is an economic system characterized by cooperative enterprises, common ownership, and state ownership. Communism is a socioeconomic system structured upon the common ownership of the means of production and characterized by the absence of social classes.

Marxist criminology views the competitive nature of the capitalist system as a major cause of financial crime. It focuses on what creates stability and continuity in society, and it adopts a predefined political philosophy. Marxist criminology focuses on why things change by identifying the disruptive forces in capitalist societies, and describing how power, wealth, prestige, and perceptions of the world divide every society. The economic struggle is the central venue for the Marxists. Marx divided society into two unequal classes and demonstrated the inequality in the historical transition from patrician and slave to capitalist and wage worker. It is the rulers versus the ruled. Marx also underlined that all societies have a certain hierarchy wherein the higher class has more privileges than the lower one. In a capitalist society, where economic resources equate to power, it is in the interest of the ascendant class to maintain economic stratification in order to dictate the legal order.

Then the question emerges: Despite all privileges of the ruling class and the ruling corporations, why do they sometimes punish their own?

Reason 1: Reduce Conflict. Since white-collar crime is crime by the wealthy and powerful, it seems to contradict social conflict theory. There are no reasons why the wealthy and powerful would like to see laws that turn their own actions into regular criminal offences. When Sutherland (1939) first coined the term "white-collar crime", there were indeed reactions in the audience of upper-class people. They asked why one should define actions by privileged individuals of the influential classes as crime at the level of street crime by ordinary criminals. According to Brightman (2009), Sutherland's theory of white-collar crime first presented in 1939 was controversial, particularly since many of the academics in the audience perceived themselves to be members of the upper echelon in American society. The audience was the American Sociological Association where Sutherland gave his address and first presented his theory of white-collar crime. What Podgor (2007) found to be the most interesting aspect of Sutherland's work is that a scholar needed to proclaim that crime of the upper socio-economic class is in fact crime that should be prosecuted. It is apparent that prior to the coining of the term "white-collar crime", wealth, and power allowed many persons to escape criminal liability.

Veblen's (1899) sociological study of the "leisured classes" and their rapacious conspicuous consumption had an influence on Sutherland's (1939) research. Josephson (1962) who coined the term "robber barons" in the 1930ties was also an influential scholar at that time. Therefore, Sutherland's work on white-collar crime seems to fit with conflict theory, where he might have seen a need to reduce the level of conflict in society by defining obvious unjustified misconduct by privileged individuals as regular crime. This is in line with Arrigo and Bernard (1997), who apply conflict theory to explain initiatives for more prosecution of white-collar criminals. Seron and Munger (1996: 187) quoted that "The plain fact is that in a new stage of capitalism, class divides as ruthlessly as it did in the age of the Robber Barons."

Reason 2: Government Influence. Another reason for starting to define capitalists and other persons of respectability and high social status as regular criminals when they abuse their powers for personal or organizational profit is the need of governments to gain some kind of control over the business sector and the market economy. Business and professional elites had achieved political influence beyond what most democratic governments found acceptable. Even worse, some enterprises were so powerful that they became almost untouchable for government interventions. They were too powerful to fail, and too powerful to jail (Pontell et al., 2014).

Criminological attention on the activities of business enterprises and other organizations, their creativity and power, remains in a conflict with political influence of business executives, capitalists, and members of the professional elites. Haines (2014: 20) discusses corporate fraud as an example, where she argues that:

> Criminalization of corporate fraud deflects attention to one of these actors, the business and its directors, without clear recognition of the role played by government itself.

Haines (2014) argues that governments critically, in close consultation with the professions, enact legal and regulatory reforms that engender confidence in both the accuracy of accounts and materiality of money while also further institutionalizing their underlying ambiguities. Hence, even as governments are excited to sanction corporate criminals with more vigor, they are at the same time implicated in the creation of corporate criminals. Corporate fraud implies that there has been a criminal misrepresentation of a financial or business state of affairs by one or more individuals for financial gain, where banks, shareholders, and tax authorities are among the victims. Yet, misrepresentation is a matter of opinion rather than accuracy. For example, estimating values of products in stock is no exact science. If nobody wants to buy products in stock, they have no value. While governments work at arm's length through external auditors, law enforcement is reluctant to prosecute unless misrepresentation of the value of a business is completely out of range.

Reason 3: "Our" Laws. A third reason for the prosecution of the wealthy and powerful individuals and corporations is that their own laws did not intend to target members of their own class. The lawmakers had others in society in mind. Caught by surprise, that members of their own class violate their own laws, leads the ruling class to turn laws against their own allies. When those allies demonstrate non-conforming and deviant behavior, others in the ruling class take on the task of prosecuting deviating members of the elite. "As we are reminded today, those who make the laws don't have the right to break the laws", Richard Frankel, the specialist agent in charge of the Criminal Division of the New York office of the Federal Bureau of Investigation, said at a news conference.

FBI held its news conference as Sheldon Silver, the speaker of the State Assembly in New York, faced prosecution for corruption. State prosecutors charged Silver with having exploited his position as one of the most powerful politicians in the state of New York to obtain millions of dollars in bribes and kickbacks. Prosecutors accused Silver's law practice of being a fiction where the sources of large payments of bribes were hiding (Rashbaum and Kaplan, 2015: A24). Silver was arrested on

Manhattan on a five-count indictment in January 2015. US attorney Preet Bharara alleged that the Manhattan democrat used New York's ethics laws to hide his scheme – allowing him to become wealthy off his position in power (Spector, 2015).

Silver resigned a few weeks later as speaker (McKinley, 2015). At the same time, Malcolm A. Smith, a former majority leader of the New York State Senate, was convicted of federal corruption charges including bribery, wire fraud, and extortion (Vega, 2015).

Reason 4: Deviant Behavior. A fourth reason might be disappointment within the ruling class. The ruling class in society faces decisions over which values to enforce. When individuals in their own upper-level class violate some of these values, then the majority defines it as a crime. Those who violate values of fair competition among capitalists and market access, for example, are potential criminals, even if they belong to the same class as those condemning them.

President George W. Bush's connections to Enron and CEO Kenneth Lay were well documented in major American newspapers. However, when Enron emerged as a deviant organization with a bad apple CEO, Lay and other top executives were prosecuted. Lay died of a heart attack before his conviction (Bendiktsson, 2010).

Reason 5: Crime Victims. A fifth and final reason might be the victim of crime. If the victim of white-collar crime were another person in the upper class, then the ruling class would like to protect that person. Victimization of upper-class members by other upper-class members can be considered a crime. Upper-class members need protection against deviant individuals in their own class. It is an inter-group conflict in the dominant class (Wheelock et al., 2011). Maybe Madoff can serve as an example. Rich Jews placed their money in Madoff's investment fund with the promise and expectation that the rate of return would be extraordinarily good. Instead, they lost their money. Wealthy people were victims of Madoff's Ponzi scheme. The government had to sanction such behavior by Madoff, and he received a record prison sentence of 150 years (Ragothaman, 2014).

3 Corporate Deviance Accounts

Corporations occasionally find themselves mired in scandals that threaten their reputation, profitability, and even survival (Fisse and Braithwaite, 1988; Goldstraw-White, 2012; Gottschalk and Benson, 2020; Piazza and Jourdan, 2018). For example, cartels (Goncharov and Peter, 2019), tax evasion (Balakrishnan et al. 2019; Dyreng et al. 2019; Guenther et al. 2019), misleading disclosure to investors (Jennings, 2019), or other forms of misrepresentation in accounting (Albrecht et al., 2001; Qiu and Slezak, 2019) can cause financial crime scandals. There is obviously a violation of ethics and lack of corporate social responsibility (Davidson et al. 2019), and scandals are often revealed after whistleblowing (Gao et al., 2015; Gao and Zhang, 2019).

A corporate scandal is "an unexpected, publicly known, and harmful event that has high levels of initial uncertainty, interferes with the normal operations of an organization, and generates widespread, intuitive, and negative perceptions" externally (Bundy and Pfarrer, 2015: 350). A scandal is a publicized instance of transgression that runs counter to social norms, typically resulting in condemnation and discredit and other consequences such as bad press, disengagement of key constituencies, the severance of network ties, and decrease in key performance indicators (Piazza and Jourdan, 2018). A scandal can be an act of elite deviance that might include financial, physical and morally harmful behavior committed by privileged members of the organization and potentially in cooperation with the state (Roth, 2020).

In attempting to respond to and manage these crises, corporations and their executives develop and publicize explanations of their involvement that are designed to forestall or at least mitigate the potential risks to reputation, profitability, and sustainability that exposure of a scandal poses (Bundy and Pfarrer, 2015; Scott and Lyman, 1968; Whyte, 2016). The explanation for a scandal that a corporation puts out technically constitutes what linguists and sociologists call an account, which is a statement made by an actor to explain unanticipated or untoward behavior that is subject to some sort of evaluative inquiry by other actors (Scott and Lyman, 1968). While there is no shortage of advice from public relations experts as crisis managers regarding how accounts should be structured (see, for example, Albrecht, 1996; Hearit, 2006), there has been relatively little research on the actual accounts developed by corporations during actual scandals (Huisman 2010; Schoultz and Flyghed, 2016). Further, there has been even less research on how such accounts may change over time (Schoultz and Flyghed, 2019a). Understanding corporate accounts is important because of the devastating social and economic effects that failed accounts can have on communities that depend on successful corporations for employment, tax revenues, charitable activities and other community enhancing benefits. It is equally important to understand the other side of the coin, that is, how corporations manage to survive

https://doi.org/10.1515/9783110766950-004

scandals even though they sometimes impose tremendous social and economic harm on society.

Emerging Corporate Scandals

When scandals first emerge into public view, corporations often do not fully understand them as negative events, as there is uncertainty regarding exactly what happened, the potential significance of the events, and how stakeholders and outside observers will respond to it. Most importantly, there is a concern whether an individual or the corporation as a whole will face responsibility and sanctions (Bandura, 1999; Schoultz and Flyghed, 2016). Scandals have become a key mechanism used by news media, pressure groups and social movements to demand inquiries and investigations into alleged corruption, incompetence, and immorality.

A corporation knows that media coverage is important in shaping public perceptions of the organization, including stakeholder perceptions (Gamache and McNamara, 2019: 921):

> The media has become society's dominant information provider and plays an important role in directing public attention.

According to Greer and McLaughlin (2017), existing research indicates that scandals can have a corrosive impact on the reputational standing, credibility and legitimacy of organizations. Scandals thus represent crises for involved organizations, executives, and offenders.

Benson (2019) argues that corporate responses to criminal allegations usually involve attempts to either deny any wrongdoing, or employ neutralizations as a way to explain their activities:

> Typically, it is the officers and directors of the firm who attempt to justify the corporation's actions to the public, the media, their shareholders, and if necessary, even before the court. These exercises in corporate self-defense are aimed at protecting the corporation's image and legitimacy and belong to a broader category of offender neutralizations and denials. Furthermore, these corporate neutralizations and denials of harm and wrongdoing can be allowed and aided by state actors, for example, through allowing a firm to pay a hefty fine, yet admits to no wrongdoing or through enabling/allowing corporate harm via de-regulation.

Protecting corporate image and image repair is a key focus in many scandalized corporations. For example, Demaline (2021) found that managers commonly employ multiple image repair tactics during U.S. Securities and Exchange Commission (SEC) investigations. Management's disclosure concerning an SEC investigation frequently focuses on adding positive information to the disclosure (bolstering) and discussing plans to solve the problem.

Some organizations attempt to conduct business as usual after corporate white-collar scandals (Bittle and Hébert, 2020; Dodge, 2020; Francis and Ryer, 2020;

Huisman, 2020; Wingerde and Lord, 2020). These companies do whatever it takes to defend themselves against accusations of misconduct and crime. Some organizations attempt to reconstruct the business and align their defense strategies, accordingly, as was the case at Siemens in Germany (Eberl et al., 2015). Corporate crime "can be defined as illegal acts or omissions that are the result of deliberate decision-making or culpable negligence within a legitimate formal organization and are committed on behalf of the corporation, or in pursuit of its formal goals" (Tombs and Whyte, 2020).

In Sweden, Schoultz and Flyghed (2016) found that Swedish transnational corporations neutralize allegations of crime. Their examples are TeliaSonera telecommunications and Lundin petroleum, which both neutralized by appeal to higher loyalties. Both corporations tried to explain why they had been doing illegitimate business despite the risks that this had involved.

Some organizations adapt their communications to what they believe is already known about the scandal. This approach is similar to suspects in police interrogations, where defense lawyers help suspects tell only those parts of the story that seem beneficial to the accused, and that already seem known to the counterpart. As corporate officers over time notice that more information about the scandal is leaking to stakeholders and the public, then corporate spokespersons may adapt their communicated accounts accordingly.

This book frames corporate white-collar crime scandals in a time perspective. The scandal starts with detection, for example when a whistleblower alerts internally or externally about observations of misconduct and crime. The scandal evolves into an investigation, for example, when the scandalized corporation hires fraud examiners to conduct an internal investigation. The scandal continues with blame games and departure of blamed executives. In the end of the scandal, reconstruction of the organization occurs, where the new board introduces change management measures that need implementation (Trullen et al., 2020), as was the case at Siemens in Germany (Eberl et al., 2015). Alternatively, the corporation collapses, as was the case at Enron in the United States (Williams, 2008).

Emerging Corporate Accounts

Corporations sometimes hire fraud examiners from local law firms and global auditing firms when financial scandals emerge (Gottschalk and Benson, 2020). Reports of investigations by fraud examiners are an important source of information regarding corporate accounts after scandals (Brooks and Button, 2011; Button et al., 2007a, 2007b; Button and Gee, 2013; Schneider, 2006; Williams, 2005, 2014). At the end of their inquiry, fraud examiners write a report of investigation and hand it over to the client organization as their property. Unfortunately, most client organizations keep reports secret and confidential, and they are not willing to make them publicly available (Gottschalk and Tcherni-Buzzeo, 2017).

This research was able to find and retrieve thirteen reports from Canada, Denmark, Japan, New Zealand, Nigeria, Norway, Sweden, and most from the United States that all are concerned with executive deviance related to financial scandals. In the reports, we searched for corporate accounts as communicated explanations, justifications and excuses for wrongdoing. Furthermore, we studied accounts as they evolved from exposure of corporate scandals in the media to internal fraud investigations. We were also interested in the destiny of executives who received blame for deviance. Termination of eleven out of thirteen executives occurred before and after reports of investigations became public.

Deviance is "the failure to obey group rules" (Becker, 1963: 8). Deviance is "a form of behavior that violates organizational norms and that consequently negatively impacts the well-being of the organization and its members" (Michalak and Ashkanasy, 2013: 20). Deviance is detrimental to organizational performance in several ways, including damaged reputation, exposure to lawsuits, and financial loss (Dilchert et al., 2007).

This chapter addresses the issue of how accounts based on neutralizations and justifications evolve over time as events from exposure of a corporate scandal move along. We are comparing corporations' initial reactions to exposure of wrongdoings to what is later contained in internal reports of investigations that they commission. We discuss the function of corporate neutralization techniques and argue that corporate accounts can mediate action over time. We study accounts that corporations communicate after the fact, that is afterwards to excuse or justify offenses.

For example, Whyte (2016) found that Chrysler, Toyota, and Volkswagen all communicated accounts initially that were based upon the systematic deception of the public and systematic attempts to resist any recall to safeguard customers. Schoultz and Flyghed (2016) found that Telia Sonera and Lundin Petroleum both communicated accounts implying appeal to higher loyalties. Both of these Swedish companies framed their communications that while they were present in areas where financial and environmental crime occurs, they justified their presence by the societal benefits of their business activities. The initial account from Wells Fargo after the sales practices scandal at their Community Bank was that the bank had fired 5,300 employees for secretly opening unauthorized deposit and credit card accounts (Rothacker, 2016).

In addition to the dynamic nature of accounts after corporate scandals, we are also looking at the outcomes of these scandals in terms of the employment of the corporate leaders. In 2014, following a report from a whistleblower and internal audit letters, it became clear that money laundering of criminal proceeds from Russia occurred in Danske Bank's Estonian branch. At about the same time, the board promoted Thomas Borgen to the position of chief executive officer (CEO) at the Danish bank, despite the fact that he was responsible for the Estonian branch and some other bank divisions in his previous position at the bank. When the Estonian scandal reached the public and politicians, the board felt obligated to start an internal investigation and hired Danish law firm Bruun Hjejle to conduct a fraud examination. Four years later, when Bruun Hjejle (2018) presented their report of investigation, Borgen had to resign as the CEO at the bank (Milne and Binham, 2018). The following year, Danish prosecutors charged ex-Danske Bank CEO Thomas Borgen over the Estonia case (Milne, 2019a). The body of Danske Bank's former Estonian chief Aivar Rehe, who was at the heart of the € 200 billion money-laundering scandal, was "found dead in an apparent suicide" in September 2019 (Milne, 2019b).

In this chapter, we present thirteen reports of investigations by fraud examiners as our empirical basis to identify accounts of corporate scandals. In a perspective of time, fraud examiners conduct their internal investigations after the exposure of a corporate scandal and before potential cases in the criminal justice system.

The chapter starts by describing corporate accounts, followed by the research method of content analysis of investigation reports (Bell et al., 2018; Berg, 2007; Bernard, 2002; Hsieh and Shannon, 2005; Krippendorff, 1980; McClelland et al., 2010; Patrucco et al., 2017; Saunders et al., 2007). Next, we use one of the thirteen cases in detail to illustrate accounts at public exposure and later accounts by fraud examiners. The case is concerned with inappropriate sales practices at Wells Fargo's Community Bank (Rothacker, 2016; Shearman Sterling, 2017; Wieczner, 2017). Then this chapter presents research results for all thirteen cases. In the following chapter 2, the same set of thirteen cases illustrates the extent of match and mismatch in corporate responses compared to situational attributions for the scandals.

From Exposure to Investigation

An account is a form of speech for explanations of negative events that the corporation wants to communicate. An account is a statement made to explain unanticipated or untoward behavior (Scott and Lyman, 1968). There are two general forms of accounts: (1) justifications and (2) excuses. In a justification, the actor admits responsibility for the act in question but denies its pejorative and negative content. In an excuse, the actor admits the act in question is wrong, but denies having full responsibility for it. Offenders can use accounts to narrow the gap between expectation and behavior and to present their acts in a favorable light. Related to the justification and the excuse is the apology. In an apology, the offender admits violating a rule, accepts the validity of the rule, and expresses embarrassment and anger at self (Benson, 1985).

Related to the justification and the excuse is the apology. In an apology, the actor admits violating a rule, accepts the validity of the rule, and expresses embarrassment and anger at self (Goffman, 1971). In a way, the actor "splits himself into two parts, the part that is guilty of the offense and the part that disassociates itself from the delict and affirms a belief in the offended rule" (Goffman, 1971: 113). As we show below, because corporations can literally split themselves in two, they are especially well equipped to make effective use of apologies as a way of getting past the damaging effects of being involved in a scandal.

Ideally, corporate accounts of a crisis represent an organization's response strategy, which is the set of coordinated communication and actions used to influence external stakeholders and the public in their perceptions of the crisis. A response strategy serves to minimize the social approval loss, the legitimacy deterioration, as well as the reputation loss. Bundy and Pfarrer (2015) suggest that a response strategy should accept crisis responsibility to the extent expected from the environment to avoid crisis-response mismatch.

Bundy and Pfarrer (2015: 347) define social approval as "perception of general affinity toward an organization", legitimacy as "assessment of an organization's appropriateness", and reputation as "assessment of an organization's ability to deliver value". In giving an account, the offender is addressing an audience and attempting to explain the offense (Benson, 1985).

Bundy and Pfarrer (2015) describe response strategies on a continuum from defensive to accommodative. A defensive response strategy attempts to avoid social approval loss by eliminating an organization's suggested association with a crisis. Examples range from outright denial of responsibility, via attacking accusers and shifting blame onto other entities, to perceive being a victim of an incident. In contrast, an accommodative response strategy attempts to manage social approval loss by acknowledging an organization's causal role in a crisis and thereby reducing external negative perceptions of the company. Examples range from outright acceptance of responsibility to communicated regrets and apologies. As will become evident from our case studies, only NNPC in Nigeria had a defensive response strategy by rejecting accusations of oil revenue manipulation and attacking a prominent accuser (PwC, 2015). None of the other cases had an initial accommodative response strategy. We find most of our cases close to the center of the continuum, where response strategies attempt to reframe how external observers judge a crisis, while the company neither accepts nor denies responsibility.

All crises are uncertain events that generate initial negative reactions. An effective response strategy should match external observers' situational attributions of the crisis to prevent cognitive dissonance among observers (Bundy and Pfarrer, 2015: 352):

> A crisis with higher situational attributions of responsibility should be matched with a response strategy that accepts more responsibility, and a crisis with lower situational attributions of responsibility should be matched with a response strategy that accepts less responsibility (. . .) An organization that is underconforming by being defensive in response to a crisis with higher situational attributions risks being perceived as unethical and manipulative.

Fisse and Braithwaite (1988: 469) did a study on the impact of scandals on corporations. They found that "the impact of enforcement can easily stop with a corporate pay-out of a fine or monetary penalty, not because of any socially justified departure from the tradition value of individual accountability, but rather because that is the cheapest or most self-protective course for a corporate defendant to adopt".

More recently, Goldstraw-White (2012) and Whyte (2016) have studied accounts. Goldstraw-White (2012) suggests that greed is always the motive for corporate offences. She defines greed as socially constructed needs and desires that can never be completely covered or contended. Greed can be a strong quest to get more and more of something, and there is a strong preference to maximize wealth, as wealth is also a symbol of success. Convenience is always the trigger for corporate offences. He defines convenience as the savings in time and effort as well as avoidance of strain and pain to exploit possibilities and avoid threats.

Accounts typically include application of all five neutralization techniques suggested by Sykes and Matza (1957): the denial of responsibility, the denial of injury, the denial of victim, the condemnation of the condemners, and the appeal to higher loyalties. Accounts also tend to include more recently suggested neutralization techniques such as the claim of blunder quota, the claim of legal mistake, the claim of normality of action, and the claim of entitlement to action. Furthermore, offenders sometimes introduce the claim of solution to a dilemma, the necessity of crime, the claim of role in society, and the perception of being a victim (Kaptein and Helvoort, 2019; Siponen and Vance, 2010).

Account giving supports the human desire to maintain the perception of the self as a rational, moral actor – that is an actor of integrity and accountability. By denial of deviance (Whyte, 2016), the denial projects the condemned behavior as the cultural norm. It does not need to be justified since the deviance is not outside expectations that should be normal. It conforms to norms within the business or the industry in which they operate.

Bandura (1999) identified the ways that corporations can disengage themselves from the harmful consequences of their actions. Moral disengagement can occur by belittled labeling, advantageous comparison, displacement of responsibility, diffusion of responsibility, disregard or distortion of consequences, and dehumanization of victims.

Corporate accounts are concerned with limiting the probability and magnitude of social approval loss when responding to a crisis. A crisis is an unexpected, publicly known, and harmful event that is associated with uncertainty. A crisis is a fundamental threat to a corporation. Ambiguity of cause, effect, and means of resolution often characterize a crisis. Most corporate crises originate from failures within the organization. Scholars denote that organizational crises require timely responses (König et al., 2020).

Bundy and Pfarrer (2015) suggest that the more an organization's response strategy matches evaluators' situational attributions of crisis responsibility, the lower the mean and variance of social approval loss. Furthermore, for an organization with higher social approval, a response strategy that accepts less crisis responsibility, relative to an average-approval organization, will generate a lower mean and variance of social approval loss than a response strategy that accepts the same or more crisis responsibility. Third, for an organization with lower social approval, a response strategy that accepts less crisis responsibility, relative to an average-approval organization, will generate a lower mean and variance of social approval loss than a response strategy that accepts the same or more crisis responsibility. Finally, managers of a higher- or lower-approval organization will be more likely to accept less crisis responsibility, relative to managers of an average-approval organization.

Initial corporate accounts occur at the onset of a crisis. A typical characteristic of the initial situation is typically high levels of uncertainty both within the organization and with expected reactions externally. As argued by Bundy and Pfarrer (2015: 351), "crisis often have multiple explanations, ambiguity regarding responsibility and potential damages, and several feasible solutions". As a crisis evolves and the scandal grows in size, there will typically be more information available that reduces the uncertainty of what actually happened. In light of new, significant, and credible information, it is natural for an organization to modify or switch its response.

Content Research Method

The research method applied in this empirical study of investigation reports is content analysis (Bell et al., 2018; Saunders et al., 2007). Content analysis is any methodology or procedure that works to identify characteristics within texts attempting to make valid inferences (Krippendorff, 1980; Patrucco et al., 2017). Content analysis assumes that language reflects both how people understand their surroundings and their cognitive processes. Therefore, content analysis makes it possible to identify and determine relevant text in a context (McClelland et al., 2010).

Private and public organizations often hire fraud examiners from global auditing firms and local law firms to investigate suspicions of executive deviance related to white-collar crime (Brooks and Button, 2011; Button et al., 2007a, 2007b; Button and Gee, 2013; Schneider, 2006; Williams, 2005, 2014). At the end of their inquiry, fraud examiners write a report of investigation and hand it over to the client organization as their property. Unfortunately, clients tend to keep reports secret (Gottschalk and Tcherni-Buzzeo, 2017). Only a few reports are publicly available, and they are often hard to find. After searching the Internet for some time, we were able to identify and retrieve 20 reports written in English. Seven of the reports were focusing on individual wrongdoing rather than corporate wrongdoing. Thirteen reports were focusing on corporate scandals. These are the thirteen reports that this research uses to search for corporate accounts:

1. Canada: Town of Pelham in Canada was involved in irregular payments in a development project. KPMG (2017) conducted a fraud examination and wrote an investigation report to explain how irregular payments occurred. The report is 100 pages.

2. Denmark: Danske Bank's Estonian branch was involved in a money laundering scandal. Non-residents used the bank to transfer criminal proceeds. Danish law firms Bruun Hjejle (2018) conducted a fraud examination and wrote an investigation report about the non-resident portfolio at Danske Bank's Estonian branch. The report is 87 pages.

3. Japan: Olympus Corporation in Japan was involved in an accounting scandal where losses for failing financial investments remained hidden in worthless credits. Auditing firm Deloitte (2011) conducted a fraud examination and wrote an investigation report about inappropriate accounting. The report is 243 pages.

4. Japan: Toshiba Corporation in Japan was also involved in an accounting scandal where work in progress and finished goods were inflated thus assigned higher values. Auditing firm Deloitte (2015) conducted a fraud examination and wrote an investigation report about inappropriate accounting. The report is 90 pages.

5. New Zealand: Fuji Xerox in New Zealand was involved in aggressive sales practices coupled to inappropriate accounting where customers felt forced to sign new contracts before old contracts had expired, and new contracts entered accounting as sales. Auditing firm Deloitte (2017) conducted a fraud examination and wrote an investigation report about inappropriate sales and accounting practices. The report is 89 pages.

6. Nigeria: NNPC is the national petroleum company in Nigeria. The company withheld transfers of oil revenues to the government and claimed it covered costs. Auditing firm PwC (2015) conducted a fraud examination and wrote an investigation report on financial transactions between the company and the government. The report is 199 pages.

7. Norway: Telenor in Norway was a major shareholder of VimpelCom, which was involved in a corruption scandal in Uzbekistan to obtain mobile phone licenses. Auditing firm Deloitte (2016) conducted a fraud examination and wrote an investigation report about reluctance among Telenor executives to react on information from whistleblowers regarding the corruption scandal. The report is 54 pages.

8. Sweden: Nordea is a bank in Sweden. The bank has a subsidiary in Luxembourg. When the Panama Papers revealed money flows to and from tax havens, investigative journalists discovered misconduct in Luxembourg. For example, the bank backdated contracts for customers for tax evasion purposes. Law firm Mannheimer Swartling (2016) conducted a fraud examination and wrote an investigation report on the bank practice of wealth management for its customers. The report is 42 pages.

Table 3.1: Corporate investigations because of corporate scandals.

#	CORPORATE INVESTIGATION	CORPORATE SCANDAL
1	Canada: Town of Pelham (KPMG, 2017)	Cover-up of Can$17 million dollars in unaccounted debt.
2	Denmark: Danske Bank's Estonian branch (Bruun Hjejle, 2018)	Money laundering of crime proceeds from Russia.
3	Japan: Olympus Corporation (Deloitte, 2011)	Fraud scheme of investment accounting violating Financial Instruments and Exchange Act and Companies Act. It was a tobashi scheme, which is a type of financial fraud where a client's losses hide in an investment firm by shifting them between the portfolios of other (genuine or fake) clients.
4	Japan: Toshiba Corporation (Deloitte, 2015)	Accounting fraud that was overstating profits by US$1.2 billion.
5	New Zealand: Fuji Xerox (Deloitte, 2017)	Inappropriate accounting practices overstating profits and illegal credit risks.
6	Nigeria: National petroleum company NNPC (PwC, 2015)	Crude oil revenues generated by the corporation withheld or unremitted to the federal accounts. A former governor of the Central Bank of Nigeria, Lamido Sanusi, raised the allegation that a huge amount had disappeared.
7	Norway: Telenor in Norway had ownership in VimpelCom (Deloitte, 2016)	VimpelCom involved in corruption in Uzbekistan, and Telenor knew about it.
8	Sweden: Nordea in Sweden had a subsidiary in Luxembourg (Mannheimer Swartling, 2016)	Illegal backdating of contracts and tax evasion revealed in the Panama Papers from tax havens.
9	USA: Lehman Brothers (Jenner Block, 2010)	Misconduct but no crime related to fiduciary duty of care by failing to observe risk management, went bankrupt.
10	USA: General Motors (Jenner Block, 2014)	Disregard of ignition switch failure in Cobalt car that caused injuries and deaths, reluctance to correct for financial reasons.
11	USA: WorldCom (PwC, 2003)	Fraud and conspiracy at false financial reporting, went bankrupt
12	USA: Wells Fargo's Community Bank (Shearman Sterling, 2017)	Improper and unethical sales practices violating specific statutory provisions.
13	USA: Enron Corporation (Wilmer Cutler Pickering 2003)	Misleading and illegal practices to hide and embezzle funds, securities and wire fraud.

9. USA: Lehman Brothers went bankrupt because of deviant risk taking in financial operations. Jenner Block (2010) conducted a fraud examination and wrote an investigation report about bank practices. The report is 239 pages.
10. USA: General Motors were reluctant to correct ignition switch failure for financial reasons. Jenner and Block (2014) conducted a fraud examination and wrote an investigation report about management practices. The report is 325 pages.
11. USA: WorldCom went bankrupt after inappropriate accounting to keep the share price at a level acceptable to the CEO, who had deposited his shares in a bank for loans to finance private properties. Auditing firm PwC (2003) conducted a fraud examination and wrote an investigation report about the collapse of WorldCom. The report is 345 pages.
12. USA: Wells Fargo's Community Bank had aggressive sales practices where bank customers received services that they had not ordered. Law firm Shearman Sterling (2017) conducted a fraud examination and wrote an investigation report about management and employees in the sales model. The report is 113 pages.
13. USA: Enron Corporation went bankrupt after inappropriate accounting practices. Enron was an energy, commodities, and services company. A whistleblower revealed that Enron's reported financial condition reflected an institutionalized, systematic, and creatively planned accounting fraud, known since as the Enron scandal. Law firm Wilmer Cutler Pickering (2003) conducted a fraud examination and wrote an investigation report about illegitimate accounting practices. The report is 218 pages.

Table 3.1 summarizes these thirteen cases in terms of corporate investigations of corporate scandals. Accounting scandals caused five out of thirteen crises that seem to satisfy Hurley et al.'s (2019: 233) description of audit quality dependent on who hires the auditor:

> Our design shifts auditors' accountability from managers, who have directional goal preferences, to investors, who prefer judgment accuracy. We find that removing auditors' economic accountability to managers and replacing it with psychological accountability to investors significantly increases audit quality.

This research was also interested in the initial corporate account concerning each scandal (Gottschalk and Benson, 2020). Initial accounts are important, because stakeholders as well as the public quickly begin to associate a crisis with an individual organization, such as the Enron scandal (Bundy and Pfarrer, 2015). An organization's initial response is influential in anchoring first impressions externally. The initial account might be an active statement about unknown internal circumstances, or a response to allegations already out there in the public. This research needed to find the very first corporate communication about the scandal, and we decided to use the first media coverage of a corporate message as the initial corporate account. As argued by Bundy and Pfarrer (2015), social disapproval of corporate crisis emerges quickly in negative media coverage that challenges, criticizes, or condemns an organization's activities, behaviors, or values.

As argued by Greer and McLaughlin (2017), the media sometimes portray scandals as a distinctive mode of tabloid infotainment that focuses primarily on celebrity individuals and businesses. Scandals are an important coverage area for the media, and the activities of investigative journalists play a crucial role. Their distinctive practices and rhythms of work often determine the story line over time. Scandals have become a prized news commodity that validates the professional watchdog conception of investigative journalism (Barak, 2007; Burns and Orrick, 2002; Campbell, 1997; Knottnerus et al., 2006; Murphy, 2010; Rosoff, 2009; Welch et al., 1998; Zavyalova et al., 2012).

We identified the university library system of databases as a reliable source, where we selected the database 'Newsbank' with the function 'Access World News' (AWN), which archives stories from thousands of U.S. and global news sources. We applied the feature 'More Search Options' to enter keywords regarding corporation, executive, misconduct, and year. We scrolled backwards in the search results to the very first news article mentioning the scandal in terms of a statement from the organization.

For the destiny of executives, we did regular Google-searches to find the most recent information about each of them. As an example, already mentioned, Milne (2019a, 2019b) reported in the newspaper 'Financial Times' that Danish prosecutors charged ex-Danske Bank CEO Thomas Borgen over the Estonian case, and that the police found the body of Danske Bank's former Estonian chief Aivar Rehe after an apparent suicide in September 2019.

Wells Fargo Case Study

Before we move into research results for all thirteen cases, we tested the database system first for Wells Fargo's Community Bank, since this is one of the more recent scandals in the United States (Shichor and Heeren, 2021; Wieczner, 2017). The earliest media coverage of the scandal we found in the newspaper 'Charlotte Observer' published September 10, 2016. Charlotte was Wells Fargo's biggest employee hub with more than 23,000 employees in a wide variety of business lines. Already the heading of the newspaper article caught our attention; "Banking – Wells Fargo gives few details about firing" (Rothacker, 2016):

> Wells Fargo has said it fired 5,300 employees for secretly opening unauthorized deposit and credit card accounts – conduct that resulted in $185 million in fines announced Thursday – but the bank isn't providing many details. Wells spokesman Mary Eshet said Friday that the employees included "both managers and team members."

At this initial stage of accounts, Wells Fargo blamed employees for the wrongdoing. Employees were simply too greedy for financial rewards under the incentive compensation program. Wells Fargo further communicates that they have acted by firing several thousand employees over the last years. The bank is sorry they failed adequately to oversee sales practices. An interpretation of the initial account is that it is scapegoating and denial of responsibility (Gangloff et al., 2016). A scapegoat is a person who is blamed for the wrongdoings, mistakes, or faults of others, in this case the wrongdoings of top management. The account mentions chief executive Carrie Tolstedt, but it relates only to her earlier announcement of her own retirement.

Fraud investigators from law firm Shearman Sterling (2017: 2) presented their report of investigation the following year. Now the blame shifted from greedy employees over on management with an aggressive sales model, as stated in the principal findings of the report:

> The root cause of sales practice failures was the distortion of the Community Bank's sales culture and performance management system, which, when combined with aggressive sales management, created pressure on employees to sell unwanted or unneeded products to customers and, in some cases, to open unauthorized accounts. Wells Fargo's decentralized corporate structure gave too much autonomy to the Community Bank's senior leadership, who were unwilling to change the sales model or even recognize it as the root cause of the problem. Community Bank leadership resisted and impeded outside scrutiny or oversight and, when forced to report, minimized the scale and nature of the problem.

Shearman Sterling (2017: 20) mention Carrie Tolstedt 141 times in their 113-pages report, all of the time in critical terms:

> The scorecards, instituted by Tolstedt when she took over the Community Bank, measured how an employee or manager was performing compared to the sales plan. Scorecards were segmented by business drivers and updated on a daily basis, and employees and managers could check their progress against the sales plan at any time and were actively encouraged to do so. Certain managers made meeting scorecard requirements their sole objective, a tactic referred to as "managing to the scorecard." As a result, employees reporting to these managers were consistently pressured to meet scorecard goals.

While investigators blamed Tolstedt, she still blamed individual employees (Shearman Sterling, 2017: 103):

> Tolstedt emphasized that a large organization could not be perfect, and that the sales practice problem was a result of improper action on the part of individual employees.

While the initial blame one year earlier was on individual employees, the communicated corporate account was now to blame Tolstedt for having introduced a sales model that caused inappropriate sales practices. As a corporation, Wells Fargo was still denying responsibility for the misconduct. However, not only did Tolstedt resign, also Wells Fargo's CEO John Stumpf resigned shortly after because the account fraud scandal continued as an ongoing controversy.

In the current research perspective of addressing the issue of how accounts based on neutralizations and justifications evolve over time as events from exposure of a corporate scandal move along, we see a shift in the blame (Lee and Robinson, 2000; Resodihardio et al., 2015; Xie and Keh, 2016), but no shift in corporate responsibility. Denial of responsibility continued. According to Sykes and Matza (1957), this is a common neutralization technique where the corporate offender disclaims responsibility for action and argues that the corporation is not responsible for what happened. The corporation as an alleged offender here claims that the corporation does not meet one or more of the conditions of responsible agency. The corporation committing a deviant act defines itself lacking responsibility for own actions. In this neutralization technique, the corporation rationalizes that the action in question is beyond corporate control. The offender may view the corporation as a billiard ball, helplessly propelled through different situations. The corporation denies responsibility for the event or sequence of events. This technique denies responsibility where the corporation accepts that wrongdoing has occurred but denies their own involvement or responsibility. The corporation may refer to some other actor as the responsible party or explain how a number of social actors jointly produced the misconduct. The corporation can also deny intent as a way of denying responsibility by referring to an event as an accident, where the corporation had no intent of producing harm. Similarly, the corporation can deny control over the situation where wrongdoing occurred. The corporation can transfer responsibility to others by the blame game or by scapegoating. The corporation will try to change expectations by referring to their limited formal responsibility.

Content Research Results

In Table 3.2, we have included a short version of the accounts as presented above for Wells Fargo as the twelfth case study.

Initial corporate accounts are dependent on what is already in the public domain in terms of rumors and allegations. In our first case from Canada, local media had for a long time presented allegations against town management, so the initial response was to refuse the allegations. In the Canadian case, there was a tendency to conspiracy theories in the public domain, and thus the initial accounts seem justified. The initial accounts were further justified by fraud examiners, who concluded that no violation of the Municipal Act had occurred.

At Olympus Corporation, the newly appointed CEO Michael Woodford detected the tobashi fraud scheme that had been going on in the company for many years. The former CEO Tsuyoshi Kikukawa was now the chair of the board in the company. Kikukawa ousted Woodford and denied any wrongdoing. The initial corporate account was that they denied telling any details, and only generally admitting to weak corporate governance (Nakamoto, 2011). A similar response occurred some

Table 3.2: Initial accounts and investigation accounts after scandals.

#	BUSINESS	INITIAL CORPORATE ACCOUNTS	INVESTIGATION ACCOUNTS
1	Canada: Town of Pelham in Canada involved in irregular payments and hiding debts in development project scandal.	"Pelham planning director Barb Wiens, however, said the deal wasn't the quick flip Hummel described." (Sawchuk, 2017). Refusing allegations.	"The Town had broad authority to use the Municipal Credits to finance the excess dedications, as long as the agreements were structured in a way that did not contravene the Municipal Act." (KPMG, 2017). Examiners did not address whether or not violation of the Municipal Act had occurred.
2	Denmark: Danske Bank's Estonian branch involved in money laundering scandal.	"The Danish bank has admitted to 'major deficiencies in control and governance' at its Estonian branch." (Moscow Times, 2017). "In press release of 21 September 2017, Danske Bank acknowledged that it was "major deficiencies in controls and governance that made it possible to use Danske Bank's branch in Estonia for criminal activities such as money laundering". The press release referred to the findings of a "root-cause analysis" prepared for the bank by US-based consultancy Promontory Financial Group, LLC ("Promontory")." (Bruun Hjejle, 2018). Not yet admitting bank services for money laundering.	"With regard to the Non-Resident Portfolio, it has been found that, from 2007 through 2017, a number of former and current employees, both at the Estonian branch and at Group level, did not comply with legal obligations forming part of their employment with the bank. Most of these employees are no longer employed by the bank. For employees still with the bank, the bank has informed us that appropriate action has been or will be taken. We are not in a position to share an assessment of an individual unless requested by the individual in question. We have been requested by the Board of Directors, the Chairman and the Chief Executive Officer ("CEO") to share their assessments. According to assessments made, the Board of Directors, the Chairman and the CEO have not breached their legal obligations towards the bank." (Bruun Hjejle 2018). Admitting bank services for money laundering by non-residents in Estonia.

| 3 | Japan: Olympus Corporation in Japan involved in inappropriate accounting practices scandal. | "Olympus' admission that it had covered up losses on securities investments dating back to the 1990s by booking them as acquisition fees of up to $1.4bn between 2006 and 2008 has once again thrown the spotlight on the weak corporate governance of Japanese companies. The company declined to provide details of how it kept those losses off its books for so long, but the revelation that a practice most closely associated with the bursting of Japan's bubble economy in the 1990s had been going on as recently as a few years ago, stunned the investment community." (Nakamoto, 2011). Tobashi still not mentioned. | "Olympus used SG Bond Plus Fund for 'tobashi' of part of the losses it suffered as the result of failures in financial management techniques in the 1990s. To cover up losses to which 'tobashi' had been used, Olympus and OFUK purchased warrants attached to FA and dividend preferred shares in association with the Gyrus acquisition; ultimately Olympus planned to use Funds for back-flow of funds." (Deloitte, 2011). Tobashi scandal. |
| 4 | Japan: Toshiba Corporation in Japan involved in inappropriate accounting practices. | "Toshiba withdrew its earnings guidance and scrapped its year-end dividend payout on Friday, saying it had found improper accounting on some of its infrastructure projects. The announcement came after the company said last month that it was looking into irregularities that had come to light in an internal probe. Since then, shares of Toshiba have fallen 5.7 per cent. The company declined to provide further details on which infrastructure projects were being questioned." (Inagati, 2015). Disclaim knowledge of the irregularities. | "For some projects, it has been found that certain members of top management were aware of the intentional overstating of apparent current-period profits and the postponement of recording expenses and losses, or the continuation thereof, but did not give instructions to stop or correct them. Moreover, with regard to some projects for which the percentage-of-completion method was used, it has been recognized that, although the Company requested approval to record provisions for contract losses, certain top management either rejected it or instructed the recording to be postponed." (Deloitte, 2015). Fake completion rates encouraged by executives. |

(continued)

Table 3.2 (continued)

#	BUSINESS	INITIAL CORPORATE ACCOUNTS	INVESTIGATION ACCOUNTS
5	New Zealand: Fuji Xerox in New Zealand involved in inappropriate sales and accounting practices.	"The Serious Fraud Office will take no action against office products firm Fuji Xerox after closing its inquiry into the company's affairs. Several senior industry players were understood to have been interviewed by the market watchdog. But yesterday, Fuji Xerox said it welcomed the SFO's decision. Fuji Xerox New Zealand managing director Gavin Pollard said the company had always been confident there were no grounds for any action, and it was pleased the matter was closed. 'We co-operated fully with the SFO with its inquiries on a voluntary basis as we were eager to resolve this matter as quickly as possible'. NZ First began putting pressure on the Government about the company in October, questioning whether Northland schools were encouraged to sign certain printing contracts." (Hamish, 2016). Denied all allegations only one year before fraud examiners exposed misconduct.	"In the interviews in this Investigation, a number of interviewees (APO-related people) said the pressure from FX to attain business results (especially to achieve sales) was very intense. In particular, people who were involved in budget allocations and personnel evaluations at FXAP from around 2009 through 2015 uniformly made statements to the effect that with the economic decline and slowdown of growth in Japan, there were expectations from all of FX for the China and Asia region to act as a driving force to restore business performance, and the regions attracted their attentions (. . . .) That the APO Finance Department, in addition to having accounting and finance check functions, also performed the role of performance management, can be raised as one of the main causes of the inappropriate accounting practices carried out at FXNZ and FXA." (Deloitte, 2017). Investigators blame top management in Japan and New Zealand for the misconduct.
6	Nigeria: National petroleum company NNPC in Nigeria withheld transfers of oil revenues to the government.	"The NNPC claimed that the country's chief banker was ignorant on matters of oil earnings and remittances. It accused Mr. Sanusi of Nigeria's version of the capital sin: Playing politics." (Reporter, 2013). A former governor of the Central Bank of Nigeria, Lamido Sanusi, raised the allegation that a huge amount had disappeared.	"For the period reviewed, we identified possible errors in the computation of crude oil prices at the NNPC that resulted in a $3.6 million shortfall in incomes to the Federation account." (PwC, 2015). Sanusi at alleged $49.8 billion, while investigators only found $3.6 million missing.

| 7 | Norway: Telenor in Norway had ownership in VimpelCom in the Netherlands that was involved in corruption in Uzbekistan. | "Norwegian telecom giant Telenor was allegedly involved in a corruption scandal in Uzbekistan with ties to President Islam Karimov's daughter, Norwegian media reported Saturday. According to documents published by Norway's Klassekampen daily, VimpelCom, an Uzbek firm partially owned by Telenor, paid \$25 million (20 million euros) in bribes to obtain telecom licenses in the Central Asian nation. The money allegedly went from a subsidiary of VimpelCom to Takilant Limited, owned by Gayane Avakyan, a friend of Karimov's oldest daughter, Gulnara Karimova. 'Bank statements document how the money was transferred from a previously unknown company in the British Virgin Islands as VimpelCom purchased licenses to the mobile market in the former Soviet state,' Klassekampen wrote on its website. Telenor owns 33 percent of VimpelCom and has 43 percent of the voting rights in the company. 'We are a minority shareholder in VimpelCom, so it's up to VimpelCom to take responsibility for answering any questions that relate to their operations', Telenor communications head Glenn Mandelid told AFP. 'Telenor has zero tolerance for corruption, both when it comes to our own operations and also to the companies that we are part owners in'." (Agence France, 2014). Denial of responsibility to act. | "In due consideration to what is stated above, we are notwithstanding of the opinion that certain employees at Telenor at certain point in time should have handled the 2011 concerns differently. The individuals in question are senior employees of Telenor and with high-ranking leadership positions and/or with professional education and experience. Due to this, our assessments of such individuals have been based what we believe should be expected of such individuals as leaders, as Telenor Nominees and as individuals with professional background and experience. The facts and circumstances in this case do in our view not solicit an approach where the actions and decisions of individuals are assessed against formal legal frameworks." (Deloitte, 2016). Criticism of lack of action, but no crime. |

(continued)

Table 3.2 (continued)

#	BUSINESS	INITIAL CORPORATE ACCOUNTS	INVESTIGATION ACCOUNTS
8	Sweden: Nordea in Sweden had a subsidiary in Luxembourg revealed by the Panama Papers in backdating documents.	"Nordea, the Nordic region's biggest bank, says it doesn't help wealthy customers evade taxes in response to reports linking it to the Panamanian law firm at the center of a media investigation into offshore accounts." (Associated Press, 2016). The Panama Papers disclosed involvement in tax havens, but the bank first denied responsibility for what customers might do in tax havens.	"The investigation has found deficiencies in the procedures regarding renewal of Powers of Attorney (POA). In at least seven cases the investigation has shown that backdated documents have been requested or provided during the last six years, which is illegal when it aims at altering the truth." (Mannheimer Swartling, 2016). The Panama Papers disclosed involvement in tax havens, and the investigation documents law violations in the Luxembourg branch of Nordea.
9	USA: Lehman Brothers went bankrupt because of alleged risky management.	"Lehman's shares fell $7.51, or 19 percent, to $31.75 after Chief Executive Officer Richard Fuld said in a statement that the Federal Reserve's decision to lend to brokers and accept securities as collateral "improves the liquidity picture and, from my perspective, takes the liquidity issue for the entire industry off the table." (Onaran, 2008). This was half a year before CEO Fuld had to file for bankruptcy. Obviously, he knew that it would not work, but his communicated account was that liquidity was fine again.	"The business decisions that brought Lehman to its crisis of confidence may have been in error but were largely within the business judgment rule. But the decision not to disclose the effects of those judgments does give rise to colorable claims against the senior officers who oversaw and certified misleading financial statements – Lehman's CEO Richard S. Fuld, Jr., and its FCOs Christopher O'Meara, Erin M. Callan and Ian T. Lowitt." (Jenner Block, 2010). Fraud examiners directly blame the top executives for their decision-making and misleading financial statements.

| 10 | USA: General Motors' reluctant to correct ignition switch failure for financial reasons. | "The company said it knows of five front-impact crashes in which six people died and air bags did not deploy in vehicles. GM said affected vehicles' ignition switches can turn off in a crash. That causes the engine to shut down, and as a result, air bags fail to activate. 'All of these crashes occurred off-road and at high speeds, where the probability of serious or fatal injuries was high regardless of air bag deployment,' GM spokesman Alan Adler said. 'In addition, failure to wear seat belts and alcohol use were factors in some of these cases.' (. . .) GM said the National Highway Traffic Safety Administration never investigated the issue. The automaker learned of it through field reports." (Shepardson and Burden, 2014). They claim they learned of the ignition switch failure from field reports, but the later investigation tells that many knew of the failure long before field reports of accidents emerged. | "From the outset, the Cobalt ignition switch had significant problems that were known to GM personnel. Designed to be a new generation ignition switch first introduced in the Saturn ion, the switch was so plagued with problems that the engineer who designed it labeled it then 'the switch from hell'. (. . .) In 2005, various committees within GM considered proposed fixes, but those were rejected as too costly. (. . .) Despite learning about what GM's outside counsel called a 'bombshell' in April 2013, it was not until February 2014 that GM issued the first recall." (Jenner Block, 2014). GM did not fix it for cost reasons. |

(continued)

Table 3.2 (continued)

#	BUSINESS	INITIAL CORPORATE ACCOUNTS	INVESTIGATION ACCOUNTS
11	USA: WorldCom went bankrupt after inappropriate accounting.	"In a conference call with investors and analysts, Ebbers and other executives sought to dismiss concerns about WorldCom's accounting practices, debt load and cash flow. The CEO also said he will not sell WorldCom shares to pay down his personal debt." (Porretto, 2002). One year later, WorldCom was bankrupt, accounting practices were wrong, and Ebbers had sold shares to pay down his personal debt.	"Numerous individuals – most of them in financial and accounting departments, at many levels of the Company and in different locations around the world – became aware in varying degrees of senior management's misconduct. Had one or more of these individuals come forward earlier and raised their complaints with Human Resources, Internal Audit, the Law and Public Policy Department, Andersen, the Audit Committee, individual Directors and/or federal or state government regulators, perhaps the fraud would not have gone on for so long. Why didn't they? The answer seems to lie partly in a culture emanating from corporate headquarters that emphasized making the numbers above all else; kept financial information hidden from those who needed to know; blindly trusted senior officers even in the face of evidence that they were acting improperly; discouraged dissent; and left few, if any, outlets through which employees believed they could safely raise their objections." (PwC, 2003). A corporate culture where executives did what Ebbers told them to do.

| 12 | USA: Wells Fargo's Community Bank had inappropriate sales practices. | "Wells Fargo has said it fired 5,300 employees for secretly opening unauthorized deposit and credit card accounts – conduct that resulted in $185 million in fines announced Thursday – but the bank isn't providing many details." (Rothacker, 2016). No corporate responsibility account so far. "The head of the community bank during the period under scrutiny was Wells Fargo veteran Carrie Tolstedt, who announced in July that she had decided to retire at the end of the year at age 56." (Rothacker, 2016). No personal 'responsibility account so far. | "Wells Fargo's decentralized corporate structure gave too much autonomy to the Community Bank's senior leadership, who were unwilling to change the sales model or even recognize it as the root cause of the problem." (Shearman and Sterling, 2017). Executive management rather than employees get the blame. "Carrie Tolstedt, head of the Community Bank, and certain of her senior leaders paid insufficient regard to the substantial risk to Wells Fargo's brand and reputation from improper and unethical sales practices even as they failed to recognize the potential for financial or other harm to customers." (Shearman and Sterling, 2017). Tolstedt was extremely ambitious and caused the misconduct with her sales model. |
| 13 | USA: Enron Corporation went bankrupt after inappropriate accounting practices. | "Absolutely no accounting issue," Lay told analysts, "no trading issue, no reserve issue, no previously unknown problem issues" is behind the departure. There will be 'no change in the performance or outlook of the company going forward', he added" (Deseret News, 2001). Skilling left the company, but accounting scandal denied by Lay. | "Individually, and collectively, Enron's Management failed to carry out its substantive responsibility for ensuring that the transactions were fair to Enron – which in many cases they were not – and its responsibility for implementing a system of oversight and controls over the transactions with the LJM partnerships. There were several direct consequences of this failure: transactions were executed on terms that were not fair to Enron and that enriched Fastow and others; Enron engaged in transactions that had little economic substance and misstated Enron's financial results; and the disclosures Enron made to its shareholders and the public did not fully or accurately communicate relevant information. We discuss here the involvement of Kenneth Lay, Jeffrey Skilling, Richard Causey, and Richard Buy." (Wilmer Cutler Pickering, 2003). Top executives were the architects of the accounting scandal that led to bankruptcy. |

years later at Toshiba Corporation where irregularities "had come to light" and "the company declined to provide further details" (Inagati, 2015).

New Zealand is an interesting case where the serious fraud office decided to take no action against Fuji Xerox after closing its inquiry into the company's affairs in 2016. The communicated account at that time was that "the company had always been confident there were no grounds for any action, and it was pleased the matter was closed" (Hamish, 2016). Some had been questioning early signing of certain printing contracts. Only one year later, investigators concluded that early signing had indeed occurred after massive pressure from top management (Deloitte, 2017).

The Nigerian case started with an allegation of $49.8 billion stolen, while the investigation found that only $3.6 million was missing. Therefore, corporate accounts remained consistent at accusing the critical Sanusi of playing politics while being ignorant on matters of oil earnings (Reporter, 2013).

Telenor in Norway was a minority shareholder in VimpelCom in the Netherlands, which had obtained telecom licenses in Uzbekistan by bribing the daughter of the president. Initially, Telenor denied any responsibility by the following account: "We are a minority shareholder in VimpelCom, so it's up to VimpelCom to take responsibility for answering any questions that relate to their operation" (Agence France, 2014). Two years later, the account was quite different, as Deloitte (2016) released their report. Two top executives at Telenor, who received information from a whistleblower about the corruption case at VimpelCom several years ago, had to resign.

Half a year before Lehman Brothers filed for bankruptcy, CEO Fuld communicated that the bank had solved its liquidity problem (Onaran, 2008). Two years later, Jenner Block (2010) concluded that risky and deviant decision-making by Fuld and others had caused bankruptcy. One decade after the internal investigation, Crosina and Pratt (2019) studied organizational mourning among former Lehman Brothers bankers.

Corporate Executive Destiny

This chapter compares fraud examiners' accounts of potential misconduct and crime with initial corporate statements, and the following chapter determines the extent of match or mismatch between these two elements. Further, this chapter also investigates the consequences of financial crime scandals for executives. The findings show that in eleven out of thirteen cases, the companies somehow separated themselves from the senior officials in the aftermath of the scandals, and only two remained in their positions, as listed below.

This and the following chapter thus study the crisis and response, as well as the destiny of leading executives following corporate white-collar crime scandals. In addition to the dynamic nature of accounts after corporate scandals, we are thus also looking at the outcomes of these scandals in terms of the employment of the corporate leaders:

1. Cari Pupo, Pelham, covered up debt in the property development project in the town (Sawchuk, 2017). KPMG (2017) blamed treasurer Pupo for misrepresenting finances for the development project, although there was no violation of the Municipal Act. Burket (2018) wrote then that she "was set up to take the fall". The town terminated the employment of Pupo. She lost the blame game (Lee and Robinson, 2000; Resodihardio et al., 2015; Xie and Keh, 2016).

2. Thomas Borgen, Danske Bank, had ignored rumors and whistleblowing concerned with money laundering in the Estonian branch (Moscow Times, 2017). When Bruun Hjejle (2018) published their report, Borgen had to resign from the position of CEO (Milne and Binham, 2018). Half a year later, police detectives searched Borgen's home in Norway, and Danish police charged him in the money laundering case (Milne, 2019a, 2019b). At that time, he already faced prosecution in the United States for investor fraud (Høgseth, 2019).

3. Tsuyoshi Kikukawa, Olympus, received the blame as the main architect of the fraud scheme from Deloitte (2011). Kikukawa has his name mentioned 81 times in the report. According to the report, he as the CEO and later chair, managed investments that made it look like the company had substantial financial claims. Kikukawa resigned as chairperson of the board when the investigation report became public. Kikukawa had been the CEO before Michael Woodford took on the position (Nakamoto, 2011). Shortly after taking on the position, Woodford blew the whistle on fraud (Neate, 2012): "Former Olympus chief executive tells of the risks he ran in exposing fraud scandal at the digital camera company".

4. Hisao Tanaka, Toshiba, was CEO. He announced his resignation in the face of the accounting scandal tied to about US$1.2 billion in overstated profits (Inagati, 2015). He announced his resignation the day after the investigation report became public. Evidence of improper accounting appeared in Deloitte's (2015) report.

5. Neil Wittaker, Fuji Xerox, was the managing director in New Zealand. Whittaker has his name mentioned 31 times in the investigation report by Deloitte (2017). Whittaker organized leasing practices that enabled early profits to emerge in accounting statements (Hamish, 2016). He "suddenly left the company, with the print vendor showing the IT veteran the door following 32 years of service" and "Neil Whittaker exits as local Fuji Xerox MD in shock departure" (Henderson, 2016). Whittaker disappeared out of the business in May 2016, while fraud examiners from Deloitte (2017) completed their investigation one year later in June 2017.

6. Ibe Kachikwu, NNPC, continued in his position as chief executive of the national petroleum company in Nigeria. After fraud examiners from PwC (2015) completed their investigation, Kachikwu became minister of state for petroleum

resources in Nigeria (Idris, 2019): "Who would have thought that Dr Emmanuel Ibe Kachikwu, Nigeria's Minister of State for Petroleum Resources would achieve success at the troubled ministry?" The NNPC case started with seemingly unfounded allegations from former governor of the Central Bank of Nigeria, Sanusi, against Kachikwu (Reporter, 2013).

7. Pål Wien Espen and Richard Olav Aa, Telenor, resigned from their group executive positions at the Norwegian telecommunication company when Deloitte (2016) presented their report of investigation. The two executives allegedly did not respond adequately to a whistleblower who informed them of VimpelCom corruption (Agence France, 2014). Attorney Espen later became a partner in a Norwegian law firm, while economist Aa was hired as chief financial officer by a major Norwegian company.

8. Gunn Wærsted, Nordea, resigned from her group executive position in the bank before fraud examiners from law firm Mannheimer Swartling (2016) presented their investigation report. She was responsible for wealth management involving tax havens (Associated Press, 2016). She resigned officially to concentrate on a board chair position at another company, so her resignation did not seem linked the scandal (Ekeberg, 2016; Grinde, 2016; Kristjansson, 2016; Trumpy, 2016).

9. Richard Fuld, Lehman Brothers (Onaran, 2008), lost his job because of the bankruptcy, and not because of the investigation by Jenner Block (2010). Fuld was on Time's list of 25 People to Blame for the Financial Crisis (http://content. time.com/time/specials/): "The Gorilla of Wall Street, as Fuld was known, steered Lehman deep into the business of subprime mortgages, bankrolling lenders across the country that were making convoluted loans to questionable borrowers (. . .) Fuld raked in nearly $500 million in compensation during his tenure as CEO, which ended when Lehman did". Nine years later, in 2017, "Dick Fuld makes quiet comeback on Wall Street" by joining a group of matrix wealth management into private equity and short selling.

10. Bill Kemp, General Motors, was senior lawyer in the automobile company. He was one out of several who received blame for the lack of reaction to the ignition switch failure (Shepardson and Burden, 2014). He was responsible for safety issues within the legal department at GM, but he ignored signals concerning the Cobalt car that caused several deaths (Jenner Block, 2014). GM terminated his employment. Fraud examiners from Jenner Block did not find CEO Mary Barra and two other top executives guilty in the ignition switch scandal, and they continued in their positions. Jenner Block (2014: 227) concluded: "All of the evidence we reviewed corroborated the conclusion that none of the three current leaders had knowledge of the problems with the Cobalt's ignition switch or non-deployment of airbags in the Cobalt until December 2013 at the earliest". Kemp was one out of several who received blame for the lack of reaction to the ignition switch failure.

11. Bernard Ebbers, WorldCom (Porretto, 2002), lost his job because of bankruptcy, and not because of the investigation the following year by PwC (2003). Along with other executives, a federal court convicted Ebbers to prison. At the age of 77 years in 2019, Ebbers was still in prison for investment fraud and conspiracy.
12. Carrie Tolstedt, Wells Fargo (Rothacker, 2016), was chief executive at Community Bank, a subsidiary of Wells Fargo. She was extremely ambitious and developed a business model that she believed in, and everyone had to follow. Shearman Sterling (2017) found that Tolstedt reinforced a culture of tight control over information about the community bank division, including sales practice issues. She retired before the accounting fraud scandal became public.
13. Kenneth Lay, Enron (Deseret News, 2001), lost his job because of bankruptcy and not because of the investigation by Wilmer Cutler Pickering (2003). Along with other executives, a federal court convicted him to prison (Knottnerus et al., 2006). Lay died in 2006.

Seven out of thirteen executives received blame in investigation reports and received termination from their companies. Three executives found themselves terminated since the companies went bankrupt. One executive resigned before the scandal became public knowledge. Only two executives experienced no negative consequences for themselves because of the scandals, where one of them at NNPC continued in his position, while the other left Nordea for a prestigious chair position independent of the scandal.

The dismissal of executives seems almost to be a standard procedure currently when there is a choice of protecting an executive while the organization continues to suffer or of protecting the organization while the executive continues to suffer as the scapegoat. A number of examples are presented later in this book, such as CEOs at Danske Bank in Denmark and Swedbank in Sweden, and executives at telecommunications company Telenor in Norway. In Spain, two executives at Acciona were convicted to prison for fraud in 2020. Acciona is a Spanish corporation involved in the development and management of infrastructure and renewable energy. The World Bank announced in 2019 the exclusion of Acciona from contracts after detection of corrupt, collusive, and fraudulent practices in the World Bank-financed national roads and airport infrastructure project in Bolivia. The debarment made Acciona ineligible to participate in World Bank-financed projects. The detected Bolivia fraud came only two years after detection of the Zaragoza fraud that was also by Acciona. Executives at Acciona gave jewels and cash to politicians and bureaucrats in the city located in northern Spain (Bentzrød, 2021).

4 Corporate Crisis-Response Match

When suspicions of corporate misconduct and crime emerge in the public, organizations respond in different ways. Their initial accounts can be defensive or accommodative, and they can reject responsibility or excuse wrongdoings (Bundy and Pfarrer, 2015). This chapter compares initial corporate responses to later findings in fraud examinations by internal investigators. This chapter applies the concept of social approval to examine the match or mismatch between situational attributions found in examination reports and initial responses from the organizations. Thirteen investigation reports regarding corporate scandals in Canada, Denmark, Japan, New Zealand, Nigeria, Norway, Sweden and the USA are subject to content analysis to interpret situational attributions by fraud examiners. Media reports are subject to content analysis to interpret initial responses from the organizations (Gamache and McNamara, 2019; Greer and McLaughlin, 2017). Research results indicate that five out of thirteen organizations were in the match zone of conformity.

Evolution of Corporate Accounts

Corporations occasionally find themselves mired in scandals that threaten their reputation, profitability, and even survival (Fisse and Braithwaite, 1988; Goldstraw-White, 2012; Gottschalk and Benson, 2020; Piazza and Jourdan, 2018). In attempting to respond to and manage these crises, corporations and their executives develop and publicize explanations of their involvement that are designed to forestall or at least mitigate the potential risks to reputation, profitability, and sustainability that exposure of a scandal poses (Bundy and Pfarrer, 2015; Scott and Lyman, 1968; Whyte, 2016). The explanation for a scandal that a corporation puts out technically constitutes what linguists and sociologists call an account, which is a statement made by an actor to explain unanticipated or untoward behavior that is subject to some sort of evaluative inquiry by other actors (Scott and Lyman, 1968). While there is no shortage of advice from public relations experts as crisis managers regarding how accounts should be structured (see, for example, Albrecht, 1996; Hearit, 2006), there has been relatively little research on the actual accounts developed by corporations during actual scandals. Further, there has been even less research on how such accounts may change over time. Understanding corporate accounts is important because of the devastating social and economic effects that failed accounts can have on communities that depend on successful corporations for employment, tax revenues, charitable activities and other community enhancing benefits. It is equally important to understand the other side of the coin, that is, how corporations manage to survive scandals even though they sometimes impose tremendous social and economic harm on society.

https://doi.org/10.1515/9783110766950-005

As emphasized in the previous chapter, a corporate scandal is "an unexpected, publicly known, and harmful event that has high levels of initial uncertainty, interferes with the normal operations of an organization, and generates widespread, intuitive, and negative perceptions" externally (Bundy and Pfarrer, 2015: 350). When a crisis or scandal goes public, corporations almost immediately have to respond to calls to explain and justify what appears to have happened. Corporations do this in different ways, as they know that media coverage is critical in shaping stakeholder perceptions (Gamache and McNamara, 2019). For example, Whyte (2016) found that when safety issues concerning their vehicles arose, Chrysler, Toyota, and Volkswagen all issued statements that were deceptive and designed to resist having to issue expensive recalls. Schoultz and Flyghed (2016) found that Telia Sonera and Lundin Petroleum – Swedish companies involved in financial and environmental crimes, respectively – admitted they were present in areas where the offenses occurred, but they justified their presence by citing the societal benefits of their local business activities. When the recent scandal at Wells Fargo emerged regarding sales practices scandal at their Community Bank, they initially blamed and fired 5,300 employees for secretly opening unauthorized deposit and credit card accounts (Rothacker, 2016). As we have shown in the previous chapter, all of these initial responses changed later.

Thus, this and the previous chapter compare corporations' initial reactions to exposure of wrongdoings to what is later contained in internal reports of investigations by external investigators that they commission. When scandals first emerge into public view, corporations often do not fully understand them as negative events, as there is uncertainty regarding exactly what happened, the potential significance of the events, and how stakeholders and outside observers will respond to it. Furthermore, Bao et al. (2019) found that managers withhold bad news in general. Most importantly, there is a concern whether an individual or the corporation as a whole will face responsibility and sanctions (Bandura, 1999; Schoultz and Flyghed, 2016). It is not surprising that corporate accounts evolve over time as more information about the event becomes public knowledge, and as the corporation assesses external reactions.

As part of crisis management, corporate boards sometimes initiate formal investigations that aim to provide a definitive account of the event. The study in this and the previous chapter examines the evolution of corporate accounts in thirteen international cases involving corporations and executives caught up in financial scandals in Canada, Denmark, Japan, New Zealand, Nigeria, Norway, Sweden, and the United States. The timeline begins when the media first report the corporate scandal and ends when the investigation report becomes publicly available. In addition to the dynamic nature of the accounts that emerge after corporate scandals, we also investigated in the previous chapter the effects of these scandals on the employment of corporate leaders (Schnatterly et al., 2018). As we show, a key part of the evolution of corporate accounts is the divergence of interests between the corporate entity and individual corporate leaders.

The development of the perspective of accounts originally had individual actors in mind, not corporate or organizational actors, although scholars recognized that organizations provide a potential resource for individuals to develop certain types of socially acceptable accounts (Scott and Lyman, 1968). For example, an organizational employee can account for an untoward act by saying that he or she was only following a superior's orders or a specific company policy. However, there are important differences between corporate and individual accounts. Public authorities and other external actors often call upon corporations to account for the untoward behavior of their members or of the corporation itself. In responding to these calls, a corporation can do something that an individual cannot and that is to ask an external party to develop an account for its actions. They do so by hiring external parties, typically law or accounting firms, to investigate the incident in question and to develop a formal account of what happened, why, and how (Gottschalk and Tcherni-Buzzeo, 2017; Schneider, 2006; Williams, 2014).

This allows corporations to defuse one of the main criticisms leveled by external evaluators at account givers, which is that accounts are self-serving. It also begins to lay the groundwork for the eventual separation of corporate from individual interests, which as we noted above is another unique feature of corporate apologies. In addition, corporate accounts usually address the activities of multiple individuals at the same time, rather a lone individual. Finally, unlike individuals corporations can engage in obfuscation in describing their actions. That is, they can claim not really to know what has happened or what they did. This strategy is not available to individuals confronted with accounting for their own individual behavior. Although, as Cohen (2001) notes, individuals can claim that they do not know exactly *why* they did what they did. Thus, corporate accounts are not identical items to individual accounts, because they have dimensions that are not available to individuals. Nevertheless, corporations use many of the same accounting techniques and strategies that individuals use to account for untoward behavior, and because of their social and economic power, they have many advantages over individuals in surviving the harmful consequences that follow the exposure of wrongdoing (Cohen, 2001).

Even though individuals, such as chief executive officers, public relations officials, board members, or investigative commissions, always perform the communication of accounts, corporate accounts nevertheless serve the purpose of benefitting the corporate actor's reputation rather than an individual's. Of course, individuals may benefit personally as a side effect of the corporate account if the account somehow exonerates the corporation from responsibility for a negative event, but victimization of individuals by a corporate account occurs if it shifts blame to the individual. Thus, as corporations respond to crises their interests may not always coincide with the interests of individual members. While a corporation cannot feel, does not have a mind, and does not think; it nevertheless finds itself treated as an actor when executives and others attempt to preserve the reputation of the corporation by communicating accounts on behalf of the corporate entity.

Response Match Research Question

A financial misconduct and crime scandal occurs when someone detects unethical and law-braking behavior among executives in a corporation. A crisis occurs when the financial misconduct and crime scandal represents an unexpected, publicly known, and harmful event that has a high level of initial uncertainty, interferes with the normal operation of the organization, and generates widespread, intuitive, and negative perceptions among stakeholders and in the public (Bundy and Pfarrer, 2015). Famous financial misconduct and crime scandals include Danske Bank in Denmark (Bruun Hjejle, 2018), Toshiba Corporation in Japan (Deloitte, 2015), Fuji Xerox Corporation in New Zealand (Deloitte, 2017), and Wells Fargo's Community Bank in the United States (Shearman and Sterling, 2017).

In addition to handling the scandal and the subsequent crisis, the corporation has to communicate messages to stakeholders and the public. Corporate accounts are communications in the form of speech or text from the corporation (Bandura, 1999; Benson, 1985; Goldstraw-White, 2012; Scott and Lyman, 1968; Whyte, 2016). Research suggests that accounts should match perceptions to avoid cognitive dissonance externally. Bundy and Pfarrer (2015) argue that social approval loss for the corporation will be minimal if the crisis communication from the corporation matches situational attributions of responsibility for the crisis from receivers. This chapter thus addresses the following research question: *How close are corporations in their crisis-response match or mismatch in their corporate accounts of financial misconduct and crime scandals?*

We have an opportunistic sample of 13 reports of investigations by fraud examiners that describe thirteen corporate financial misconduct and crime scandals. The reports are from Canada, Denmark, Japan, New Zealand, Nigeria, Norway, Sweden, and most from the United States. We define the contents of these reports as the situational attributions of responsibility for the crises. We compare these attributions with the responsibility that corporations initially communicated in their accounts. Thereby we identify the extent of match or mismatch between accounts and attributions in each case.

Response Literature Review

Bundy and Pfarrer (2015) define a continuum of response strategies from defensive to accommodative. While a defensive strategy accepts no or little responsibility for a scandal, an accommodative strategy acknowledges the organization's causal role in a scandal. Response strategies in the center of the continuum attempts to reframe how the environment perceives a crisis, while not accepting or denying responsibility. The purpose of a response strategy is to manage social approval loss, minimize damage to corporate legitimacy, and prevent reputation decline. Social approval is perception of general affinity toward an organization; legitimacy is assessment of an organization's appropriateness, while reputation is assessment of an organization's ability to deliver value.

Corporate accounts are the result of an explicit or implicit response strategy. An account is a form of speech for explanations of negative events that the corporation wants to communicate (Benson, 1985; Scott and Lyman, 1968). Some initial accounts serve the purpose of deception of the public (Schoultz and Flyghed, 2016; Whyte, 2016). In giving an account, the offender is addressing an audience and attempting to explain the offense (Benson, 1985).

All crises are uncertain events that generate initial negative reactions. An effective response strategy should match external observers' situational attributions of the crisis to prevent cognitive dissonance among observers (Bundy and Pfarrer, 2015).

Goldstraw-White (2012) studied accounts and suggests that greed is always the motive for corporate offences. She defines greed as socially constructed needs and desires that can never be completely covered or contended. Convenience is always the main characteristic of white-collar offenses. Accounts then typically include application of all five neutralization techniques suggested by Sykes and Matza (1957): the denial of responsibility, the denial of injury, the denial of victim, the condemnation of the condemners, and the appeal to higher loyalties (Maruna and Copes, 2005). Accounts also tend to include more recently suggested neutralization techniques such as the claim of blunder quota (Galvin and Simpson, 2020), the claim of legal mistake (Kaptein and Helvoort, 2019), and the claim of normality of action (Kennedy, 2020). Furthermore, the claim of entitlement to action (Cullen et al., 2020; Dodge, 2020), the claim of solution to a dilemma (Jordanoska, 2018; Rooij and Fine, 2020), and the necessity of crime (Cohen, 2020) are often present. Finally, the claim of role in society (Bernat and Whyte, 2020), and the perception of being a victim (Burns and Meitl, 2020; Siponen and Vance, 2010) are often present as well.

Accounts, neutralizations, and moral disengagement are related forms of linguistic behavior because the content of a neutralization technique can form the basis of an account (Maruna and Copes, 2005). For example, if an individual neutralizes the inner feelings of guilt associated with the contemplation of a deviant act by denying responsibility for the act to himself or herself, he or she can later also deny responsibility to an audience of evaluators. By neutralizing guilt feelings, offenders do not feel accountable, ashamed or responsible (Chen and Moosmayer, 2020).

Thus, accounts, neutralizations, and moral disengagement serve different functions and their temporal ordering is different. Neutralizations and moral disengagement involve verbalizations that actors make to themselves beforehand in order to excuse themselves from standard moral prescriptions against certain types of untoward behavior. Their function is to allow the actor to engage in deviance while still maintaining a positive self-image (Benson, 1985; Maruna and Copes, 2005; Sykes and Matza, 1957). Accounts, on the other hand, are presentations made after the behavior has occurred and represent communications to others. Their function is to protect the actor's reputation and social standing from negative evaluations by others. Account giving supports the human desire to maintain the perception of the self as a rational, moral actor, an actor of integrity (Whyte, 2016). Bandura (1999) identified the ways that corporations can disengage themselves from the harmful consequences of their actions.

An important motive for corporate accounts is restoring stakeholder trust. Trust is a vital element at all levels of business operations and relationships, and the concept of trust is, "a psychological state comprising the intention to accept vulnerability based upon positive expectations of the intentions or behavior of another" (Rousseau et al., 1998: 395). Trust grows over time but is easily destroyed and difficult to repair (Kraus et al., 1992).

"A crisis with higher situational attributions of responsibility should be matched with a response strategy that accepts more responsibility" (Bundy and Pfarrer, 2015: 353), and "in the latter stages of a crisis, a truly misleading defensive strategy may offer few benefits" (Bundy and Pfarrer, 2015: 363). When we compare corporations' initial reactions to exposure of wrongdoings, we have to keep in mind that much more information might be available at later stages. Uniformed individuals deliver their initial accounts with their own reputational interests in mind. What is later contained in internal reports of investigations that corporate leaders have commissioned normally has a much more solid information base compared to the onset of a crisis. The interests of the organization may have diverged from those of the individuals who first responded to the crisis. Complete knowledge of responsibility is rare at the onset of a crisis, and it may take a long time before an organization and stakeholders agree on the facts. In the beginning, there are mainly rumors, allegations, and perceptions of what happened, how it happened, who did what to make it happen or not happen, and why it happened. Uncertainty decreases over time and consequently the space for making sense of events is reduced (Bundy and Pfarrer, 2015: 364): "An organization therefore may switch its response strategy based on new information and feedback from evaluators."

A later corporate account that is significantly different from an early account – sometimes leading to dismissal of executives and board directors (Ghannam et al., 2019) – is not necessarily a result of manipulation or other unethical communication strategies. It might as well be the case that new information gave reason to communicate an updated corporate account. The release of authoritative information that conflicts with an organization's initial response can trigger a switch in a corporate account (Bundy and Pfarrer, 2015: 364): "Because such information is difficult to contest, it is likely that any organization would alter its message to be consistent with the message evaluators will perceive as more credible."

Nevertheless, an organization may face extreme reactions to its switching response strategies, especially when a switch comes as a major surprise. A non-consistent response throughout a scandal can itself increase the loss of social approval for the organization. In contrast, consistent corporate accounts throughout the scandal might create trust in the organizational handling of the crisis. The design of our study in this chapter serves to determine how the accounts of corporations mired in scandals actually do change over time.

However, as we showed in the previous chapter, initial accounts sometimes appeared more as obfuscations rather than as denials, justifications, excuses, or apologies. By obfuscation, we mean that the initial public statements neither admit nor deny that anything untoward has happened. Rather, the statement vaguely suggests that something may have happened, but nobody knows for sure because details of the event are missing.

Response Match Research Method

The research method applied in this empirical study of news reports as well as investigation reports is content analysis (Bell et al., 2018; Saunders et al., 2007), as described in the previous chapter. Content analysis is any methodology or procedure that works to identify characteristics within texts attempting to make valid inferences (Krippendorff, 1980; Patrucco et al., 2017). Content analysis assumes that language reflects both how people understand their surroundings and their cognitive processes. Therefore, content analysis makes it possible to identify and determine relevant text in a context (McClelland et al., 2010).

As mentioned in the previous chapter, private and public organizations often hire fraud examiners from global auditing firms and local law firms to investigate suspicions of executive deviance related to white-collar crime (Brooks and Button, 2011; Button et al., 2007a, 2007b; Button and Gee, 2013; Schneider, 2006; Williams, 2005, 2014). At the end of their inquiry, fraud examiners write a report of investigation and hand it over to the client organization as their property. Unfortunately, clients tend to keep reports secret (Gottschalk and Tcherni-Buzzeo, 2017). Only a few reports are publicly available, and they are often hard to find. After searching the Internet for some time, we were able to identify and retrieve 20 reports written in English. Seven of the reports were focusing on individual wrongdoing rather than corporate wrongdoing. Thirteen reports were focusing on corporate scandals. Table 4.1 summarizes these thirteen cases in terms of internal investigations of corporate scandals.

Table 4.1: Corporate investigations because of corporate scandals.

#	CORPORATE INVESTIGATION	CORPORATE SCANDAL
1	Canada: Town of Pelham was involved in irregular payments in a development project. KPMG (2017) conducted a fraud examination and wrote an investigation report to explain how irregular payments occurred. The report is 100 pages.	Cover-up of Can$17 million dollars in unaccounted debt.
2	Denmark: Danske Bank's Estonian branch was involved in a money laundering scandal. Non-residents used the bank to transfer criminal proceeds. Danish law firms Bruun Hjejle (2018) conducted a fraud examination and wrote an investigation report about the non-resident portfolio at Danske Bank's Estonian branch. The report is 87 pages.	Money laundering of crime proceeds from Russia.
3	Japan: Olympus Corporation was involved in an accounting scandal where losses for failing financial investments remained hidden in worthless credits. Auditing firm Deloitte (2011) conducted a fraud examination and wrote an investigation report about inappropriate accounting. The report is 243 pages.	Fraud scheme of investment accounting violating Financial Instruments and Exchange Act and Companies Act. It was a "tobashi" scheme, which is a type of financial fraud where a client's losses hide in an investment firm by shifting them between the portfolios of other (genuine or fake) clients.
4	Japan: Toshiba Corporation was also involved in an accounting scandal where work in progress and finished goods were inflated thus assigned higher values. Auditing firm Deloitte (2015) conducted a fraud examination and wrote an Investigation report about inappropriate accounting. The report is 90 pages.	Accounting fraud that was overstating profits by US$1.2 billion.
5	New Zealand: Fuji Xerox was involved in aggressive sales practices coupled to inappropriate accounting where customers felt forced to sign new contracts before old contracts had expired, and new contracts entered accounting as sales. Auditing firm Deloitte (2017) conducted a fraud examination and wrote an investigation report about inappropriate sales and accounting practices. The report is 89 pages.	Inappropriate accounting practices overstating profits and illegal credit risks.

Table 4.1 (continued)

#	CORPORATE INVESTIGATION	CORPORATE SCANDAL
6	Nigeria: NNPC is the national petroleum company in Nigeria. The company withheld transfers of oil revenues to the government and claimed it covered costs. Auditing firm PwC (2015) conducted a fraud examination and wrote an investigation report on financial transactions between the company and the government. The report is 199 pages.	Crude oil revenues generated by the corporation withheld or unremitted to the federal accounts. A former governor of the Central Bank of Nigeria, Lamido Sanusi, raised the allegation that a huge amount had disappeared.
7	Norway: Telenor in Norway was a major shareholder of VimpelCom, which was involved in a corruption scandal in Uzbekistan to obtain mobile phone licenses. Auditing firm Deloitte (2016) conducted a fraud examination and wrote an investigation report about reluctance among Telenor executives to react on information from whistleblowers regarding the corruption scandal. The report is 54 pages.	VimpelCom involved in corruption in Uzbekistan, and Telenor knew about it.
8	Sweden: Nordea is a bank in Sweden. The bank has a subsidiary in Luxembourg. When the Panama Papers revealed money flows to and from tax havens, investigative journalists discovered misconduct in Luxembourg. For example, the bank backdated contracts for customers for tax evasion purposes. Law firm Mannheimer Swartling (2016) conducted a fraud examination and wrote an investigation report on the bank practice of wealth management for its customers. The report is 42 pages.	Illegal backdating of contracts and tax evasion revealed in the Panama Papers from tax havens.
9	USA: Lehman Brothers went bankrupt because of deviant risk taking in financial operations. Jenner Block (2010) conducted a fraud examination and wrote an investigation report about bank practices. The report is 239 pages.	Misconduct but no crime related to fiduciary duty of care by failing to observe risk management, went bankrupt.

Table 4.1 (continued)

#	CORPORATE INVESTIGATION	CORPORATE SCANDAL
10	USA: General Motors were reluctant to correct ignition switch failure for financial reasons. Jenner and Block (2014) conducted a fraud examination and wrote an investigation report about management practices. The report is 325 pages.	Disregard of ignition switch failure in Cobalt car that caused injuries and deaths, reluctance to correct for financial reasons.
11	USA: WorldCom went bankrupt after inappropriate accounting to keep the share price at a level acceptable to the CEO, who had deposited his shares in a bank for loans to finance private properties. Auditing firm PwC (2003) conducted a fraud examination and wrote an investigation report about the collapse of WorldCom. The report is 345 pages.	Fraud and conspiracy at false financial reporting, went bankrupt
12	USA: Wells Fargo's Community Bank had aggressive sales practices where bank customers received services that they had not ordered. Law firm Shearman Sterling (2017) conducted a fraud examination and wrote an investigation report about management and employees in the sales model. The report is 113 pages.	Improper and unethical sales practices violating specific statutory provisions
13	USA: Enron Corporation went bankrupt after inappropriate accounting practices. Enron was an energy, commodities, and services company. A whistleblower revealed that Enron's reported financial condition reflected an institutionalized, systematic, and creatively planned accounting fraud, known since as the Enron scandal. Law firm Wilmer Cutler Pickering (2003) conducted a fraud examination and wrote an investigation report about illegitimate accounting practices. The report is 218 pages.	Misleading and illegal practices to hide and embezzle funds, securities and wire fraud.

We were also interested in the initial corporate account concerning each scandal, as listed in the previous chapter. Initial accounts are important, because stakeholders as well as the public quickly begin to associate a crisis with an individual organization, such as the Enron scandal (Bundy and Pfarrer, 2015). An organization's initial response is influential in anchoring first impressions externally. The initial account might be an active statement about unknown internal circumstances, or a response to allegations already out there in the public. We needed to find the very first corporate communication about the scandal and decided to use the first media coverage of a corporate message as the initial corporate account. As argued by Bundy and Pfarrer (2015), social disapproval of corporate crisis emerge in negative media coverage that challenges, criticizes, or condemns an organization's activities, behaviors, or values.

As described in the previous chapter, we identified the university library system of databases as a reliable source, where we selected the database 'Newsbank' with the function 'Access World News' (AWN), which archives stories from thousands of U.S. and global news sources. The stories form a written history of an event as it occurs (Newsbank, 2018). We applied the feature 'More Search Options' to enter keywords regarding corporation, executive, misconduct, and year. We scrolled backwards in the search results to the very first news article mentioning the scandal in terms of a statement from the organization. In addition, from the investigation reports it was possible to identify approximately, when news about the scandals first appeared in the media.

Response Match Research Findings

This chapter addresses the following research question: *How close are corporations in their crisis-response match or mismatch in their corporate accounts of financial misconduct and crime scandals?* A previous table in this book has illustrated in qualitative text terms the extent of match or mismatch between initial corporate accounts and investigation accounts. We assume that investigation accounts represent perceptions in the public in terms of corporate responsibility for a deviant act, while initial corporate accounts represent a response strategy from the organization that is attempting to prevent or limit the loss of social approval, legitimacy, and reputation.

To enable a quantitative analysis, we apply a figure suggested by Bundy and Pfarrer (2015), where it is possible to combine situational attributions with response strategy as illustrated in Figure 4.1.

We define an arbitrary scale for both situational attributions and responses. Situational attribution can range from 1 (fraud examiners conclude that the corporation has no responsibility for the event) to 5 (fraud examiners conclude that the corporation carries full and complete responsibility for the event). Corporate response can range from 1 (corporation denies any responsibility for the event) to 5 (corporation acknowledges full and complete responsibility for the event). The difference between these two numbers for each case represents the extent of match. Zero is the ultimate match, while four is a complete mismatch.

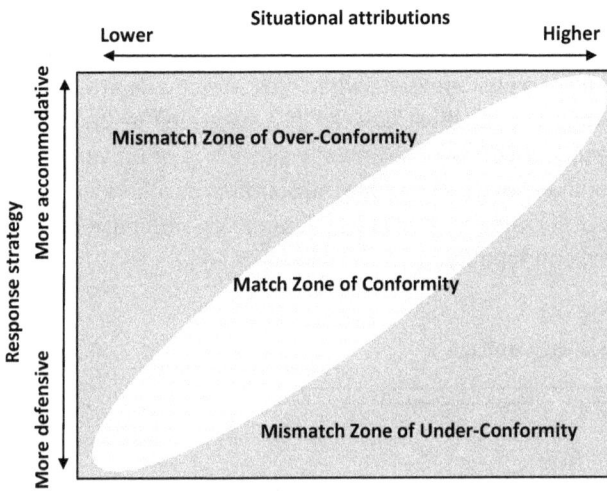

Figure 4.1: The crisis-response match (adapted from Bundy and Pfarrer 2015).

The numbers in Table 4.2 are simple estimates based on research knowledge about each case. The numbers represent exploratory research that need confirmation by multiple raters of the same thirteen case studies in future research.

Table 4.2: Results of simple rating of response-attribution match.

#	Business	Response	Attribution	Match
1	Town of Pelham expansion in Canada (KPMG, 2017)	1	2	1
2	Danske Bank in Denmark (Bruun Hjejle, 2018)	2	5	3
3	Olympus Corporation in Japan (Deloitte, 2011)	1	4	3
4	Toshiba Corporation in Japan (Deloitte, 2015)	2	4	2
5	Fuji Xerox Corporation in New Zealand (Deloitte, 2017)	3	4	1
6	Nigerian National Petroleum Corporation in Nigeria (PwC, 2015)	1	2	1
7	VimpelCom by Telenor in Norway (Deloitte, 2016)	2	3	1
8	Nordea bank in Sweden (Mannheimer Swartling, 2016)	2	4	2
9	Lehman Brothers in the USA (Jenner Block, 2010)	3	2	−1
10	General Motors in the USA (Jenner Block, 2014)	2	5	3
11	WorldCom Corporation in the USA (PwC, 2003)	2	5	3
12	Wells Fargo's Community Bank in the USA (Shearman Sterling, 2017)	1	4	3
13	Enron Corporation in the USA (Wilmer Cutler Pickering, 2003)	1	5	4

Figure 4.2 illustrates the numbers in Table 4.2, where five out of thirteen corporate accounts are within the match zone of conformity. The figure is interesting, as all strategies for corporate responses were defensive, while most situational attributions tended to be medium or high. The figure illustrates the idea suggested by Bundy and Pfarrer (2015) that an accommodative response strategy as such is of no value. The response strategy has to be adapted to the situational attributions by others to be successful. Corporate accounts that match external expectations can minimize the loss of social approval, legitimacy, and reputation.

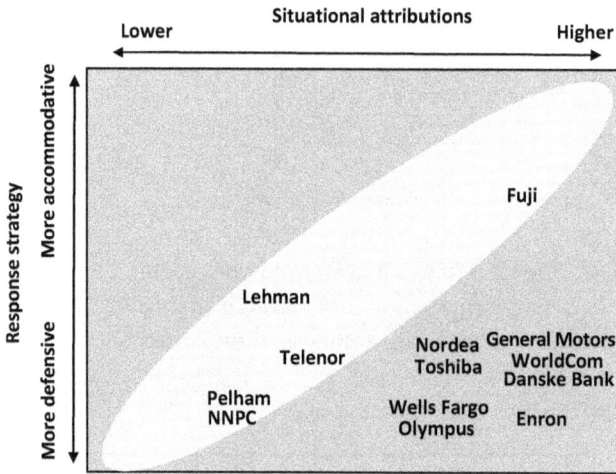

Figure 4.2: The crisis-response match for our sample based on simple rating.

It is important to emphasize that the numbers in Table 4.2 and Figure 4.2 are only exploratory to illustrate the possibility of analyzing corporate responses to scandals by comparing responses at two different points in time by the corporations and their investigators respectively.

We can expand our empirical study by including the variable of information increase followed by a subsequent uncertainty reduction. As argued by Bundy and Pfarrer (2015), initial corporate accounts occur at the onset of a crisis, where a high level of uncertainty both internally and externally is common. As a crisis evolves and the scandal grows in size, more information will usually emerge. An organization may therefore switch its response, especially when information that is more credible becomes available. The report prepared by external investigators hired by the company presents the kind of credible and authoritative information that might conflict with an organization's initial framing of the event. If the investigators have detected information that the organization had no way of knowing,

Table 4.3: Effect of information correction on response-attribution match.

#	Business	Scandal Response Match	New Examination Information	Revised Response Match
1	Town of Pelham expansion in Canada (KPMG, 2017)	1	0	1
2	Danske Bank in Denmark (Bruun Hjejle, 2018)	3	1	2
3	Olympus Corporation in Japan (Deloitte, 2011)	3	0	3
4	Toshiba Corporation in Japan (Deloitte, 2015)	2	0	2
5	Fuji Xerox Corporation in New Zealand (Deloitte, 2017)	1	0	1
6	Nigerian National Petroleum Corporation in Nigeria (PwC, 2015)	1	1	0
7	VimpelCom by Telenor in Norway (Deloitte, 2016)	1	1	0
8	Nordea bank in Sweden (Mannheimer Swartling, 2016)	2	1	1
9	Lehman Brothers in the USA (Jenner Block, 2010)	−1	0	−1
10	General Motors in the USA (Jenner Block, 2014)	3	0	3
11	WorldCom Corporation in the USA (PwC, 2003)	3	0	3
12	Wells Fargo's Community Bank in the USA (Shearman Sterling, 2017)	3	1	2
13	Enron Corporation in the USA (Wilmer Cutler Pickering, 2003)	4	0	4

then information shortage rather than deception caused the initial response to be different from examiners conclusions.

We introduced this information in our analysis by reviewing the investigation reports to determine whether new significant information emerged after the initial exposure of the scandal. Our content analysis here focuses on determining whether the reports use information from sources, such as documents, accounts, and interviews that seemed unknown to the corporation at first. We introduce the new information variable in Table 4.3. A zero in the column for new information indicates that no significant new information is present in a report after fraud examination. A one in the column indicates that some new information emerged. The third column indicates a corrected crisis-response match where we subtracted the new information number from the initial crisis-response match.

Based on available information from investigation reports and the media, the analysis shows that that significant new information emerged in five of our twelve cases. Consequently, the response match improves for these cases as illustrated in Figure 4.3. This result suggests that in at least some of the cases examined here, the initial response from corporate agents was in some way deceptive. In other words, at some level of the organization, managers understood the nature of the scandal, but corporate agents did not necessarily know and chose to engage in impression management and present the scandal in such a way that its potential negative effects on the organization's reputation would be minimized.

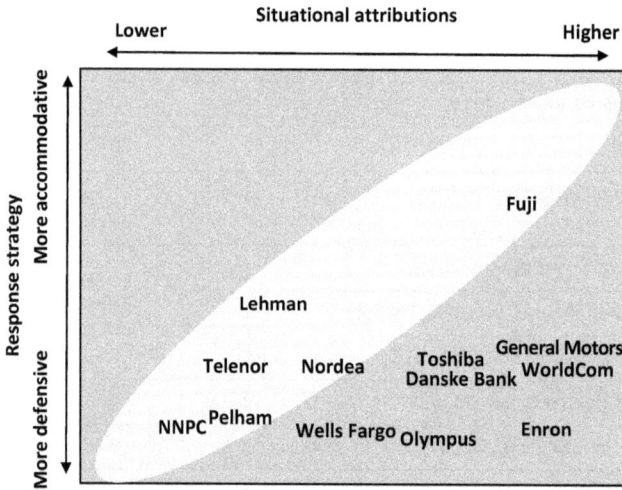

Figure 4.3: Corrected crisis-response match for our sample based on simple rating.

Theoretical Contribution

This and the previous chapter present and analyze accounts from thirteen corporate scandals based on Bundy and Pfarrer's (2015) zones of conformity. What emerges from our empirical study is the impression of convenience when corporations attempt to tackle an evolving scandal in their communications (Chan and Gibbs, 2020; Gottschalk, 2020; Hansen, 2020; Kireenko et al., 2019; Braaten and Vaughn, 2019). Convenience is a term used to describe the potential savings in time and effort, as well as the potential avoidance of suffering and pain (Engdahl, 2015). Convenience is the state of being able to proceed with something with little effort or difficulty, avoiding pain and strain (Mai and Olsen, 2016). A convenience-oriented person is one who seeks to accomplish a task in the shortest time with the least expenditure of human energy (Berry et al., 2002).

Convenience orientation varies among entities, as some are more concerned than others are about time saving, effort reduction, and pain avoidance (Higgins, 1997). Convenience comes at a potential cost to the entity in terms of the likelihood of detection of more serious wrongdoing over time. In other words, reducing time and effort now entails a greater potential for future cost. Paying for convenience is a way of phrasing this proposition (Farquhar and Rowley, 2009).

Convenience is a phenomenon that most of us practice in many aspects of human life. For example, convenience stores and convenience shopping is associated with easy access to goods and services (Sari et al., 2017). A theory of convenience applies to a number of areas where people prefer alternatives that are associated with savings in time and effort, and with avoidance of pain and problems. For example, a convenience theory of cheating suggests that cheating is a preferred alternative in certain situations. Convenience is an explanation for white-collar crime. Convenience manifests itself in the financial motive, the organizational opportunity, and the personal willingness for deviant behavior.

Sundström and Radon (2015) argue that a convenient individual or organization is not necessarily neither bad nor lazy. On the contrary, people see it as smart and rational to be convenient. From a resource matching perspective, convenience directly relates to the amount of time and effort (resources) that you have to dedicate to accomplish a task. However, convenience is a more comprehensive construct than simply examining ease of use perceptions that also addresses the amount of effort in an interaction. Ease of use is the degree to which an alternative action is free of effort. Convenience addresses the time and effort exerted before, during, and after an action or avoidance of action (Collier and Kimes, 2012).

As a relative construct, convenience is in line with decision-making among alternatives, where accounts can imply denial, justification, excuse or apology. What is considered most convenient is decided by the corporation (Chan and Gibbs, 2020; Gottschalk, 2020; Hansen, 2020; Kireenko et al., 2019; Braaten and Vaughn, 2019). Because of the overwhelming workload combined with a need to prioritize own time, convenience is often at the core of thinking among chief executives in organizations (Bigley and Wiersma, 2002).

The theory of accounts initially described and explained how individual actors react when people observe or accuse them of behaving in an untoward manner. According to the theory, accounts are crucial to maintaining social order, because they help smooth over conflict and dissension that may arise when someone behaves in an abnormal or unexpected way. For example, as individuals, people expect us to obey the law and when we do not, we have to in some way justify, excuse, or apologize for our infractions if we hope to have any chance of receiving trust and acceptance from others in the future. As with individuals, business corporations find a multitude of social and legal expectations in their surroundings. For instance, among other things, they face the expectation to conduct their businesses honestly, to treat their customers, employees, investors, and competitors fairly, and not to damage the environment excessively. When they violate these expectations, they face a potential loss of social approval and acceptance. Hence, like individuals, they must in some way account for their indiscretions when they become public.

In this and the previous chapter, we have shown that when corporations fall into scandals, they initially pursue one of three strategies to account for their actions – denial of wrongdoing, obfuscation, or denial or responsibility. In our sample of twelve cases, these initial responses were not successful in that they did not quell public interest and condemnation of the corporations involved. So, the corporations eventually appointed or hired outsiders to investigate the scandals and prepare reports that in theory were supposed to fully explain what happened and why. These reports can be treated as accounts that are similar to the accounts developed by individuals, but they also have unique characteristics in that the account is not prepared directly by the actor and because corporations can do something that individuals cannot do when they apologize, and that is literally to split themselves in two.

Corporate entities can apologize for wrongdoing, while at the same time blaming it on individual members. Hence, the entity survives but not some of its individual members. In our sample, this was a common pattern. In our view, this pattern differs in an important way from accounts of atrocities that political entities tend to provide.

As Cohen (2001: 77) notes, when political entities must account for their involvement in an atrocity, they develop accounts that mirror the internal logic of individual accounts. They put forth narratives that acknowledge that something has happened, but they refuse to accept how outsiders are characterizing the act or their role in it. For example, officials of the U.S. government have disputed that waterboarding is "torture" (Beam, 2008; DeFrank, 2009). Members of political entities also frequently deny knowledge of an atrocity as a way of denying responsibility for it (Cohen, 2001). What political entities do not is to apologize for the atrocity. At least they do not apologize within a contemporary period, though they may apologize after enough time has passed so that all of the original participants are either dead or out of office. For example, it was not until 2008 that the U.S. House of Representatives passed a resolution apologizing for the enslavement and racial segregation of African Americans.

Like political entities, corporations start by denying responsibility or disputing the characterization of a wrongful act. However, unlike political entities, they often later acknowledge their wrongdoing, apologize for it, and resolve to mend their ways going forward (Schoultz and Flyghed, 2019a, 2019b). As proof of their sincerity, corporations reassign, degrade or fire previously trusted senior leaders. It is beyond the scope of the present research to theorize fully why this happens, but we speculate that a root cause involves the difference between citizens and consumers. Nationhood represents an important aspect of the identities of citizens, so when political leaders acknowledge and apologize for wrongdoings, it reflects negatively on the identities of its citizens. Thus, political leaders must be exceedingly careful about acknowledging wrongdoing. On the other hand, the identities of consumers connect less strongly to the companies they trade with than are the identities of citizens in their nations. Hence, corporations can afford to apologize without worrying about offending their customers; indeed, they often must do so, if they want to keep consumers happy.

Future Research Ideas

It is important to acknowledge limitations to the presented research. There is a small sample of cases, which necessarily makes our results provisional. Future research should expand the number of cases. In addition, our sample was limited to cases in which a formal investigative report was produced and released, and not all scandals end with formal reports. There may be something unique about the scandals examined here in that they led to formal reports, and this same factor may have influenced the nature of the accounts provided by the corporate entities. A potential avenue for future researchers is to investigate whether information on the evolution of corporate accounts can be traced in the news media even if there is no formal report and then linked to the theoretical perspective advanced by Bundy and Pfarrer (2015).

Future research needs to apply a multiple-rater approach to a more thoroughly developed scale. Future research also needs to verify the underlying assumption suggested in a research proposition by Bundy and Pfarrer (2015: 357):

> The more an organization's response strategy matches evaluators' situational attributions of crisis responsibility, the lower the mean and variance of social approval loss.

The research article by Bundy and Pfarrer (2015) is a purely theoretical paper presenting four research propositions. This chapter has demonstrated a potential path to conduct an empirical test of their crisis-response match figure.

There are thus several more avenues for future research. First, it is the use of an opportunistic sample. We have provided no reason for the 13 cases selected or their representation across countries, simply because we have no reason for it either than this is what we found. Furthermore, there is a need for a stronger theoretical motivation for this kind of study, and the current research does not address most of the literature on white-collar crime. Our approach may seem a very narrow one that limits the overall contribution of this study to the broader field of criminology.

Based on a theoretical article published in the "Academy of Management Review" regarding social approval loss after corporate scandals (Bundy and Pfarrer, 2015), this chapter has illustrated how corporate accounts in the media and in fraud investigations might empirically test suggested research ideas. Specifically, the crisis-response match is an interesting combination of initial corporate responses and later findings by fraud examiners. Based on a simple rating scheme, we find that five out of thirteen organizations were in the match zone of conformity. It is interesting to note that the initial response strategy suggested is not to be as accommodative as possible. Rather, minimization of social approval loss occurs if the initial response matches situational attributions from stakeholders and the public.

An avenue for future research might be to study corporate responses as a reaction to media coverage. In the current research, corporate responses are mainly driven by internal politics, blame games and surfacing of new information. Gamache and McNamara (2019: 920) suggest there is a reciprocal effect where media coverage influences the targets of the coverage:

> The reciprocal effects model views the relationship between the media and the subject of media coverage as having feedback, or reciprocal, effects. (. . .)

> The reciprocal effects model includes both direct and indirect effects. The central mechanisms suggest that the behavior of media subjects stimulate media reports, which in turn directly influence the cognitions, appraisals, emotions, and behaviors of those subjects. Subjects of negative media coverage pay close attention to media assessments and tend to overestimate the influence of these reports. Indirect effects come from the influence that the media has on the general public and other stakeholders who, in turn, influence the media subjects. Finally, the effects of the media coverage shape the subjects' subsequent decisions and action.

Gamache and McNamara (2019: 921) suggest that the reciprocal effects model is particularly important for exploring the impact of negative media coverage, which is certainly the case when corporate white-collar crime scandals become publicly known:

> The negativity effect suggests that negative information has a greater impact on people than equally intense positive information, or, in short, that "bad is stronger than good". Bad news or negative feedback is more impactful than good information in part because bad information is processed more thoroughly. This is believed to be primarily a result of evolutionary processes, as bad news is more closely associated with survival threats. Importantly for the media context, negative information is likely to be more salient when both positive and negative information is available.

Another potential avenue for future research also stimulated by Gamache and McNamara (2019: 921) is their suggestion that executives "have been known to distance themselves from journalists who provide negative coverage of the firm". One motive for such executive behavior might be that negative media coverage can have a widespread impact even in shaping customer disloyalty and employee amoral. However, the strategy of ignoring negative journalists can jeopardize the scandal as the communication disappears far out of the match zone of conformity.

A third potential avenue for future research, again stimulated by Gamache and McNamara (2019: 936), is their suggestion that temporal focus shapes how much an organization pays attention to negative media reactions:

> More specifically, we argue and find that CEOs high in past focus tend to be highly influenced by negative media coverage while this coverage has a substantially lower influence on CEOs high in future focus.

Translated into our context of accounts, this finding suggests that it might be easier to move into the match zone of conformity for organizational spokespersons when they represent a corporate culture of strong future focus.

An interesting avenue for future research is financial restatements as a crisis-response strategy to improve the extent of match between situational attributions and corporate responses. Following the Sarbanes-Oxley Act in the United States two decades ago, the number of financial restatements increased dramatically. Each restatement indicates that financial information previously issued by management and relied upon by investors and other stakeholders, was incorrect (Cianci et al., 2019: 299):

> Restatements, by definition, indicate that a previous earnings report, thought to be correct, was, in fact, materially misstated. Because company management is responsible for preparing financial statements, the occurrence of a restatement is indicative of a reporting failure by company management, which, in turn, raises concerns about the financial reporting process and the individuals responsible for that process. In this way, restatements, especially those involving intentional misstatements (i.e., fraud), erode trust in company management and damage management's reputation.

In our perspective of obtaining match and avoiding mismatch by entering the match zone of conformity, financial restatements can just as well represent a mismatch contribution as a match contribution, since surprising restatements are likely to cause an increase in situational attributions. Cianci et al. (2019) studied how investors respond to restatements. They found that corporate pe-restatement reputation and post-restatement announcement of corrective actions combine to influence investors' corporate fraud prevention assessments, which in turn mediate investors' degree of trust in the corporation (Cianci et al., 2019: 306):

> Specifically, when management does not announce a corrective action in response to a restatement, investors trust management with a poor pre-restatement reputation less than management with a good pre-restatement reputation because investors do not believe that such management values preventing fraud.

Thus, it appears that corporate pre-restatement reputation and corporate announcement of corrective actions in response to a restatement can act to determine investors' situational attributions concerning the scandal. Pre-restatement corporate reputation and the announcement of corporate corrective actions can lessen the negative consequences from issuing a restatement and thereby reduce the mismatch and potentially help the match depending on a number of other factors.

By announcement of corrective actions, the corporation attempts reputation-building tasks such as strengthening internal governance. While such actions may positively affect the post-restatement match, they can be costly to the corporation (Cianci et al., 2019: 297):

Accordingly, it is important for managers to understand the extent to which announcing such actions, is likely to mitigate investors' negative response to the restatement.

While there are costs associated with corrective actions, it seems to be an important mechanism to restore investor confidence and thus reduce the mismatch and improve the match. Corrective actions may even mitigate the damage from restatements.

Part II: **Empirical Studies**

5 Telia Telecom in Sweden

Swedish researchers Schoultz and Flyghed (2020a, 2020b, 2021) studied corporate crime in three Swedish corporations. They identified corporate initial responses such as "we didn't do it" to later responses such as "we've learned our lesson" (Schoultz and Flyghed, 2020a), they noticed denials and confessions (Schoultz and Flyghed, 2020b), and they identified responses such as "we have been thrown under the bus" (Schoultz and Flyghed, 2021).

The three companies were Lundin Petroleum, Stora Enso, and Telia Company. Ever since Lundin Petroleum was awarded a contract for a block in southern Sudan, the company's operations have faced allegations of participating in crime against humanity. A report led to the initiation of a police investigation in Sweden into violations of international law. Stora Enso is a Finnish-Swedish paper and pulp manufacturer operating around the world. The allegations directed at Stora Enso involve the company's actions in relation to local landowners in Brazil and China (Schoultz and Flyghed, 2020a).

Telia Corporate Corruption Story

The case of Telia Company, which is the focus of this chapter, is concerned with corporate corruption. Telia bribed the daughter of the president in Uzbekistan to obtain licenses for mobile phone communication in the country. When detected, Telia agreed to pay $965 million to resolve charges relating to violations of the Foreign Corrupt Practices Act in the United States. At the same time, the public prosecutor in Sweden charged three executives at Telia of bribery in connection with the company's entry in Uzbekistan (Schoultz and Flyghed, 2020a).

Telia were not the only company bribing Gulnara Karimova, the daughter of Uzbek president Islam Karimov. The Dutch telecommunication company Vimpel-Com did the same, and they had to enter into a deferred prosecution agreement with the US Department of Justice, where VimpelCom admitted, accepted, and acknowledged that it was responsible for acts of its officers, directors, employees, and agents. The Norwegian chief executive at VimpelCom, Jo Lunder was charged for corruption by Norwegian police. Two executives at Telenor in Norway had to leave their positions after ignoring whistleblowers from VimpelCom, where Telenor had a substantial share of the ownership (Deloitte, 2016).

Corruption is defined as the giving, requesting, receiving, or accepting of an improper advantage related to a position, office, or assignment (Ashforth et al., 2008). The improper advantage does not have to be connected to a specific action or to not doing this action (Artello and Albanese, 2021). It will be sufficient if the advantage can be linked to a person's position, office, or assignment. An individual or group

https://doi.org/10.1515/9783110766950-006

is guilty of corruption if they accept money or money's worth for doing something that he is under a duty to do anyway, that he is under a duty not to do, or to exercise a legitimate discretion for improper reason. Corruption is to destroy or pervert the integrity or fidelity of a person in his discharge of duty, it is to induce to act dishonestly or unfaithfully, it is to make venal, and it is to bribe (Lord et al., 2018). Corruption involves behavior on the part of officials in the public or private sectors, in which they improperly and unlawfully enrich themselves and/or those close to them, or induce others to do so, by misusing the position in which they are placed. Corruption is an undesirable and destructive aspect of social life (Pertiwi, 2018). Corruption covers a wide range of illegal activity such as kickbacks, embezzlement, and extortion. Corruption entails "mistreatment of suppliers, customers, or competitors" (Kolthoff, 2020: 434).

In 2006, Telia sought to expand into the central Asian telecommunications market (Schoultz and Flyghed, 2020b: 4):

> The growth strategy was well-anchored in Telia and among the company's owners, which include the Swedish state. Telia entered Uzbekistan in 2007, a country controlled by the authoritarian President Islam Karimov and his family (up until his death in 2016), who over the years has been shown to have very little respect for human rights. Uzbekistan was known as a country in which it was almost impossible to implement international investments without the involvement of the governing regime. In information presented to the Telia board in 2007, Uzbekistan was described "as the most difficult and politically most uncertain country" but was at the same time understood to be the "commercially most interesting".
>
> As a result of the region's human rights record, Telia's presence in Uzbekistan was from the start criticized by human rights organizations, investors and the Swedish media. The criticism related to Telia's partner in Uzbekistan and this partner's connections with president Karimov, also to claims that Telia's equipment was being used for the purpose of surveilling the political opposition in several authoritarian countries.

Telia's response to the allegations involved a wide range of neutralizations and denials as described later in this chapter. The company stated that they were aware of the corruption problems in Uzbekistan while at the same time giving assurance s that the company had zero tolerance for corruption (Schoultz and Flyghed, 2020b).

The Telia corruption case was detected by investigative journalists at the Swedish public broadcasting corporation. Then the Telia affair in Uzbekistan became a public scandal in 2012 (Schoultz and Flyghed, 2020b: 5):

> Following revelations focused on how the company was participating in surveillance operations conducted by the secret services linked to several oppressive regimes, the investigative TV shows moved on to look at the 2007 acquisition by Telia of a 3G license, frequencies and number series, in order to become established as a telecom operator in Uzbekistan. Information was presented describing extensive financial transactions with a letter-box entity, Takilant. The journalists could show that Takilant was owned by an assistant to the president's daughter, Gulnara Karimova. By the time that Telia purchased the license in Uzbekistan,

Gulnara Karimova's racketeering activities in the telecommunications market had been documented in several high-profile news publications.

Convenient Financial Motive

The financial motive for Telia was to make money in Uzbekistan by providing mobile phone services in the country. In many organizations, ends justify means (Campbell and Göritz, 2014). If ends in terms of ambitions and goals are difficult to realize and achieve in legal ways, illegal means represent an alternative in many organizations (Jonnergård et al., 2010). Among most executives, it is an obvious necessity to achieve goals and objectives, while it is an obvious catastrophe failing to achieve goals and objectives. Welsh and Ordonez (2014) found that high performance goals cause unethical behavior. Dodge (2009: 15) argues that it is tough rivalry making executives in the organization commit crime to attain goals:

> The competitive environment generates pressures on the organization to violate the law in order to attain goals.

Individual executives would like to be successful, and they would like their workplace to be successful. Being associated with a successful business is important to the identity of many executives. They explore and exploit attractive corporate economic possibilities in both legal and illegal ways, so that their organization can emerge just as successful, or as even more successful, than other organizations. Profit orientation becomes stronger in goal-oriented organizations whose aim tends to be an ambitious financial bottom line. A strong emphasis on goal attainment might indeed lead organizational members to engage in illegal acts (Kang and Thosuwanchot, 2017). The corporate crime motive for Telia was possibilities for profits as illustrated in Figure 5.1.

Convenient Organizational Opportunity

The organizational opportunity to involve themselves in corruption was based on legitimate access to crime resources as illustrated in Figure 5.1. A white-collar offender has typically legitimate access to resources to commit and conceal crime (Williams et al., 2019). A resource is an enabler applied and used to satisfy human and organizational needs. A resource has utility and limited availability. A white-collar offender has usually access to resources that are valuable (application of the resource provides desired outcome), unique (very few have access to the resource), not imitable (resource cannot be copied), not transferrable (resource cannot be released from context), combinable with other resources (results in better outcome), exploitable (possible to apply in criminal activities), and not substitutable (cannot be replaced by a different resource). According to Petrocelli et al. (2003), access to resources equates access to power. Others are losers in the competition for resources (Wheelock et al., 2011). In the conflict perspective suggested by Petrocelli et al. (2003), the upper class in society exercises its power and controls the resources.

Opportunity is dependent on social capital available to the criminal. The structure and quality of social ties in hierarchical and transactional relationships shape opportunity structures. Social capital is the sum of actual or potential resources accruing to the criminal by virtue of his or her position in a hierarchy and in a network. Social capital accumulated by the individual in terms of actual and potential resources, which are accessible because of profession and position, creates a larger space for individual behavior and actions that others can hardly observe. Many initiatives by trusted persons in the elite are unknown and unfamiliar to others in the organization. Therefore, white-collar criminals do not expect consequences for themselves.

Berghoff and Spiekermann (2018: 291) argue that all economic transactions depend on a certain degree of trust, without which transaction costs would simply be too high for economic activity:

> White-collar criminals abuse the good faith of various stakeholders, from customers to the general public, from shareholders to the authorities. Therefore, white-collar crime often coincides with the breach of trust.

Offenders take advantage of their positions of power with almost unlimited authority in the opportunity structure (Kempa, 2010), because they have legitimate and often privileged access to physical and virtual locations in which crime is committed, are totally in charge of resource allocations and transactions, and are successful in concealment based on key resources used to hide their crime. Offenders have an economic motivation and opportunity (Huisman and Van Erp, 2013); linked to an organizational platform and availability, and in a setting of people who do not know, do not care or do not reveal the individual(s) with behavioral traits who commit crime. Opportunity includes people who are loyal to the criminal either as a follower or as a silent partner, for example, when the follower perceives ambitious goals as invariable.

As illustrated in Figure 5.1, Telia attempted to conceal corruption in criminal market structures dominated by corruption. Criminal market structures cause external collapse. Collapse represents a convenient situation for everybody ready to commit white-collar crime. Some industries have criminal market structures, where a corporation simply adapts to illegitimate practices (Chang et al., 2005; Geest et al., 2017).

Convenient Deviance Willingness

The executive decision to bribe the president's daughter was a rational choice. Rationality here means that expected benefits exceed expected costs, where detection consequences including potential punishment are cost elements that are multiplied by the low probability of detection. The rational choice assumption about offending is based on a normative foundation where advantages and disadvantages are subjectively compared (Müller, 2018).

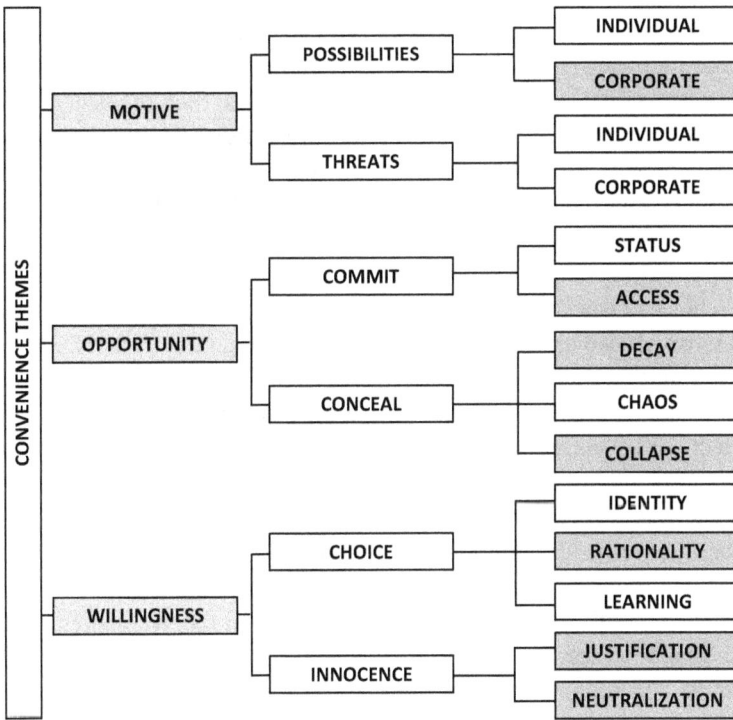

Figure 5.1: Convenience themes for Telia Telecom corruption.

When there is no perceived likelihood of detection, then there is no deterrence effect to prevent offences (Comey, 2009). If there is a certain perceived likelihood, then willingness might depend on the perceived consequences. For potential white-collar offenders it can be frightening to think of time in jail or prison. Research has shown that some white-collar offenders suffer from special sensitivity in prison, while others have special resilience in prison (Logan, 2015; Logan et al. 2019), which means that they cope better with incarceration than other inmates. Deterrence comes from whether or not an offender has to go to prison, rather than the severity of sanction in terms of imprisonment length. Generally, the severity of punishment has shown to have no effect on recidivism (Mears and Cochran, 2018).

Rational choice is concerned with benefits of crime exceeding costs (Pratt and Cullen, 2005), where the perceived likelihood of incarceration is a cost element. Another cost element is media exposure, where investigative journalists often are the first to disclose suspected white-collar crime and the offenders. Press reporters' detection of misconduct and crime "represented an important ingredient of the nineteenth-century newspaper" (Taylor, 2018: 346), and this is certainly also the case so far in the twenty-first century media.

The economic model of rational self-interest is all about weighing up the pros and cons of alternative courses of action. Organizations are less likely to comply if they conclude that following laws and rules is less profitable than violating those laws and rules (Peeters et al., 2020). When the desire increases, then the benefits in the rational benefit-cost comparison increase that in turn influences willingness. The rational choice perspective simply states that when benefits exceed costs, we would all do it. The perspective is explicitly a result of the self-regarding preference assumption, where rationality is restricted to self-interested materialism (Paternoster et al., 2018).

The rational choice perspective suggests that anyone might be an offender when the benefits of a crime exceed expected costs of crime (Pratt and Cullen, 2005). Rational choice assumes that the standard economic model of individual preferences will determine whether crime is committed. The greater the benefits of crime and the smaller the costs of crime, the more attractive it is to commit criminal acts. The economic model of rational self-interest does not imply that every individual in the same situation will conclude and act in the same way. There will be different choices in the same situation because rationality is a subjective matter. For example, the objective detection risk will be the same for individuals in exactly the same situation, but the subjective detection risk will vary with individual variations in risk willingness and risk perception. Similarly, the threat of imprisonment works fewer deterrents on some than on others. The economic perspective is thus concerned with the influence of rational self-interest in explaining white-collar criminality (Pillay and Kluvers, 2014). The economic model of rational self-interest is all about weighing up the pros and cons of alternative courses of actions. The model considers incentives and probability of detection (Welsh et al., 2014). This applies to both private and professional life. Human behavior finds motivation in the self-centered quest for satisfaction and avoidance of suffering (Hirschi and Gottfredson, 1987).

Neutralization of Corporate Crime

In their analysis of the temporalization of neutralizations of corporate crime, Schoultz and Flyghed (2020b) found that the three Swedish companies had to work hard to legitimate their actions as a result of allegations of criminal activity. While Telia moved from literal denial to confession, Lundin Petroleum stayed with its literal denial in parallel with a strong condemnation of the condemners, while Stora Enso denied responsibility for environmental harm. Neutralization techniques do not cause corporate crime, but they allow it conveniently to happen.

Schoultz and Flyghed (2020a) found evidence of a number of neutralization techniques in their analysis: denial of the act, denial of responsibility for the act, denial of evidence, denial of involvement, avoidance and minimization of the allegations, condemnation of the condemner, denial of intent, denial of control, diffusion of responsibility, defense of necessity, and scapegoating. By scapegoating, the responsibility for the act or event is transferred from the corporation to one or a few public figures, such as dismissed senior company executives or lower-level managers. From a corporate perspective, scapegoating has been effective in several business scandals in Sweden, where former chief executive officers had to retire with complete attribution of blame for the scandals. Thereby, the company might claim that the problem is solved.

The initial response by Telia executives was denial of knowledge as to who had benefited from the purchase of 3G licenses in Uzbekistan. The immediate response was literal denial which includes denial of the act, where the corporate action or inaction is repudiated (Schoultz and Flyghed, 2020b).

The first theoretical approach to corporate neutralizations was developed by Sykes and Matza (1957) who suggested five types of techniques of neutralization: denial of responsibility, denial of injury, denial of the victim, condemnation of the condemners, and appeals to higher loyalties. Later, the list of neutralization techniques has grown, and these are the most frequently cited neutralization techniques in the research literature for corporate offenders:

1. *Disclaim responsibility for crime: Not responsible for what happened.* The offender here claims that one or more of the conditions of responsible agency did not occur. The person committing a deviant act defines himself or herself as lacking responsibility for his or her actions. In this technique, the person rationalizes that the action in question is beyond his or her control. The offender views himself as a billiard ball, helplessly propelled through different situations. He denies responsibility for the event or sequence of events.

2. *Refuse damage from crime: There is no visible harm from the action.* The offender seeks to minimize or deny the harm done. Denial of injury involves justifying an action by minimizing the harm it causes. The misbehavior is not very serious because no party suffers directly or visibly because of it.

3. *Refuse victim from crime: There is nobody suffering from the action.* The offender may acknowledge the injury but deny any existence of victims or claims that the victim(s) are unworthy of concern. Any blame for illegal actions are unjustified because the violated party deserves whatever injury they receive.

4. *Condemn those who criticize: Outsiders do not understand relevant behavior.* The offender tries to accuse his or her critics of questionable motives for criticizing him or her. According to this technique of condemning the condemners, one neutralizes own actions by blaming those who were the target of the misconduct. The offender deflects moral condemnation onto those ridiculing the misbehavior by pointing out that they engage in similar disapproved behavior. In addition, the offender condemns procedures of the criminal justice system, especially police investigation with interrogation, as well as media coverage of the case.

5. *Justify crime by higher loyalties: It was according to expectations.* The offender denies the act was motivated by self-interest, claiming that it was instead done out of obedience to some moral obligation. The offender appeals to higher loyalties. Those who feel they are in a dilemma employ this technique to indicate that the dilemma must be resolved at the cost of violating a law or policy. In the context of an organization, an employee may appeal to organizational values or hierarchies. For example, an executive could argue that he or she has to violate a policy in order to get things done and achieve strategic objectives for the enterprise.

6. *Claim blunder quota: It was a necessary shortcut to get things done.* The offender argues that what he or she did is acceptable given the situation and given his or her position. The person feels that after having done so much good for so many for so long time, others should excuse him or her for more wrongdoings than other people deserve forgiveness. Others should understand that the alleged crime was an acceptable mistake. This is in line with the metaphor of the ledger, which uses the idea of compensating bad acts by good acts. That is, the individual believes that he or she has previously performed a number of good acts and has accrued a surplus of good will, and, because of this, can afford to commit some bad actions. Executives in corporate environments neutralize their actions through the metaphor of the ledger by rationalizing that their overall past good behavior justifies occasional rule breaking.

7. *Claim legal mistake: This should never pop up as illegal in the first place.* The offender argues that the law is wrong, and what the person did should indeed not pop up as illegal. One may therefore break the law since the law is unreasonable, unfair, and unjustified. The offender may argue that lawmakers sometimes criminalize behaviors and sometimes decriminalize more or less randomly over time. For example, money involved in bribing people were treated as legal expenses in accounting some decades ago, while corruption today is considered a misconduct and therefore criminalized.

8. *Claim normality of action: Everyone else does and would do the same.* The offender argues that it is so common to commit the offense, so that it one can hardly define it as an offense at all. The offense is no deviant behavior since most people do it or would do it in the same situation. The offender might even

suggest that what may constitute deviant behavior is when people in the same situation obey the law.

9. *Claim entitlement to action: It is sometimes a required behavior in this position.* The offender claims to be in his right to do what he did, perhaps because of a very stressful situation or because of some misdeed perpetrated by the victim. This is defense of necessity, which is a kind of justification that if the rule breaking seems necessary in the mind of the offender, one should feel no guilt when carrying out the action.

10. *Claim solution to dilemma: The benefits of action outweigh costs.* The offender argues a dilemma arose whereby he or she made a reasonable tradeoff before committing the act. Tradeoff between many interests therefore resulted in the offense. A dilemma represents a state of mind in which it is not obvious for an offender what is right and what is wrong to do. For example, the criminal carries out the offense to prevent what seems to be a more serious offense from happening.

11. *Justify necessity of crime: It was necessary to carry out the offense.* The offender claims that the offense belongs into a larger picture in a comprehensive context, where the crime is an illegal element among many legal elements to ensure an important result. The offense was a required and necessary means to achieve an important goal. For example, a bribe represents nothing in dollar value compared to the potential income from a large contract abroad. Alternatively, a temporary misrepresentation of accounts could help save the company and thousands of jobs.

12. *Claim role in society: It is a natural maneuver among elite members.* The offender argues that being a minister in the government or a chief executive officer in a global company is so time-consuming that little time is available for issues that seem trivial. Shortcuts are part of the game. Some shortcuts may be illegal, but they are nevertheless necessary for the elite member to ensure progress. If someone is to blame, then subordinates are supposed to provide advice and control what the elite member is doing.

13. *Perceive being victim of incident: Others have ruined my life.* The incident leads to police investigation, prosecution, and possible jail sentence. Media is printing pictures of the offender on the front page, and gains from crime disappear as public authorities conduct asset recovery without considering the harm caused to the offender. Previous colleagues and friends have left, and so has the family. The offender perceives being a loser and made victim of those who reacted to his crime after disclosure.

14. *Gather support: Nobody thinks it is wrong.* Most colleagues, friends, and others in the upper echelon of society think what the offender did, is quite acceptable. The supporters communicate to the public, the media, and others that it is ri-

diculous that the offender becomes subject to police investigation and eventually subject to prosecution and conviction. The supporters argue that it is completely misleading to portrait the white-collar offender as a criminal. The supporters may suggest that the offender was unlucky and made an unintentional mistake. They may argue that in the eyes of the public, the offense can emerge as misconduct, but certainly not crime. The offender potentially made a shortcut for very good reasons, which is tolerable and not objectionable. Given such massive support from those who condemn the criminal justice system, the offender gathers support that cause a fundamental reduction in his or her potentially guilty mind. The guilty mind may further deteriorate as the offender hires top defense attorneys who tell the offender that it is the state or someone else who, without any acceptable or plausible reason, is out there to catch him or her for an act that certainly was no crime.

15. *Claim rule complexity*: It is impossible to understand what is right and what is wrong. Some laws, rules and regulations are so complex that compliance is random. The regulatory legal environment is supposed to define the boundaries of appropriate organizational conduct. However, legal complexity is often so extreme that even specialist compliance officers struggle to understand what to recommend to business executives in the organization.

Lehman et al. (2019: 6) define rule complexity in terms of components and connections:

> First, a rule is more complex to the extent that it comprises more components that together describe the actions and outcomes necessary for compliance. A rule with a high number of components contains more detail and requires more actions to constitute compliance. Second, a rule is more complex to the extent that it has more connections to or functional dependencies upon other rules in the same system. A rule with a high number of connections refers to actions or outcomes that may be affected by activities pertaining to another rule or set of rules.

Neutralizations are not merely after-the-fact rationalizations where offenders can live with and accept what they have done. Neutralizations imply a deterministic or causal relationship available before the offense takes place. The use of neutralization techniques function as a means of making it possible to commit violations while at the same time reducing a guilt feeling (Cohen, 2001). When potential offenders apply neutralization techniques in advance of potential criminal actions, then their willingness for criminal behaviors might increase. A simple example is speeding on the highway, where the offender can drive too fast because of neutralizations such as everyone else does it, there is something wrong with the speed limit, or nobody will get hurt anyway. Neutralizations ahead of a criminal act protect the offender from harm to his or her self-image.

Criminal Telecom Market Activities

It was not only Telia in Sweden that sought to expand into the central Asian tele-communications market in 2006. The Dutch telecommunications company Vimpel-Com was active, and so was the Norwegian company Telenor. VimpelCom bribed the daughter of the president in Uzbekistan to obtain mobile licenses similar to Telia, while Telenor approach corrupt governments in other Asian countries such as Bangladesh, Thailand, India, and Myanmar. When Telenor was questioned about the business practice in Asia, the company refused to investigate, maybe be-cause the Norwegian Sigve Brekke was promoted from the position of regional man-ager in Asia to the position of chief executive officer at Telenor. The only internal investigation that Telenor was forced to conduct because the Norwegian state is a major shareholder in the company, was concerned with Telenor's ownership in VimpelCom through board positions in the Netherlands. Telenor sought to control damage from bribery allegations (Hovland and Gauthier-Villars, 2015).

The description of VimpelCom's Uzbekistan transactions by Deloitte (2016) was based on statement of facts by United States and Dutch investigating authorities re-lated to the settlement with VimpelCom. The statement of facts can be downloaded from www.justice.gov/usao-sdny/file/826456/download. The statement was incor-porated by reference as part of the deferred prosecution agreement between US De-partment of Justice and VimpelCom, where VimpelCom admitted, accepted, and acknowledged that it was responsible for acts of its officers, directors, employees, and agents.

VimpelCom corruptly entered the Uzbek market in 2005 and 2006. In internal VimpelCom documents, foreign officials were identified only as "partner" or "local partner" rather than by name. For example, documents prepared for board meet-ings concerning partnership agreement with a shell company referred only to a "local partner" who was the 100% owner of the shell company. VimpelCom struc-tured the partnership agreement to hide the bribe payments to foreign officials.

In 2007, VimpelCom arranged to pay foreign officials, through the shell com-pany, an additional $25 million bribe to obtain 3G frequencies in Uzbekistan. The year before, VimpelCom had paid $114 million in bribes for foreign officials' understood influence over decisions made by the Uzbek government. Furthermore, VimpelCom directly or through a subsidiary, entered into fake consulting contracts, where real work did not justify the large consulting fees.

Two executives at VimpelCom closely monitored the approval process and en-sured that the shell company was paid quickly. In 2011, the two executives received an email showing that all approvals had been received also for the 4G consulting agreement. The shell company never provided any legitimate consulting services to justify its $30 million fee. In fact, the shell company's consulting reports and pre-sentations, which were prepared in supposed satisfaction of its obligations under the consulting agreement, were not needed by VimpelCom, and the reports were almost entirely plagiarized from Wikipedia entries, other Internet sources, and internal VimpelCom documents.

While Telia admitted to charges and paid $965 million, VimpelCom entered into a deferred prosecution agreement with the US Department of Justice and with the prosecution service in the Netherlands, where the company paid $835 million to the US Securities and Exchange Commission and to the public prosecution service of the Netherlands. According to the statements of facts for the agreement, the bribe related to the acquisition of 3G frequencies in 2007 was falsely recorded in VimpelCom's consolidated books and records as the acquisition of an intangible asset, namely, 3G frequencies, and as consulting expenses.

Deloitte is a multinational professional services firm. Accountants, auditors, lawyers, social scientists, IT specialists, engineers, and other professionals within Deloitte conduct private investigations and forensic services as fraud examiners. Deloitte was hired in November 2015 to investigate Telenor's involvement in and knowledge of VimpelCom's corruption scandal.

VimpelCom is a global provider of telecommunications services. Most of the company's revenue came from Russia and Italy. In the summer of 2015, the United States Justice Department claimed that VimpelCom used a network of shell companies and phony consulting contracts to funnel bribes to the daughter of the president of Uzbekistan, in exchange for access to that country's telecommunications market. In November 2015, VimpelCom CEO, Jo Lunder, was arrested on corruption charges in Oslo, Norway. The case alleged that in exchange for an operating license, VimpelCom funneled $57 million to Takilant, a company controlled by Gulnara Karimova, the daughter of Uzbek President Islam Karimov. The Securities and Exchange Commission announced in February 2016 a global settlement along with the U.S. Department of Justice and Dutch regulators that required telecommunications provider VimpelCom Ltd. to pay $835 million to resolve its violations of the Foreign Corrupt Practices Act (FCPA) to win business in Uzbekistan.

Telenor is a Norwegian multinational telecommunications company. Telenor operates in Scandinavia, Eastern Europe and Asia. The company had a 33% ownership in VimpelCom Ltd.

Telenor's board of directors assigned Deloitte to conduct a review of Telenor's handling of its ownership in VimpelCom including Telenor executives on the board of VimpelCom and Telenor's follow up as a shareholder, as well as actions and decisions by Telenor representatives and Telenor employees in relation to VimpelCom's investment in Uzbekistan.

The investigation mandate states that the review of decisions and handling should be based on an assessment of the context at the time the decisions were made and take due account of the different phases of Telenor's ownership in VimpelCom. The review should cover all Telenor employees and board members.

Since the review should cover all Telenor employees and board members, Deloitte (2016) investigators had to select. They selected the chairman of the board at

Telenor, the chief executive at Telenor, as well as Telenor executives who had been on the board of VimpelCom and some more Telenor executives:

- Chairman of the board at Telenor: Svein Aaser. He was suspected of not disclosing information about VimpelCom corruption in Uzbekistan to Telenor shareholders.
- Chief executive at Telenor: Fredrik Baksaas. He was suspected of being involved in corruption as a board member at VimpelCom for a while, and also for not disclosing information about VimpelCom corruption in Uzbekistan to Telenor board members.
- Five Telenor board members at VimpelCom: Arve Johansen, Ole Bjørn Sjulstad, Kjell Morten Johansen, Henrik Torgersen and Fridjof Rusten. They were suspected of being involved in corruption as board members at VimpelCom for a while, and also for not disclosing information about VimpelCom corruption in Uzbekistan to Telenor management.
- Two Telenor executives: Richard Olav Aa (CFO) and Pål Wien Espen (CLO). They were suspected of not having handled a whistleblower' message correctly.

These nine persons were at the core of the Deloitte (2016) inquiry. The incoming CEO at Telenor, Sigve Brekke, who took over after Fredrik Baksaas, avoided attention by the fraud examiners, although he had been responsible for market development in corrupt countries such as Myanmar, Thailand, Bangladesh, and India. Brekke replaced Baksaas as CEO independent of the VimpelCom scandal (Ekeberg, 2016; Hustadnes, 2015; Trumpy, 2016).

The interwoven nature of corruption by Telia in Sweden, Telenor in Norway, and VimpelCom in the Netherlands illustrate the criminal market structures in global telecommunication markets. To obtain licenses in corrupt countries, the most convenient way is by corruption. While the bribes typically represent minor monetary amounts compared to revenues expected from mobile licenses, the chances of gaining access to new mobile telephone markets improve significantly after corruption.

In 2018, three former executives from the global telecommunications company Telia were put on trial in Sweden in the bribery case involving the eldest daughter of the late Uzbek president Karimov. One of the defendants in court was former chief executive officer at Telia, Lars Nyberg. In a press release, acting U.S. attorney Joon H. Kim referred to the Telia case as "one of the largest criminal corporate bribery and corruption resolutions ever" (Schoultz and Flyghed, 2021).

The detection of the criminal telecom market structures involving Telia in Sweden, Telenor in Norway, and VimpelCom in the Netherlands led to public charges in the United States and in the Netherlands paid by Telia and VimpelCom. Three Telia executives had to leave their positions and faced charges in Swedish courts. However, the cases against them were dismissed. The chairperson at Telenor had to resign because of the Uzbek scandal, and so did two senior executives. The newly appointed chief executive at VimpelCom had to resign as he did not react to whistleblowing regarding corruption in Uzbekistan.

The theoretical perspective of state-corporate crime was introduced earlier in this book (Bernat and Whyte, 2020; Ken and León, 2021; Müller, 2018: Osoria, 2021; Rothe, 2020; Rothe and Medley, 2020; Tombs and Whyte, 2020; Whyte, 2014; Zysman-Quirós, 2020). The Norwegian state owns 54 percent of Telenor (Hovland et al., 2019). The state encourages Telenor to win mobile phone licenses in corrupt countries. When Telenor was about to lose its licenses in an Asian country, the state got involved. Trond Giske, the social democratic minister of industry, got on the plane from Norway to influence the local government in favor of Telenor (Norli, 2012).

6 Danske Bank in Denmark

Wealth management is a profitable service for most global banks where they take care of money values for affluent individuals, families, and firms. It is a banking service which incorporates structuring and placement of wealth to assist in preserving and protecting owner fortunes. Often, wealth management involves secrecy by placement in tax havens. Therefore, suspicions of tax evasion and money laundering are often associated with wealth management. Recent scandals involving Danske Bank in Denmark (Bruun Hjejle, 2018), Swedbank in Sweden (Clifford Chance, 2020), and Nordea bank in Sweden (Mannheimer Swartling, 2016) have provided evidence of criminal market structures in the banking sector. While the cases involving Danske Bank and Swedbank in money laundering were detected and reported by whistleblowers, the case involving Nordea in tax evasion was detected and reported by the Panama Papers. This chapter concentrates on the case of Danske Bank involved in money laundering in Estonia, while returning to the issue of criminal market structures in the banking sector towards the end of the chapter.

Danske Bank is the largest financial institution in Denmark with focus on the Nordic region and presence in sixteen countries. Danske Bank is listed on the Nasdaq OMX Copenhagen stock exchange. The bank offers financial services, life insurance and pension, mortgage credit, wealth management, real estate and leasing services.

Danske Money Laundering Story

Local law firm Bruun Hjejle (2018) investigated suspicion of money laundering at Danske Bank in Denmark. The suspicion focused on activities at Danske Bank's branch office in Estonia. Danske Bank paid 210 million Danish kroner (about US\$ 30 million) for the investigation by the law firm. The investigative knowledge strategy included mainly knowledge workers with legal training at Bruun Hjejle. In addition, forensic experts from PwC and Ernst & Young were assisting the law firm based on accounting and auditing knowledge, and the international data management software company Palantir Technologies deployed its software platform to integrate and enable analysis of the comprehensive magnitude of customer, transaction and trading data available. CERTA Intelligence and Security was also assisting in these investigative tasks.

The fraud examiners investigated thousands of customers and millions of transactions as well as trading activity. They examined the now terminated non-resident portfolio in the Estonian branch from the time of Danske Bank's acquisition of Sampo Bank completed in 2007 until the termination of the non-resident portfolio in late 2015, with some accounts closing in early 2016. The main focus was on the

https://doi.org/10.1515/9783110766950-007

customers in the non-resident portfolio and their payments and trading activities during this period. The employees and agents of the Estonian branch who handled the non-resident portfolio or could otherwise have been involved were also investigated to uncover potential internal collusion.

The fraud examiners followed the guide on investigations issued by the Association of Danish Law Firms as well as the code of conduct issued by the Danish Bar and Law Society. The investigation was assisted by Danske Bank's compliance incident management team as well as the Estonian branch's IT department.

Identified data included 87 million payments for all customers at the Estonian branch, which were transferred into Palantir's software platform to store, structure and enable data analysis. Relevant external data from other sources than the Estonian branch were also identified, collected and ingested into the software platform.

The fraud examiners conducted a large number of interviews with relevant persons. For preparation of interviews, they engaged consultants from Promontory. Interviews were conducted with employees, including members of the executive board in the bank as well as members of the board of directors. 49 individuals were interviewed, and a total of 74 interviews were conducted as part of the investigation. All interviews were conducted in accordance with rules on due process.

The fraud examiners did let suspects and others comment on their findings (Bruun Hjejle, 2018: 20):

> Based on all collected information, the conducted interviews and observations, Bruun & Hjejle assessed the potential institutional and individual accountability. All individuals subject to individual assessment were given the opportunity to review a draft assessment together with relevant material. Also, other individuals with knowledge of the events relevant to the accountability investigation, but not subject to individual assessment, were given the opportunity to review relevant material. Comments and proposed amendments received were subsequently evaluated and reflected where deemed appropriate.

One of the reasons why corporate control functions did not work was because the branch operated computer systems different from computer systems at the headquarters. Not only was the IT platform different, but local bank executives also operated in the local language which executives from the headquarters did not understand.

Money laundering is the process of removing illegitimate proceeds from attachment to crime such as drug trade and trafficking and introducing the proceeds in the legal economy such as real estate and business enterprises. Danske Bank was such a financial institution used by organized criminals and others to delete traces of the origin of large sums of money. Especially in Danske Bank's branch office in Estonia, proceeds were transferred from Russian oligarchs and the Russian mafia, state officials in Aserbajdsjan, weapon smugglers in Ukraine, criminals in Pakistan, and other suspected places of origins (Hecklen et al., 2020).

Chief executive Thomas Borgen at Danske Bank had ignored rumors and whistleblowers regarding money laundering in the Estonian branch, where most of the money came from Russian oligarchs and organized criminals. Borgen had to resign from his position when the Bruun Hjejle report was published. Later, he was investigated by Danish police and sued by Danske Bank shareholders (Corcoran, 2019; Milne, 2019a; Milne and Binsham, 2018; Sivertsen, 2018; Moscow Times, 2017). The body of Danske Bank's former Estonian chief Aivar Rehe, who was at the heart of the € 200 billion money-laundering scandal, was "found dead in an apparent suicide" in September 2019 (Milne, 2019b).

Convenient Financial Motive

Wealth management is a profitable business for financial institutions. Especially Russian oligarchs and Russian organized criminals are willing to pay substantial bank fees to remove their funds out of Russia and into European banks where the political situation is stable, and the banking sector is predictable. By moving their wealth into the Western banking systems, wealthy Russians and others can also remove traces of the origins of their funds. For Danske Bank, this was thus possibilities for extraordinary corporate profits as indicated in Figure 6.1.

The financial motive for Danske Bank was to make money in Estonia by providing financial services to citizens and enterprises in Eastern Europe. A business enterprise is always looking for attractive corporate economic possibilities. Profit-driven crime is a result of a desire for more gain (Naylor, 2003). We thus develop an understanding of profit-driven crime in mainly economic rather than in sociological terms. The profit-driven crime prospective suggests a typology that shifts the focus from actors to actions. Rather than focusing on profit-driven crime as a logical sequence of actions, it deconstructs the crime into its inherent characteristics, which differ radically according to whether an offense is predatory, market-based or commercial in nature. Among the main characteristics is whether transfers of property occur by force, free-market exchange or fraud, whether those transfers involve redistribution of wealth, distribution of income, or redistribution of income; and whether the crime occurs in a non-business, underground network, or legitimate business setting. The profit-driven crime perspective answers the how-question, rather than who-question or why-question concerned with white-collar crime.

In his perspective of profit-driven crime by Naylor (2003), predatory offences involve redistribution of existing legally owned wealth from one party to another. Marked-based offences involve evasion of regulations, taxes, and prohibitions. Commercial offences involve illegal methods to distribute goods and services. Predatory crime involves the illegal redistribution of existing wealth, market-based crime involves the illegal earning of new income, and commercial crime involves the illegal redistribution of legally earned income.

Wealth refers to a stock of assets that accumulates or deteriorates over time, and wealth measurement takes place at a specific point in time. On the other hand, income refers to a flow of value per unit of time. Predatory crime is crime purely of redistribution of existing wealth. Examples include bank fraud and embezzlement. Marked-based crime is crime of distribution of new income. Examples include tax evasion and here money laundering.

Convenience theory emphasizes that a white-collar offense is a crime-by-choice, where legal means less conveniently might enable satisfaction of needs. Convenience theory stresses that there are always alternatives to crime. The theory thus contradicts one part of Berghoff and Spiekermann's (2018: 291) definition of white-collar crime, where white-collar crime is an illegal act "to secure financial returns that cannot be collected by legal means". While sometimes almost impossible, there will always be avenues available for legal paths to reach goals in more stressful and painful, yet legitimate ways.

Motivation plays a central role in convenience theory insofar as it is convenient for corporations to expand possibilities for success by pursuing illegitimate financial gain when legitimate alternatives are less attractive and threats to success (Langton and Piquero, 2007), or threats of detection and punishment can be easily avoided (Naylor, 2003). Similarly, offenders may save time and energy while avoiding possible uncertainty or pain if they choose illegitimate over legitimate opportunities to climb the hierarchy of needs for status and success (Maslow, 1943), to avoid failure or a fear of falling (Bucy et al., 2008), to realize the American dream of prosperity for local bank executives in Estonia (Schoepfer and Piquero, 2006), to satisfy the need for acclaim as narcissists (Chatterjee and Pollock, 2017), or to restore the perception of equity and equality (Leigh et al., 2010). Thus, convenience theory offers a unique theoretical integration of multiple perspectives of offender motivations for illegal behavior. Figure 6.1 illustrates that local Danske Bank executives had individual motives in addition to corporate motives.

Goal setting is a common practice in the field of organizational behavior, where the pursuit and achievement of ambitious and high-performance goals tends to encourage unethical behavior (Welsh et al., 2019). The possibility of extra profit resulting from financial crime enables the offender to emphasize desired outcomes over feasible threats, including detection and punishment. It is the convenience associated with extra profit, rather than the convenience of illegal profit, that is important in the motive dimension of convenience theory. However, under certain circumstances, additional benefits may result from pursuing illegal extra profit rather than legitimate extra profit in general, since illegal funds avoid the attention of external and internal control mechanisms, including corporate compliance functions (Kawasaki, 2020). Illegitimate financial gain can thus find its ways into pursuing desired outcomes and avoiding threats that funds obtained legitimately cannot. This phenomenon is at the core of convenience in the motive dimension of convenience theory.

Convenient Organizational Opportunity

Controls and guardianship did not work at the branch office because of a separate IT platform with computer systems designed and programmed in software that the headquarters did not understand. This convenient concealment mechanism is illustrated in Figure 6.1 by decay and chaos.

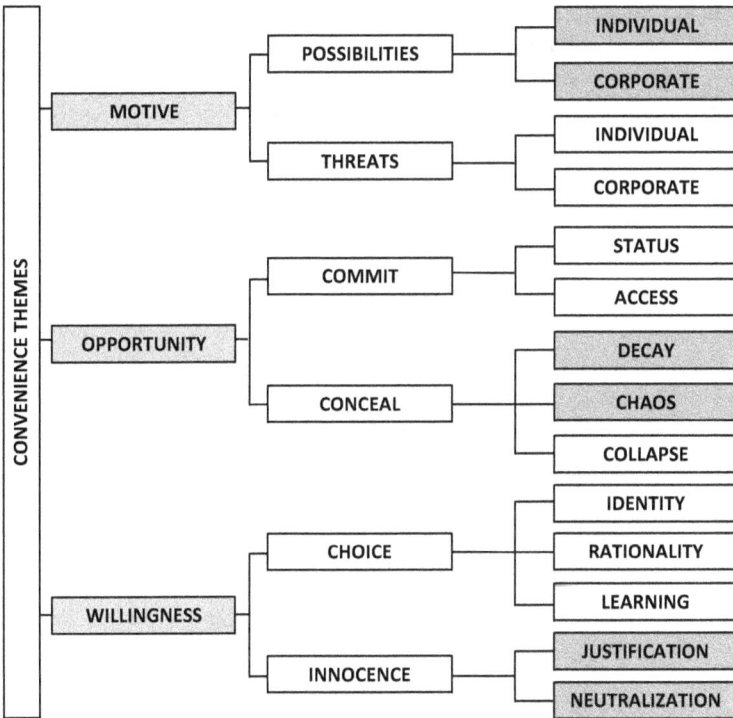

Figure 6.1: Convenience themes for Danske Bank money laundering.

Corporations have unique opportunities to engage in white-collar crime, but the link between crime and opportunity remains an underexplored area of criminology (Schnatterly et al., 2018). A convenient opportunity arises when individuals or groups may be enabled to engage in illegal and unethical behavior with the reasonable expectation that they may avoid detection and punishment. Individuals can have convenient access to resources and contexts in which financial crime can be easily perpetrated, obfuscated, and explicitly concealed, particularly in organizational contexts. For example, Benson and Simpson (2018) suggested that convenience to commit white-collar crime is derived through legitimate access to premises and systems, spatial separation from the victim, and the appearance of legitimacy. Similar theoretical perspectives integrated into the opportunity dimension of convenience theory include having specialized access to routine activities (Cohen and Felson, 1979), blaming others through misleading attributions (Eberly et al., 2011), and institutional deterioration with lack of guardianship (Rodriguez et al., 2005).

Within the convenience perspective, a typical white-collar offender might also be less likely to attempt avoiding detection using the same approaches and techniques of a typical street offender. Rather, office offenders would be expected to conceal financial crime among legal transactions to make illegal conduct appear legitimate. Similarly, the offender may conceal financial crime by removing certain activities from records. A typical white-collar offender with convenient and legitimate access to commit crime is more likely to exert most energy disguising crime in the professional context (Huisman and Van Erp, 2013; McClanahan and South, 2020).

Social disorganization is the inability of an organization to realize common values of its members and maintain effective social control. Social disorganization implies that the ability of social bonds to reduce delinquent behavior is absent (Forti and Visconti, 2020; Hoffmann, 2002; Onna and Denkers, 2019). Differential reinforcement of crime convenience develops over time as individuals become vulnerable to various associations and definitions conducive to delinquency. Both Danske Bank in Denmark (Bruun Hjejle, 2018) and Swedbank in Sweden (Clifford Chance, 2020) had branch offices in Estonia where organized criminals from Russia conducted money laundering because of social disorganization between bank headquarters and local branch offices. As a result, Danske Bank and Swedbank made conveniently extra, yet illegitimate, profits.

Convenient Deviance Willingness

Justification and neutralization characterize the perception of innocence among offenders at Danske Bank. Neutralization techniques were described in the previous case study about Telia. Justification can be based on a perception of acts of wrongdoing being morally justifiable (Schnatterly et al., 2018), being based on upper echelon information selection (Gamache and McNamara, 2019), and peer pressure (Gao and Zhang, 2019).

The slippery slope perspective suggests that a business can slide over time from legal to illegal activities without really noticing. The small infractions can lead to the larger ones. An organization that overlooks the small infractions of its employees creates a culture of acceptance that may lead to its own demise (Welsh et al., 2014). The slippery slope perspective applies to a number of situations, such as seventeenth century England, where "unregulated overseas trade was a slippery slope to fraud" (Pettigrew, 2018: 313). Arjoon (2008: 78) explains slippery slope in the following way:

As commonsense experience tells us, it is the small infractions that can lead to the larger ones. An organization that overlooks the small infractions of its employees creates a culture of acceptance that may lead to its own demise. This phenomenon is captured by the metaphor of the slippery slope. Many unethical acts occur without the conscience awareness of the person who engaged in the misconduct. Specifically, unethical behavior is most likely to follow the path of a slippery slope, defined as a gradual decline in which no one event makes one aware that he or she is acting unethically. The majority of unethical behaviors are unintentional and ordinary, thus affecting everyone and providing support for unethical behavior when people unconsciously lower the bar over time through small changes in their ethical behavior.

Welsh et al. (2014) argue that interpretation of many recent scandals as resulting from a slippery slope makes sense, in which a series of small infractions gradually increase over time. Committing small indiscretions over time may gradually lead people to complete larger unethical acts that they otherwise would have judged to be impermissible.

The slippery slope perspective is in contrast to individual perspectives such as the standard economic model of rational choice. Psychological and organizational processes shape moral behavior, where individuals are motivated to view themselves in a positive manner that corresponds with their moral values. Individuals tend to rationalize minor unethical acts so that they may derive some benefit without feeling the burden of negatively to update their self-concept. For example, a minor transgression such as taking a pen home from the office may seem permissible, whereas taking money out of the company cash drawer more clearly may become stealing in the minds of observers (Welsh et al., 2014).

Criminal Bank Market Activities

Recent scandals involving Danske Bank in Denmark (Bruun Hjejle, 2018), Swedbank in Sweden (Clifford Chance, 2020), and Nordea bank in Sweden (Mannheimer Swartling, 2016) have provided evidence of criminal market structures in the banking sector. The current review of the banking sector was limited to Scandinavia, where the largest Norwegian bank DNB was involved in money laundering of corruption payments from Iceland to Namibia (Kleinfeld, 2019, 2020; Seljan et al., 2019). The largest banks in Scandinavia – Danske Bank in Denmark, DNB in Norway, and Nordea and Swedbank in Sweden – were thus all involved in recent criminal market activities (Amundsen, 2021).

While the cases involving Danske Bank (Bruun Hjejle, 2018) and Swedbank (Clifford Chance, 2020) in money laundering were detected and reported by whistleblowers, the case involving Nordea in tax evasion was detected and reported by the Panama Papers (Mannheimer Swartling, 2016), and the corruption payments through DNB were detected by investigative journalists at Al Jazeera (Kleinfeld, 2019, 2020) and the Icelandic national broadcasting service (Seljan et al., 2019). A criminal banking sector in Scandinavia is probably no exception from banking sectors elsewhere in the world.

While the case of Danske Bank has been presented above, a short review of the other Scandinavian cases is presented below. Starting with DNB in Norway, the broadcasting corporation Al Jazeera investigated allegations and published the report entitled "Anatomy of a bribe: A deep dive into an underworld of corruption – An Al Jazeera investigation into the corrupt power brokers and global business elites defrauding the Namibian people" (Kleinfeld, 2019). The alleged corruption payments from the Icelandic fishing corporation Samherji traveled via the Norwegian bank DNB to state officials in Namibia to obtain fishing rights off the coast of Namibia (Amundsen, 2021; Schultz, 2019; Schultz and Trumpy, 2019a, 2019b). According to Reuters (2019), Samherji transferred more than $70 million through a shell company in the tax haven Marshall Islands from 2011 to 2018. Samherji transferred the money through bank accounts in DNB. The bank's largest shareholder is the Norwegian state, which holds 34% stake in the bank (Ekroll et al., 2019; Kibar, 2020a, 2020b).

The scandal at Swedbank in Sweden was similar to the scandal at Danske Bank in Denmark. It was all about money laundering convenience for non-resident Russian clients. While CEO Thomas Borgen had to leave his position when the investigation report by Bruun Hjejle (2018) was published, CEO Birgitte Bonnessen had to leave her position when the investigation report by Clifford Chance (2020) was published (Johannessen and Christensen, 2020; Makortoff, 2019; Milne, 2020). The next in line to leave the CEO position at Danske Bank because of money laundering was Chris Vogelzang. He was previously the CEO at the bank Abn Amro in the Netherlands that was investigated by Dutch police for money laundering activities (Solgård, 2021).

The firing of chief executives during a scandal is a way of scapegoating (Gangloff et al., 2016), where key individuals can be attributed blame. When the scapegoats have left the organizations and new CEOs are in place, banks attempt to create a clean image of their business. However, there is not necessarily reason to believe that the new CEO will react differently in a similar situation compared to the former CEO.

Just like Danske Bank, Swedbank benefited from having oligarchs and other Russians as customers without implementing anti-laundering procedures (Amundsen, 2021). The motive for violating anti-money laundering (AML) laws was to make extraordinary profits by corporate crime. The whistleblowers at Swedbank contacted the Swedish public broadcasting corporation. On February 20, 2019, the program "Uppdrag gransking" (Assignment investigation) began a series of programs alleging that customers of Swedbank's Baltic subsidiaries in Estonia, Latvia, and Lithuania had engaged in suspicious transactions indicative of money laundering. Following the first program, Swedbank engaged law firm Clifford Chance (2020) to investigate the allegations that investigative journalists had presented and more broadly into Swedbank's Baltic banking business from January 2007 through March 2019.

The Nordea scam was also revealed by investigative journalists. Their source was the Panama Papers, which consisted of 11.5 million leaked documents that detailed financial and attorney-client information for more than 214,000 entities in tax havens. Law firm Mannheimer Swartling (2016) was hired by Nordea to investigate the allegations. They found illegal backdating of contracts by Nordea wealth management that was headed by Gunn Wærsted (Kristjánsson, 2016):

> The big bank is one of the many banks that were caught with their pants down in the Panama Papers leak. The bank's internal investigation establishes that offenses were committed in the Luxembourg branch, as the bank helped customers backdate documents. The bank also provided customers with annual reports that could be used to mislead tax authorities. Wærsted denies knowing about this but defends the practice of creating straw companies in tax havens, as long as they were used for "legitimate tax planning".

Gunn Wærsted was not only head of wealth management at Nordea. She was also chairperson at the Luxembourg branch. Shortly after the scandal became public, Wærsted resigned from her position at the bank (Kaspersen and Eriksen, 2015).

Similar to corporate crime in the telecom services market involving companies like Telia, Telenor, and VimpelCom, corporate crime in the bank services marked involve companies such as Danske Bank, DNB, Nordea, and Swedbank.

Criminal bank market activities in this chapter have focused on financial services concerned with money laundering and tax evasion. Another example of a criminal bank market activity is the rigging of the LIBOR as a form of market manipulation. Manipulation of the LIBOR (London InterBank Offered Rate) involves misrepresentations, false statements, artificial transactions, and trading schemes that influence participants in financial markets. Banks as perpetrators achieve financial gain that would not be possible in the absence of such deceptive practices (Jordanoska and Lord, 2020).

McGrath (2020) found that the banking culture can be characterized by aggressive risk-taking. Banks are lending money in an irresponsible manner to property developers, on the basis of fragile security without leveraging themselves properly or diversifying sufficiently into other forms of lending. Cheap and easy credit fuel an old-fashioned asset bubble. Irresponsible risk-taking in the banking sector is part of the criminal bank market. Regulators are too trusting of the banks they are supposed to regulate.

The theoretical perspective of state-corporate crime was introduced earlier in this book (Bernat and Whyte, 2020; Ken and León, 2021; Müller, 2018: Osoria, 2021; Rothe, 2020; Rothe and Medley, 2020; Tombs and Whyte, 2020; Whyte, 2016; Zysman-Quirós, 2020). The Norwegian state owns 34 percent of the bank DNB. When the Panama Papers revealed that the bank helps wealthy clients hide their fortune in tax havens, and that the bank helps backdating contracts when desired by bank clients, the state did nothing to intervene. The government only asked for a review of the case, and the review was conducted by the law firm that served the bank and that was paid for by the bank (Hjort, 2016). Similarly, when investigative journalists detected that DNB helped Icelandic fishing company Samherji launder money on its way to bribe Namibian officials, the Norwegian state did nothing (Reuters, 2019; Schultz and Trumpy, 2019a, 2019b).

In April 2021, the Danish prosecutor decided to close the case against former CEO Thomas Borgen while continuing the criminal investigation of Danske Bank. The former Danske Bank CEO was no longer charged in the money laundering scandal. In order for individuals to be convicted under the money laundering act in Denmark, it is required that there is solid evidence that they have shown gross negligence. The Danish prosecutor was unable to find such evidence for Thomas Borgen. Henrik Ramlau-Hansen and Lars Stensgaard Mørch, two other former Danske Bank executives, also had their charges dropped (Klevstrand, 2021).

In May 2021, Norwegian bank DNB got harsh criticism from the financial supervisory authority of Norway. The bank had to pay a fine of NOK 400 million (about USD 45 million) that chief executive officer Kjerstin Braathen accepted. The public authority fund significant deficiencies in the bank's compliance with the money laundering act (Norum, 2021).

The Next Danske Bank Scandal

Danske Bank admitted in September 2020 that they had known for years about the bank's practice of collecting outdated and excessive debt from customers. Denmark's financial watchdog Finanstilsynet (2020) launched the previous month an inquiry into how Danske Bank had wrongly collected debt from up to 106,000 customers since 2004. The bank blamed IT system errors (Reuters, 2020):

> "There has been knowledge about at least parts of the problem in different parts and levels of the organization, including leaders, during the years", Denmark's largest bank said in a statement. "Despite attempts to manage the problems, the underlying data flaws were never fully addressed, and unfortunately this has caused the issues to continue for several years", it said.

Blaming IT system errors and data flaws is not any more an acceptable excuse for digitized business enterprises such as banks. A computer system is programmed by people according to specifications. If bank managers have provided misleading specifications to computer programmers, then it is a matter of human error. If computer programmers have developed wrongful algorithms and coding, then it is a matter of human error. A computer system never creates errors by itself.

Danske Bank is the largest financial institution in Denmark with focus on the Nordic region and presence in sixteen countries (Plesner, 2020). Danske Bank is listed on the Nasdaq OMX Copenhagen stock exchange. The bank offers financial services, life insurance and pension, mortgage credit, wealth management, real estate, and leasing services.

The data migration from an old computer system to the Debt Collection System (DCS) in 2004 contained pre-existing incorrect data in relation to outstanding amounts owed by certain customers. Over time an increased level of reliance on and trust in the DCS, a decreased level of institutional knowledge among those involved in the debt collection process, and a declining level of reference to historic paper records have contributed to the persistence of errors in handling the debt of some of the bank's customers.

Employees at different levels in the organization, including managers, at various points in time had known about the problem to varying degree. The executive management was informed of the systemic flaws affecting the bank's collection systems in May 2019.

A decade earlier, in 2009, Danske Bank launched an initiative known at Lean, which aimed to streamline existing businesses processes in an attempt to become more efficient in case handling. The focus on Lean meant that the employees in the debt collection area were under increasing pressure to rely on the data in DCS when carrying out debt collection and not to spend time looking at files in physical archives. This increased the transitioning into almost complete reliance on the data in DCS, and it implied the elimination of prior manual controls of the flawed data in DCS that had prevented, at least to a certain extent, the data flaws from ultimately impacting the customers wrongfully.

While a correction team was established in 2007 with the purpose of manually correcting the cases in DCS on a continuous basis, the team was closed down again in 2016. The team leader argued then that also new cases included incorrect calculations. Bank management ignored this warning and decided not to allocate people to the task of correcting cases. The correction team was re-established in 2019.

Fraud examiners suggested four root causes for the fraudulent debt collection. The first root cause is that accrued interest, fees, and costs on debt was incorrectly aggregated into a single amount and added to the principle amount. The implications of root cause 1 are that the systems do not distinguish between the different types of claims despite that in the context of time-barring principles such claims are subject to different time-barring periods.

The second root cause is incorrect debt origination date. The statutory limitation period starts counting from the date the specific debt fall due. When a debt was transferred into DCS, however, the systemic statutory limitation period was effectively set to the date of the transfer – and not the actual due date. The incorrect origination date in DCS made the debt appear younger than it actually is. This meant that it was difficult, using DCS, to identify and control at which point in time the statutory period of limitation should be interrupted to avoid the debt becoming time barred. The bank may thus have collected debt that at the time of the collection process was time-barred.

The third root cause is the same treatment of guarantors and co-debtors. The bank may have pursued to collect the full debt from each of the debtors, co-debtors, and guarantors. In absence of a manual adjustment in DCS, this meant that if a settlement agreement had been made with a debtor, the system would still attempt to collect the full amount from co-debtors and guarantors.

The fourth and final root cause was separate bank accounts for the principal debtor and related actors such as guarantors. Each account reflects the full debt as being owed. The full debt was consequently recorded on more than one account. Procedures required debtor accounts to be adjusted manually following debtor payments, accrued interest, and other financial items related to the debt. One customer might thus have repaid the debt in full, while the now non-existing debt was still registered as owed by the co-debtor and guarantor.

The total number of potentially impacted customers was 106,000. Under Danish law, if a person or entity has paid an amount due to a mistake, misunderstanding or as a result of an error, the consequence is that the victim is eligible of a restitution against the offender.

Examiners address the issue of how the bank handled information on identified errors by providing very general answers. The report describes a number of projects and activities, such as the data quality project, group risk management and compliance, and program Athens. It seems that rather than solving problems by correcting programming flaws, groups and projects were organized to discuss the issues. An example is the following sentence where a number of actors are mentioned, but there is no mention of actions (Plesner, 2020: 10):

> The bank engaged EY to assist with program Athens and to provide the bank with an analysis and verification of system flaws identified by Plesner.

Examiners thus document a bureaucratic approach to solving technical problems. The manual effort required to review computer code seems ignored. The only manual effort described is concerned with actual transactions in terms of new manual controls regarding calculations for each customer. No new debt collection cases with effect from 2019 were to be initiated without manual calculation being done before. If the manual calculation resulted in different figures compared to the systems figures, then figures in the system were corrected. The bank was thus incapable of solving the underlying systems error, instead system results were corrected.

The manual correction team was 4 people but grew quickly by 21 people to further accelerate the recalculation process. Consultants from Ernst & Young were also engaged to assist with the recalculations. In addition to the new manual control to stop new cases being brought to court before a recalculation, it was late 2019 also decided to withdraw all current court cases, including debt relief cases, private and business estate and bankruptcy court cases where the bank was uncertain about the real status for customers. It was decided to compensate all customers for their losses resulting from the identified root causes. To further minimize the risk of over-collection of debt, the bank decided to suspend approximately 17,000 customers' debt collection cases until they had been recalculated as part of the ongoing efforts to remediate the identified errors in the bank's debt collection system. These were the cases in which more than 60% of the principal amount had been repaid for which reason there was a higher risk that overcollection would take place before the cases had been reviewed. The collection would resume when each case had been reviewed and potential errors corrected. Furthermore, interest would not accrue while collection was suspended.

It was not until 2020 that the real problems in computer systems were addressed. Then an IT implementation plan was set in motion, which included a number of technical safeguards and improvements to the implicated IT system in order to enhance existing and set up additional checks and controls.

Examiners were asked to find out how many customers have been affected by the errors. As a starting point, a total of 402,000 customers with 600,000 accounts were processed.

Examiners found that the total number of possibly impacted customers across systems, and who were at risk of potentially having made overpayments, was 106,000. On the other hand, examiners found that a total of 105,000 customers had not made any payments to the debt when entering the debt collection system. People who were eligible of repayments because of overpayments had so far received on average one or two thousand Danish kroner, but they were probably entitled to higher amounts.

While the bank was recalculating accounts for potential overpayments, customers received no information about it. At the time of the investigation in 2020, only 17,000 out of 106,000 customer cases had been recalculated. Therefore, no customers had been contacted so far (Plesner, 2020: 15):

> All customers identified as having been affected by the root causes will be contacted directly by Danske Bank to disclose exactly what has gone wrong, what Danske Bank is doing to ensure that the customer receives proper redress, and what the customer can expect to happen next.

As of September 1, 2020, only 326 customers had received a compensation payment from Danske Bank. The total value of compensation paid to these customers was the equivalent of less than 40,000 US dollars.

The fraudulent debt collection by Danske Bank represents corporate crime to benefit the business and not any specific individual at the bank (Bittle and Hebert, 2020), as illustrated in Figure 6.2.

In many organizations, ends justify means (Campbell and Göritz, 2014). If ends in terms of ambitions and goals are difficult to realize and achieve in legal ways, illegal means represent an alternative in many organizations (Jonnergård et al., 2010). Among most executives, it is an obvious necessity to achieve goals and objectives, while it is an obvious catastrophe failing to achieve goals and objectives. Welsh and Ordonez (2014) found that high performance goals cause unethical behavior. Dodge (2009: 15) argues that it is tough rivalry making executives in the organization commit crime to attain goals:

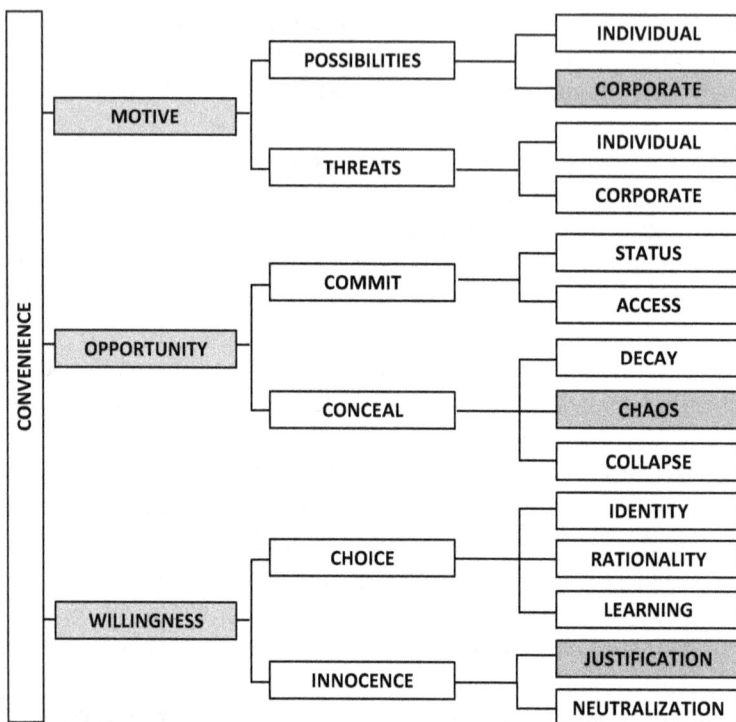

Figure 6.2: Convenience themes for Danske Bank fraudulent debt collection.

> The competitive environment generates pressures on the organization to violate the law in order to attain goals.

Individual executives would like to be successful, and they would like their workplace to be successful. Being associated with a successful business is important to the identity of many executives. They explore and exploit attractive corporate economic possibilities in both legal and illegal ways, so that their organization can emerge just as successful, or as even more successful, than other organizations. Profit orientation becomes stronger in goal-oriented organizations whose aim tends to be an ambitious financial bottom line.

There was a lack of oversight and guardianship that best can be labeled chaos, as indicated in Figure 6.2. Nobody understood or tried to understand computer code. Bank executives noticed that there were some strange things happening when migrating into a new system, but they continued to study the symptoms rather than the causes. As evidenced by many internal investigation reports by fraud examiners after white-collar crime scandals, internal auditors, external auditors, compliance committees and other internal and external control units do not function properly (e.g., Bruun Hjejle, 2018). Oversight and control functions tend to be formal units without any insights into the substance of business activities and transactions in computer systems. They tend to review procedures rather than transactions within procedures. Therefore, ineffective control functions are often an important part of the opportunity structure for white-collar crime.

Lack of justification can occur when an offender ignores information related to misconduct and crime. There is simply no need for justification. The upper echelon perspective suggests accordingly that white-collar offenders such as bank executives selectively attend to information when evaluating own decisions. As argued by Huang et al. (2020) in the upper echelon perspective, elite member's cognitions, values, and perceptions, which are formed by previous experiences, can significantly affect the process of strategic choices. White-collar offenders may receive feedback from a range of actors while selectively ignoring some of the feedback by not paying attention to it (Gamache and McNamara, 2019: 920):

> However, corporate executives operate in an environment where they receive feedback from a range of actors, yet we have a limited understanding of whether and to what extent these "soft performance feedback cues" influence their decision making.

Members of the upper echelon of society where we find white-collar offenders may thus combine neutralization techniques with disregard of negative information related to them personally. They try to choose what information they pay attention to and how they interpret that information.

7 Trafigura Trading in the UK

This case study illustrates the growing interest in environmental crime by corporate offenders (Van Erp, 2020). The case study documents escalation of commitment to environmental crime and deviant behavior. Commitment to goals can escalate to such an extent that it encourages deviant behavior even after detection of crime. This case study illustrates how detection of environmental crime in one country led to environmental crime in another country. The Probo Koala tanker ship was to deliver another shipment of coker gasoline waste to the Ivory Coast, and her sister ship, Probo Emu, both owned by Trafigura, was preparing for the same journey. Trouble started when the illegal waste shipment was detected. Trafigura management quickly found an alternative destination for the waste, where an explosion harming local citizens occurred. The case of redirecting the tanker ship to Norway is studied as a dark project by application of convenience theory, which suggests that offenders have financial motives, organizational opportunities, as well as willingness for deviant behavior caused by escalating commitment to illegal behavior to reach goals such as getting rid of the hazardous waste.

Escalation of commitment is defined as "decision-making in the face of negative feedback about prior resource allocations, uncertainty surrounding the likelihood of goal attainment, and choice about whether to continue" (Keil et al. 2007: 392). While escalation of commitment is a well-known phenomenon, many researchers have focused primarily on studying escalation behavior in laboratory experiments, thereby studying the antecedents or causes of escalation of commitment (e.g., Biyalogorsky et al., 2006; Conlon and Garland, 1993; Schmidt and Calantone, 2002). Sleesman et al. (2018) state that previous escalation literature focused largely on psychological and individual aspects, where only a fraction of the literature is highlighting contextual factors. This results in a poor understanding of the rich and complex dynamics underlying escalation behavior in organizations (Sleesman et al., 2018).

As such, existing research offers little to explain how escalation behavior starts, intensifies, and sometimes, spirals out of control. With 'out of control' we refer to commitment to a project that drives project managers to intensify illegal behavior (Welsh et al., 2020), i.e., the dark side of organizational leadership (Linstead, 2014). When time or costs turn out to be insufficient for the project, escalating unethical or illegal activities may occur in an attempt to attain the project's goals (e.g., Locatelli et al., 2017; Schweitzer et al., 2004; Welsh et al., 2020).

In this chapter, we explore what can drive a project beyond the edge, that is: how commitment to a project, over time, can escalate to such a degree that the project engages in further unethical or illegal practices. To analyze this question, we focus on an extreme case of Vest Tank, a so-called dark project: a project that was

https://doi.org/10.1515/9783110766950-008

illegal from the start (Gormley, 2009; Gulating, 2013, 2015; Maksimentsev and Maksimentseva, 2020; Nordhordland, 2010; Pedersen, 2017).

The increased focus on sustainable development goals and environmental crime has made handling and disposal of waste more difficult and more expensive than ever before. The potential financial gains for bending the rules or concealing illegal dumping of waste can be substantial (Böhm, 2020; Huisman and Van Erp, 2013; Lynch, 2020; Van Erp et al., 2019a, 2019b). As such, this is the right context for examining dark projects. Examining such an extreme case allowed us to discover the dynamic drivers of illegal behavior in dark projects. Based on convenience theory (Braaten and Vaughn, 2019; Dearden and Gottschalk, 2020), we will discuss causes for engaging in illegal activities and examine how these causes interact and reinforce each other in system dynamics terms (Sterman, 2000). Furthermore, we will propose how these three t causes also can explain escalation of commitment in legitimate projects.

In the next sections, we will discuss our theoretical framework that is based on two streams of research, i.e., escalation of commitment and corporate crime convenience. Then, the case study is described, followed by a case analysis. In the discussion we introduce a dynamic model explaining the drivers of unethical behavior and explain how these drivers interact so that they push a project over to the darker side. Finally, we present managerial and theoretical contributions.

Escalation of Commitment

In his seminal study on this phenomenon, Staw (1976: 29) describes escalation behavior as a negative reinforcing process: "due to a need to justify prior behavior, a decision maker may increase his commitment in the face of negative consequences, and this higher level of commitment may, in turn, lead to further negative consequences". Van de Ven and Poole (1990) found that negative outcomes in an innovation project predicted subsequent expansion of actions in the wrong direction. Thus, instead of accepting an immediate loss and terminating the project, decision makers may commit new and additional resources in terms of funds, personnel, or time to it. Once investors have made commitments to a project, they are inclined to reinvest later in order to "save" their initial investment (Van de Ven et al., 2008). This could lead to a costly circle of escalation (Staw and Ross, 1978).

In their meta-analytic review of the determinants of escalation of behavior, Sleesman et al. (2012) describe four sets of antecedents. Project determinants explain that the decision to escalate or de-escalate depends on the highest expected utility. The quality of information available to decision makers is such a project determinant. Biyalogorsky et al. (2006) argue that escalation is caused by the improper use of initial positive beliefs in the face of negative new information, and Keil et al. (2000) remark that negative project status information is sometimes not available or not attended to. Simester and Zhang (2010) describe three ways of responding to unfavorable information in escalation settings: distorting, discrediting, or simply not collecting information that may reveal unfavorable news. Uncertain, ambiguous, or simply the lack of information about the project may increase escalation. Psychological determinants are the second set of antecedents of escalation behavior.

Examples of these determinants are sunk costs, self-efficacy, ego threats, and personal responsibility for the initial decision (Sleesman et al., 2012). Project managers who are personally responsible for negative outcomes are more inclined to increase investment in resources (Staw, 1976). Schmidt and Calantone (2002) argue that managers who initiate a project report a higher level of commitment to it than do those who assume leadership after the start. Social determinants of escalation describe the involvement of other parties (evaluators, commentators, rivals, observers). Decision makers subject to outside evaluation are more likely to escalate in order to save face (Brockner et al., 1981; Sleesman, et al., 2012). Finally, structural determinants of escalation describe the structural features of an organization and its interaction patterns. The principal-agent perspective is part of this category, whereby managerial incentives to escalate diverge from the interests of the organization (Sleesman et al., 2012). This may occur especially in a context that is conducive to adverse selection, as when the manager has private knowledge and so can pursue a personal agenda.

Sleesman et al. (2012) concluded from their literature review of these four sets of determinants that a relative dearth exists of empirical studies examining social and structural determinants. Some years later, a follow-up study was published focusing on the role of context (Sleesman et al., 2018), in particular group, organizational, and external context. The group context captures factors like autonomy and authority. High levels of autonomy may increase escalation of commitment (Sleesman et al., 2018; Weick and Sutcliffe, 2003). Organizational context focuses on organizational factors that contribute to escalation behavior, like decision making processes, organizational identity and culture, corporate governance, and incentives such as bonuses. Finally, the external context describes, for example, the stakeholder environment, and market and industry factors. Sleesman et al. (2018) conclude in their extensive review that escalation research has largely focused on a single context and that little research has explicitly examined the interaction of factors across these three contexts. In addition, besides mentioning how legal commitments may hamper the ability to terminate a project (Sleesman et al., 2018; Walker, 2000) the role of illegal and/or unethical practices in escalation of commitment is not mentioned in this review.

Although criminal organizational practices, to the best of our knowledge, have not been analyzed in the context of escalation of commitment, goal setting offers more insight into these practices. Goalsetting is often perceived in a positive light, meaning that high goals increase performance (Locke and Latham, 2013). However, there is also some evidence suggesting that high goals can lead to unethical and criminal behavior (Schweitzer et al., 2004; Simmons, 2018; Welsh and Ordonez, 2014; Welsh et al., 2019). Welsh et al. (2020) argue that this is not only because of rewards associated with goal attainment, but also because of changing morale reasoning processes related to the goal. As such, high goal commitment facilitates unethical behavior by increasing not only the motivation to achieve the goal but also the motivation to justify doing so by any means necessary (Jonnergård et al., 2010). This is also known as state moral disengagement: a process through which individuals justify unethical behavior (Moore, 2015).

Environmental Crime Case Study

The Vest Tank case that is the subject of our analysis is a case about illegal waste disposal in Norway. Handling and disposal of waste has become more difficult and expensive due to the increased focus on sustainable development goals and environmental crime. As such, the potential financial gains for bending the rules or concealing illegal dumping of waste can be substantial. Environmental harm and crime has received increased attention in recent years (Böhm, 2020; Budo, 2021; Huisman and Van Erp, 2013; Lynch, 2020). Traditionally, corporate crime cases have mainly focused on non-violent financial crime. Recently, with increased environmentalism, researchers have focused on corporate crime that can impose physical harm on people (Benson and Simpson, 2018: 129):

> These offenses are potentially much more serious in that they can and often do impose physical costs on individuals. This is not to say that the perpetrators deliberately set out to harm other people. They do not. The physical harms that they cause are unintended in the sense that they are not what the offender is trying to achieve. The motivation for the offense is not to impose harm on others but rather to gain a financial advantage.

For example, Wingerde and Lord (2020: 478) argue that the waste industry is a criminogenic industry that is vulnerable to environmental crime:

> First, this concerns the waste product itself. Waste is a product that has a negative value attached to it (. . .). Second, the industry in itself also has some characteristics that are considered to be criminogenic.

However, few individuals face convictions for environmental crime. For example, after the British Petroleum (BP) Deepwater Horizon oil spill in the Gulf of Mexico in 2010, prosecutors brought criminal charges against four British Petroleum executives, but no one ended up in prison (Fowler, 2014; Freeh, 2013; Thompson, 2017). Greife and Maume (2020) found that:

Despite recent attention to multi-billion-dollar settlements for environmental violations involving high-profile offenders such as BP and VW, criminal sanctioning of individuals and organizations for environmental offenses is uncommon.

One exception is the conviction of both the chief executive officer and the chairperson of the board at Vest Tank in Norway, as well as a chemical advisor to the company, who received prison sentences for a tank explosion caused by dangerous waste (Gormley, 2009; Gulating, 2013, 2015; Nordhordland, 2010; Pedersen, 2017). Because going to prison is such a serious matter (Dhami, 2007; Logan et al., 2019; Stadler et al., 2013), the case of Vest Tank falls into the category of dark projects. The project was concerned with getting rid of the dangerous waste after Trafigura was denied access to waste disposal at the usual site in Africa. The redirection of the Probo Emu tanker to Norway is considered the project, as described below.

The methodology applied in this case study is archival review by content analysis of court documents (Gulating, 2013, 2015; Nordhordland, 2010), media reports (Gormley, 2009; Knudssøn and Bakke, 2009; NRK, 2015; Oliver, 2010; Pedersen, 2017), and published research (Maksimentsev and Maksimentseva, 2020). Content analysis is any methodology or procedure that works to identify characteristics within texts attempting to make valid inferences (Bell et al., 2018; Braaten and Vaughn, 2019; Saunders et al., 2007). Content analysis assumes that language reflects both how people understand their surroundings and their cognitive processes (Krippendorff, 1980; Patrucco et al., 2017). Therefore, content analysis makes it possible to identify and determine relevant issues in a context (McClelland et al., 2010).

Environmental Crime Description

The Probo Koala tanker ship was to deliver another shipment of coker gasoline waste to the Ivory Coast, and her sister ship, Probo Emu, both owned by Trafigura, was preparing for the same journey. Trouble started when the government of the Ivory Coast detected illegal waste disposal and threatened to take Trafigura to court for the illegal shipment of coker gasoline waste. The company was later prosecuted and charged for 16 lethal cases and over 100,000 claims of health problems as a result of harm caused by toxic pollution (Maksimentsev and Maksimentseva, 2020: 286):

> In order to bring the story to a close and release its executives detained in a local prison in expectation of host state court rulings on criminal charges, Trafigura concluded a settlement deal, totaling 100b local francs, with host state government and local victims to pay 95b francs to civil victims and 5b francs to the Côte d'Ivoire state budget in reparation and compensatory payments, at that time an equivalent to approximately USD 198m; it also released its two top managers from the local jail after the deal was properly enacted on 12 February 2007 and countersigned by the government of Côte d'Ivoire. Also, in order to avoid proactive collective lawsuits from the extraterritorial legal attempts of 1,000 victims from the Abidjan community brought overseas to the London courts, Trafigura paid GBP 32m in an out-of-court settlement.

Courts not only in the Ivory Coast and the United Kingdom, but also in the Netherlands later considered Trafigura as liable for deeply negligent pollution and damage to the safety of the living environment of the host state citizens. The courts found the damage to be a breach of security of industrial operations and transportation of oil products with a heavy impact on human health in Africa. Contact with toxic waste, spills and sludge remaining in the soil and water along oil-transportation pipelines and around onshore and offshore oil-processing sites were considered the responsibility of both Royal Dutch Shell and Trafigura (Maksimentsev and Maksimentseva, 2020).

Rather than terminating their detected criminal activities after reactions and controversy in the West African state, Trafigura instead redirected the Probo Emu tanker ship to the tank facility Vest Tank in Norway (Knudssøn and Bakke, 2009; NRK, 2015; Oliver, 2010). By not telling the whole story about the cargo to executives at Vest Tank in Norway, the waste was accepted and treated by desulphurization, since coker gasoline has low octane and high sulphur content (Gormley, 2009).

Vest Tank was selected for two reasons. First, Vest Tank was a company specializing in the receipt and treatment of wash water from the cleaning of empty tanks on oil tankers. The company held the required environmental permits for such activities. For Trafigura, Vest Tank in Norway was in a related business that they could contact when they had trouble. For Vest Tank, Trafigura had a waste disposal problem where Vest Tank could make a profit from cleaning it. Vest Tank had entered into an agreement with Trafigura in 2006 to clean wash water from Trafigura's oil tankers. Thus, there was already a business relationship between the two companies. When Trafigura had a different waste disposal problem, Vest Tank was willing to solve that problem for their customer as well. Six Trafigura vessels arrived with coker gasoline at Vest Tank before the explosion occurred (Knudssøn and Bakke, 2009; Pedersen, 2017).

The illegal chemical process at Vest Tank started with water and caustic soda being added to the gasoline. Sulfur and some other impurities bind to the caustic soda and precipitate. The mixture is then allowed to stand and separate, and the gasoline that settles on top can be drained. However, some explosive residuals from the coker gasoline accumulated at the bottom of the tank. An attempt was made to neutralize the bottom layer by adding hydrochloric acid. This caused a flammable gas to form, which was ignited by a spark from a coal filter. The pressure from the explosion also caused the neighboring tank to burst, and the waste stored in it flowed down to the explosion site and burned up there. The fire caused a large cloud of poison that spread along the fjord in several directions. The cloud reached the village of Eivindvik three hours after the explosion. Two weeks later, it was discovered that a large proportion of Eivindvik's one thousand inhabitants were inflicted with disease. Some people developed migraine and other forms of headaches, while others suffered from nausea and vomiting (NRK, 2015).

The dark project of illegal waste disposal caused public outrage after the explosion at Vest Tank in Norway. Both the chairperson and the chief executive at Vest

Tank as defendants received prison sentences in Norwegian courts (Gulating, 2013, 2015; Nordhordland, 2010). The commodity trading and logistics company Trafigura avoided the criminal justice system. While Vest Tank corporate offenders were sentenced to prison in Norway, Trafigura corporate offenders in the Ivory Coast were released from custody in a settlement deal as explained earlier. Trafigura as a company had to pay fines in the UK, the Netherlands, and the Ivory Coast, but there were never any convictions of Trafigura executives to the best of our knowledge. Trafigura did not stop or alter their waste disposal business, but instead introduced corporate structures with responsibility for potential wrongdoings in local subsidiaries in Africa.

Environmental Crime Analysis

We apply the structural model of convenience theory to examine Trafigura's motive, opportunity, and willingness in Figure 7.1 (dark grey boxes). There was a threat to the corporation of not getting rid of the dangerous waste that caused strain, pain, and uncertainty (Langton and Piquero, 2007). Surprisingly often, environmental crime and other forms of corporate crime are not caused by the well-known phenomenon of greed (Goldstraw-White, 2012). Rather, avoidance of corporate problems is more common as well as adaption to criminal market forces (Leonard and Weber, 1970), and required cooperation with criminal networks and cartels (Goncharov and Peter, 2019).

Maksimentsev and Maksimentseva (2020: 285) suggest that executives at Trafigura made a rational judgment to avoid risks of liability in the future by transferring responsibility to local actors in Africa:

> The rational judgment from the headquarters was to thus avoid risks related to physical participation in local subsoil use and the environmental impact of criminal extracting and mining operations. This would leave any trouble from host state jurisdictions to locally incorporated special-purpose vehicles (subsidiaries and affiliates), thus anticipating that the corruption and low competencies of local (host state) public officers, prosecution, courts and enforcement agents would limit or mitigate any potential risk and negative impact of environmental crime of transnational corporations, with minimum or no material impact on mother companies, allowing them thus, according to Riley, to 'evade the risk of liability'.

Trafigura obviously considered it a rational choice to have operations through host state affiliates and subsidiaries under transnational companies holding corporate control. Similarly, they found it convenient to have a shipment destined for Vest Tank.

In the dimension of organizational opportunity of convenience theory, executives at Trafigura had opportunities both to commit and to conceal crime. They created opportunity by entrepreneurship (Ramoglou and Tsang, 2016), and they had specialized access in routine activity (Cohen and Felson, 1979) to commit crime.

They created opportunity by institutional deterioration based on legitimacy with lack of guardianship (Rodriguez et al., 2005), lack of control in principal-agent relationships (Bosse and Phillips, 2016), and rule complexity preventing compliance (Lehman et al., 2020) to conceal crime.

Scheaf and Wood (2021: 2) found that entrepreneurial fraud has stimulated a wide array of research related to white-collar crime, where they provided the following definition of entrepreneurial fraud:

> Enterprising individuals (alone or in groups) deceiving stakeholders by sharing statements about their identity, individual capabilities, elements of new market offerings, and/or new venture activities that they know to be false in order to obtain something of value.

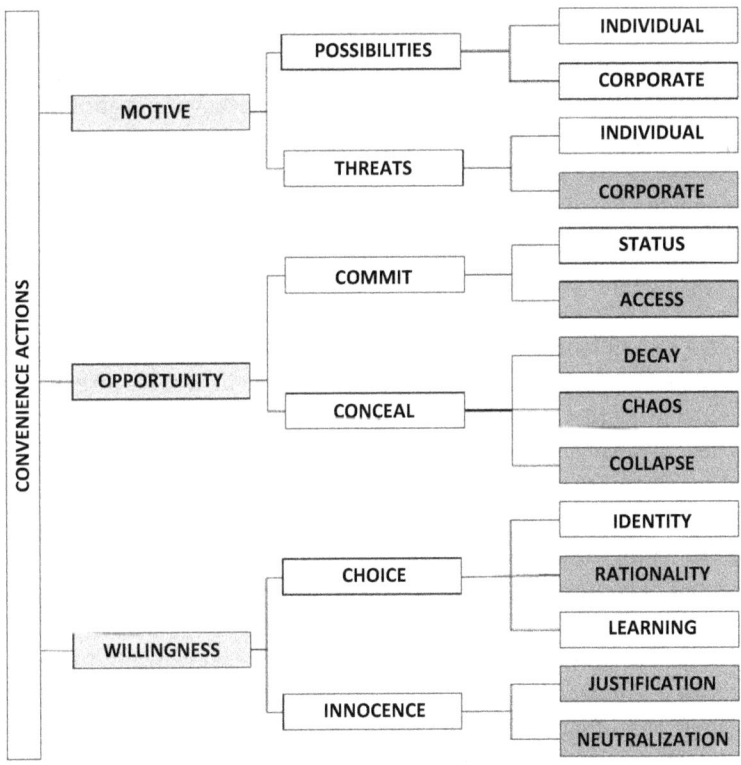

Figure 7.1: Convenience themes in the Trafigura case.

Redirecting dangerous waste to a facility that had no state approval for handling it was a rational choice in the motive dimension as well as in the behavioral dimension of convenience theory (Pratt and Cullen, 2005). Executives at Trafigura could neutralize their potential guilt by claiming a dilemma had to be solved. Offenders can argue that a dilemma arose whereby they made a reasonable tradeoff before committing the act (Schnatterly et al., 2018). Tradeoff between many interests therefore resulted in the offense. Dilemma represents a state of mind where it is not obvious what is right and what is wrong to do. For example, the offense might be carried out to prevent a more serious offense from happening, such as dumping the toxic waste in the ocean. Executives might also slide further down on the slippery slope, where they had already left the right side for the wrong side of the law (Welsh et al., 2014) while suffering from lack of self-control regarding law compliance (Gottfredson and Hirschi, 1990).

System Dynamics Model

Convenience theory explains why people choose deviant behavior over normal (legal, ethical) behavior. While the theory explains that deviant behavior is caused by motive, opportunity, and willingness, the theory is still developing regarding interactions and interdependencies between all three determinants. To analyze how these three determinants may interact over time, we have developed a causal loop diagram, inspired by the Vest Tank case as well as convenience dynamics. In developing the causal loop diagram, we applied the theoretical perspectives of commitment escalation and crime convenience. The causal loop diagram is depicted in Figure 7.2.

The arrows in a causal loop diagram indicate a causal relationship. A positive causal relationship indicates that cause and effect behave in similar directions: when the cause increases (decreases) the effect increases (decreases). A negative causal relationship means that cause and effect behave in opposite directions: when the cause increases (decreases) the effect decreases (increases). Feedback loops can be either balancing (B) or reinforcing (R). Balancing loops are self-stabilizing, and they bring equilibrium to the system. Reinforcing loops are amplifying, they spiral out of control. These loops are also known as vicious or virtuous cycles.

Starting below in the causal loop diagram, organizations set goals for projects. (Note that we focus on projects and the effect project goals can have on project managers. But goals can of course also be used for departments, groups, or processes, which will influence the behavior of department, group, or process managers.) The more ambitious these goals are, the more difficult they are to realize. As such, the ambition level of goals positively influences the complexity of the situation project managers need to deal with. Complex situations are often characterized by a lack of visibility or transparency (Skilton and Robinson, 2009; Sterman 2000). The situation may be ambiguous; information may be distorted or not readily accessible, or observable to every stakeholder in the project. Such a lack of transparency, however, creates opportunities to conceal certain activities, since it is hard for people to understand and evaluate what is going on in those situations.

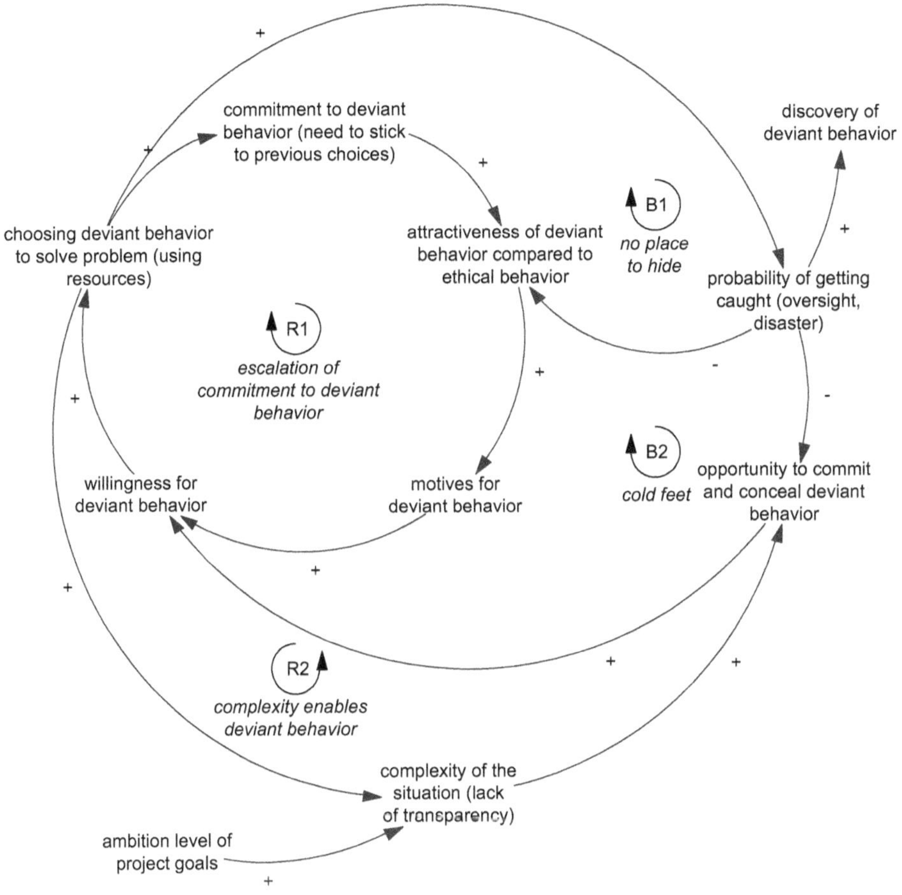

Figure 7.2: Conceptual model of the convenience theory.

For example, a project manager may deliberately choose to hide negative information about the project or twist the information to the project's advantage without the steering committee or the project owner noticing this. The opportunity for concealing "evidence" positively influences the willingness of the project manager to actually do so. This willingness is also impacted by the motives for deviant behavior. Motives can be diverse, but they are affected by the attractiveness of deviant behavior compared to normal, ethical behavior.

There may be personal financial incentives involved for getting the project to the finish line or a promotion after the project's completion. If, by bending the rules a little, these incentives are easier to reach, one may not be able to resist temptation and actually opt for the deviant behavior to solve a problem, similar to the state moral disengagement described by Moore (2015). This is a dangerous choice, because it is likely to start a path dependency, or commitment to this kind of behavior. Once the rules are bent, it is more difficult to go back to normal because this may require a confession of the crime of deviant behavior. Commitment to the path chosen leads to an increased attractiveness of deviant behavior, which increases the motives for a continuation of this behavior even more, thereby continuing down the slippery slope (Welsh et al., 2014). We have now described the first loop in our causal loop diagram: the reinforcing loop of *escalation of commitment to deviant behavior*. The loop is reinforcing because it amplifies itself, it is a vicious cycle that may spiral out of control (if nothing else happens to stop this behavior).

A side-effect of actually choosing deviant behavior in a given situation is that the entire situation gets even more complex. The project manager now needs to manage two worlds in one project: the world that everyone is allowed to see and know about and the secret world where the deviant behavior is hidden. This does not make the situation more transparent, and it may actually make it easier to continue with this kind of behavior. The two worlds make it even more difficult for steering committees or other stakeholders to understand what is going on and as such the opportunity for concealing deviant behavior increases. Now we have a second reinforcing loop of *complexity enabling deviant behavior*.

Although a lot of crime or unethical behaviors in projects may remain undiscovered forever, a large number will be discovered eventually. "Limits to growth" is a well-known archetype in system dynamics (Senge, 1990) that describes that the growth, represented by reinforcing loops in a system, and cannot continue forever. Systems reach their limits. These limits are formed by balancing feedback loops. These balancing loops either put a stop to the growth or they may even turn the growth around and cause a decline of behavior. Previously, we discussed that the more often someone bends or breaks a rule and selects deviant behavior, the more complex and the less transparent the situation becomes. But at the same time also more and more people, stakeholders, governance systems etc. are affected. The probability that eventually someone starts to notice something strange or that a warning signal turns red will increase over time. As such, the probability of getting caught increases. When this happens, the attractiveness of deviant behavior is reduced, which in turn decreases the motives for this kind of behavior. We have labeled this the balancing loop of *no place to hide*. The probability of getting caught also reduces the opportunity for concealing deviant behavior, which lowers the willingness for this behavior. We call this the balancing loop of *cold feet*.

Together, these two balancing loops can either force the project manager (or the offender of a crime) to choose legal, normal behavior over deviant behavior, or to come clean and confess to crime committed. When this happens early in the project, the project and the project manager may still be spared from disaster. Later in the project, it is more likely that crime is discovered by someone else, which probably puts an immediate stop to the project and the project manager's career. This is what happened in the Vest Tank case when the project literally exploded and revealed the crime committed.

Goal-Setting Research

This chapter uses the example of a waste disposal project to illustrate the relationship between core dimensions of convenience theory and thereby explain the dynamics that can lead to a self-reinforcing cycle in terms of an escalation of deviant behavior. It has highlighted mechanism that can spiral criminal behavior. The extension to convenience theory and its connection with escalation of commitment is a conceptual contribution to the field of dark projects. Our contribution is in line with previous research on escalation of commitment, dynamics, and self-reinforcing processes by Alvarez et al. (2011), Fleming and Zyglidopoulos (2008), Hällgren (2007), Stingl and Geraldi (2017), and Vaughan (1996). Some researchers make a distinction between commitment toward a task and commitment toward behavior, which might be explored in future research. One line of research is concerned with escalation of commitment by normalization of deviant behavior (Fleming and Zyglidopoulos, 2008; Jenkins and Delbridge, 2017; Pinto, 2014; Vaughan, 1996).

The combination of motive, opportunity, and willingness for deviant behavior may drive people to select unethical/illegal activities over ethical/legal activities. The reinforcing loops described in our causal loop diagram in Figure 7.2 suggest how deviant behavior reinforces itself. There is escalation of commitment to deviant behavior: once you have chosen to go to the dark side, it is very hard to go back. The causal loop diagram can also be used to explain decision making in projects that do not literally go to the dark side, but nevertheless are running out of control. In these projects, a project manager may have the motive, opportunity and willingness to hide some negative information about the project and to paint a more positive picture of the project to the steering committee. When the steering committee then approves and supports the continuation of the project, it will be more difficult for the project manager to reveal this negative information in a later stage and easier to continue hiding it. As such, our causal loop diagram suggests how escalation of commitment to a certain kind of behavior can lead to projects spiraling out of control. Escalation of commitment *to behavior* is different from escalation of commitment *to a project*, although the results may be the same. Therefore, our findings point to a new avenue for research on escalation of commitment.

By combining contextual factors of escalation of commitment (group, organization, external contexts), as suggested by Sleesman et al. (2018), goal-setting addition that explains that deviant behavior can be triggered when goals are (too) ambitious (Welsh et al. 2020), and finally the three elements of the theory of convenience, we show how commitment to deviant behavior can escalate. We also described two ways to break the escalation cycle. An offender may eventually realize that one has pushed the boundaries too far and that there is no way to continue with deviant behavior without getting caught. This reduces opportunity and willingness for deviant behavior. Also, the attractiveness of deviant behavior compared to legal/ethical behavior decreases that will negatively impact the motivation for deviancy. If it is not too late, this realization may stop deviant behavior in favor of legal/ethical behavior. But if it is too late, deviant behavior will be discovered and offenders will probably get caught.

In addition, our causal loop diagram shows that escalation is not a one-time event. It is a dynamic process that grows over time. The majority of previous research on escalation of commitment has focused on determinants or antecedents, but not so much on the interrelations between determinants and how they can reinforce each other (Sleesman et al., 2018). In fact, our diagram proposes that one can get stuck into a path of deviant behavior down the slippery slope (Welsh et al., 2014).

Our findings also help explain the "sweet spot" in the relationship between motivation and performance that is mentioned in goal-setting research. Ambitious goals increase motivation and as such performance, but goals that are too ambitious may enable state moral disengagement (Welsh et al., 2020). Our model in Figure 7.2 suggests that when it is not possible to lower the ambition level of goals, deviant behavior can still be avoided when the opportunities for this behavior are reduced. This can be done by increasing governance mechanisms or by removing incentives that increase motivation for deviant behavior. As such, our model contributes to the call for more research on the dynamics between motivation and performance (Welsh et al., 2020).

Finally, our findings also contribute to the convenience theory. This theory explains that motive, opportunity, and willingness cause deviant behavior. But it is underdeveloped whether these three determinants are required at the same time and if interdependencies exist between them. Our causal loop diagram in Figure 7.2 proposes that motive, opportunity, and willingness are interconnected in such a way that they can reinforce each other which creates an escalation of commitment to deviant behavior. This dynamic perspective contributes to the theory of convenience.

8 ABB Cables in Switzerland

Cartels are illegal associations of corporations who cooperate rather than compete on the same markets. Cartel members enter into agreements where they divide markets among themselves, decide on pricing, and agree on production quotas for each member. The purpose is to avoid competition to increase profits without a need for efficiency, effectiveness, and innovation. Customers of cartel members suffer by paying too much for goods and services of inferior quality (Bertrand and Lumineau, 2016; Jaspers, 2020). If cartel is the name of the game in an industry, the only way to survive might be to join the cartel, where cartel members divide markets among themselves (Freiberg, 2020; Goncharov and Peter, 2019; Nielsen, 2003).

Corporate Cartel Crime Story

When the Soviet Union turned partly into Russia and the iron curtain in East Europe fell down, then many west-European companies wanted to approach the Russian market. One of them was a small Norwegian ABB subsidiary that was in the business of producing signaling cables for car and computer manufacturers. In every BMW car there was one meter of cable produced in Norway, and in many Siemens computers, there was a short piece of cable produced in Norway. When approaching the Russian market, meetings in Moscow with interested parties were quite successful. However, when returning to Norway, the sales approach was stopped by the headquarters in Switzerland. Norwegians were told that they were not allowed to approach the Russian market. The Russian market belonged to the Finnish cable producer Nokia. In return, Nokia stayed away from Sweden and Norway, while ABB stayed away from Finland as well as Russia. This came as no surprise to the Norwegian subsidiary, since they already knew that the local cable market in Norway was divided between ITT (later Alcatel) and ABB, where some wholesalers were customers of ITT, while other wholesalers were customers of ABB.

It was no surprise to the Norwegians also because they had the same experience in other parts of the cable market. Just like they themselves were part of a cartel in the cable market, they knew that their customers were part of cartels as well. When they sold cables for electricity rather than for signals, large construction entrepreneurs such as Skanska (Landre, 2006), Peab (Gedde-Dahl et al., 2007), Veidekke (Landre, 2006; Lilleås, 2011), NCC (Landre, 2006; Lilleås, 2011), AF Group (Brandvol, 2016), and others did not really compete with each other. When the main airport in Norway at Gardermoen outside the capital of Oslo was expanded, the costs far exceed forecasts because of cartel activity. Similarly, when the Norwegian parliament buildings in Oslo were renovated and expanded, the costs far exceeded forecasts because of cartel activity. It was expended that the same would be the case when the new

https://doi.org/10.1515/9783110766950-009

government center in Oslo should be rebuilt in the late 2020ies after the terrorist attack in 2011. The named companies had experienced some minor fines and lenience
in exchange for cartel confessions to Norwegian regulatory authorities (Lilleås, 2011).
One frequent cartel pricing approach is to agree among cartel members on who is
next in line. That business provides a very expensive offer to the customer. The other
cartel members provide offers as well, but they price their offers even higher than the
business that is next in line (Goncharov and Peter, 2019).

The chief executive at ABB from 1988 to 2002 was the Swede Percy Barnevik
stationed in Zürich in Switzerland. After Barnevik's resignation, he became the center of a giant pension dispute that shook Sweden in 2003. When the new ABB board
made the pension payment public, Barnevik was forced to resign from other positions and return a large fraction of his pension to ABB (Shah, 2002). A few years
earlier, researchers compared ABB's Percy Barnevik to Virgin's Richard Branson in
terms of charisma in action by transformational abilities (Vries, 1998) as one of the
new global leaders (Katz, 1999). Barnevik's fall from grace was thus very steep.

Cartel Partners in Corporate Crime

A cartel is an association of independent firms in the same industry that strive to reduce competition by agreeing on areas such as market sharing, pricing levels, and production quotas. A cartel is collective misconduct of firms (Bertrand and Lumineau,
2016: 983):

> Instead of competing with one another, cartel members rely on each other's agreed course of
> action. Consequently, these underhanded agreements reduce the member firms' incentives to
> provide new or better products and services at competitive prices. Their clients (other businesses
> or final consumers) ultimately pay more for lower quality. Final consumers observe a reduction
> in their welfare, and businesses suffer from more expensive inputs. By artificially decreasing the
> natural level of competition in the market, cartels decrease the overall competitiveness not only
> of the cartelized industry but also of other industries. The damage to customers and other busi-
> nesses can thus be significant, particularly when cartels are able to last for years.

Bertrand and Lumineau (2016) studied cartels that were prosecuted between 2001
and 2011 by the Directorate General for Competition within the European Commission. The directorate is responsible for enforcing the European antitrust regime. The
sample consisted of 41 cartels with 463 members. The study purpose was to understand the variety of age-based experience, the separation in uncertainty avoidance,
and the power disparity in cartels. The study found evidence that the diversity of
members involved in cartels is a critical factor of the longevity of such secret activity. The cartels with the longest lifetime until detected and prosecuted were characterized by a high variety of age-based experience, by cultural similarity, and by one
firm being the leader in each cartel. Cartels survived for a shorter period of time

when group members had similar backgrounds, did not share the same values, and did not have a leader to manage the group.

Markets with crime forces can represent painful corporate economic threats. In many markets, there are cartels that regulate the supply side. A cartel is an implicit agreement between firms in the same industry to fix prices, to divide customers and markets among themselves, to fix industry outputs, to allocate territories, or to divide profits (Goncharov and Peter, 2019: 152):

> Cartel members seek to act collectively, as if they were a single monopolist, thereby maximizing the collective profit. By doing so, cartels violate competition policy and severely reduce consumer welfare through price-fixing activities that increase the price of goods far beyond the competitive level. Recent evidence shows that the average price overcharges by cartels prosecuted by U.S. and EU cartel authorities were 48.4 and 32.2 percent, respectively.

Supply to some customers occurs only from some vendors, while supply to other customers occurs only from other vendors in the cartel. There is only symbolic competition between vendors as far as they all seem to offer their products to all potential customers. Cartel members agree not only on market division but also on prices to various customers. When a public procurement officer asks for offers from all potential vendors, they may all provide an offer. However, they have agreed who is next in line by determining the relative price offer among themselves. The vendor next in line provides an expensive offer to the public procurement officer, while the remaining vendors provide offers that are even more expensive to the public procurement officer.

In Norway, large construction projects for the government and municipalities tend to suffer from cost overruns, where responsible politicians and bureaucrats typically have to leave their positions while there is suspicion of cartel arrangements among construction firms that drive construction projects into cost overruns. In the city of Oslo where a substantial cost overrun occurred when developing a reserve water source for all six hundred thousand inhabitants, the top politician Lan Marie Berg, in the position of environmental council, had to resign from her post (Lønnebotn, 2021):

> -Before we talk about Lan Marie Berg and the water supply case, I would first like to say: "Why is the cost overrun so large? My hypothesis is that there is a cartel".

> Petter Gottschalk, an economist and professor at BI Norwegian Business School, has followed the case of Oslo's new reserve water supply closely. This week it became known that the construction work will be NOK 5.2 billion more expensive than estimated, and city councilor Lan Marie Berg had to resign for not having informed the city council well enough.

> -A cartel is not a price collaboration, as many believe. Cartel activity means that you share the market and contracts among cartel members. Whose turn is it now? The cartel members agree, and the company in question submits an expensive tender. The other cartel members, the "competitors", then submit even more expensive tenders. We saw this when the airport at

Gardermoen was expanded, and the budget cracked. And it was repeated in the expansion of the Norwegian parliament Stortinget. Even when one is annoyed that it will become more expensive, other contractors would put themselves even higher in price. Cartel activities are incredibly widespread in Norway, and I will not be surprised if the construction of the new government quarter becomes twice as expensive as estimated. Due to cartel activities. Many construction enterprises have been fined for cartel activities over the years, but they continue like before, since the fines are so low.

-But this is a criminal offense, isn't it?

-Yes, when competitors communicate with each other and make agreements that affect the free market, then it is a criminal offense. But the Norwegian competition authority (Konkurransetilsynet) does not have the competence to investigate such matters, and the National authority for investigation and prosecution of economic and environmental crime in Norway (Økokrim) does not prioritize them, so it happens over again and again. The chief executive at the Storting had to leave after the budget gap there, and now Lan Marie Berg has to leave her position in Oslo.

Being a member of a cartel is illegal in most countries, yet they exist all over the world. Trying to operate outside a cartel in an industry can be painful and impossible to survive. To stay in the industry, businesses have to adapt to the usual way of business in markets with crime forces. In some markets, there is no other choice but to break the law. If a cartel completely dominates a market, then a new entrant may perceive no other choice but to join the cartel and cooperate with others on price fixing and other illegal activities. The market is such that the only way to survive is to implement financial practices similar to the ones applied by competitors. If corruption is the name of the game, every corporation in the industry has to provide bribes to stay in business.

Secrecy and concealment are at the center of cartel activities preventing detection (Bertrand and Lumineau, 2016). Therefore, Jaspers (2020) found that cartel confessions are an essential source for competition authorities in uncovering cartels. Confessions can be attractive to cartel members when leniency offers corporations the possibility to come clean about their involvement in cartels. A confessing cartel member can achieve immunity from competition authorities, especially if the cartel member is the first to notify authorities of that particular cartel and if authorities had no ongoing suspicion or investigation against the cartel.

Convenient Financial Motive

In many organizations, ends justify means (Campbell and Göritz, 2014). If ends in terms of ambitions and goals are difficult to realize and achieve in legal ways, illegal means represent an alternative in many organizations (Jonnergård et al., 2010). Among most executives, it is an obvious necessity to achieve goals and objectives, while it is an obvious catastrophe failing to achieve goals and objectives. Welsh and Ordonez (2014) found that high performance goals cause unethical behavior. Dodge (2009: 15) argues that it is tough rivalry making executives in the organization commit crime to attain goals:

> The competitive environment generates pressures on the organization to violate the law in order to attain goals.

Individual executives would like to be successful, and they would like their workplace to be successful. Being associated with a successful business is important to the identity of many executives. They explore and exploit attractive corporate economic possibilities in both legal and illegal ways, so that their organization can emerge just as successful, or as even more successful, than other organizations. Profit orientation becomes stronger in goal-oriented organizations whose aim tends to be an ambitious financial bottom line.

When an organization develops and maintains a strong systematic socialization program, employees not only identify with the organization but also its goals. When personal promotion or dismissal, as well as bonuses and benefits link directly and individually to the achievement of goals, then employees identify even stronger with organizational goals. When the socialization process couples tightly to strong accountability systems, employees perceive the pressure from individually oriented regulation to achieve organizational goals. The pursuit of goals therefore does not at all imply the absence of crime. The bottom-line focus within an organizational context might increase the frequency of financial crime on behalf of the organization for profit or enhancement. A strong emphasis on goal attainment might indeed lead organizational members to engage in illegal acts (Kang and Thosuwanchot, 2017).

Incentive systems such as bonus arrangements can lead to corporate crime such as cartel membership to meet sales targets or other targets on which bonus payments depend (Nichol, 2019).

A business organization such as ABB is always looking for attractive corporate economic possibilities as illustrated in Figure 8.1. Profit-driven crime is a result of a desire for more gain (Naylor, 2003). We thus develop an understanding of profit-driven crime in mainly economic rather than in sociological terms.

Convenient Organizational Opportunity

Cartels cause collapse of normal market mechanisms as illustrated in Figure 8.1 While cartels can represent painful corporate economic threats as discussed earlier in economical dimension of convenience theory, a cartel can represent an opportunity for those enterprises that have joined the cartel. In many markets, there are cartels that regulate the supply side. Cartel members agree not only on market division but also on prices to various customers (Goncharov and Peter, 2019).

The social exchange perspective aids explanations of how power structures in cartels and corruption networks develop and institutionalize through relationship building and social exchanges among participating enterprises. The perspective suggests that organizational activities are contingent on the actions of other organizations. The successful cartels and networks are dependent on generation of obligations and fulfillment of rewards. Relational efforts in an industry or in a community lead to repeated patterns of interactions that may develop into durable institutions of interdependencies in cartels and networks (Cropanzano and Mitchell, 2005; Lawler and Hipp, 2010).

Cartels and corruption networks are important to many global business enterprises. When the corruption case at Siemens became public, Murphy and Dacin (2011) found that the business climate encouraged corruption and fraudulent behavior as normal and acceptable. To cope with the scandal, Siemens replaced its management board (Berghoff, 2018: 423):

> Siemens is one of the world's leading electrical engineering corporations. In 2006, a massive corruption scandal erupted, concluded in 2008 with a record fine. For Siemens the largest risk was being barred from government contracts. As a consequence, it replaced virtually its entire managing board, an unprecedented procedure in the history of the company.

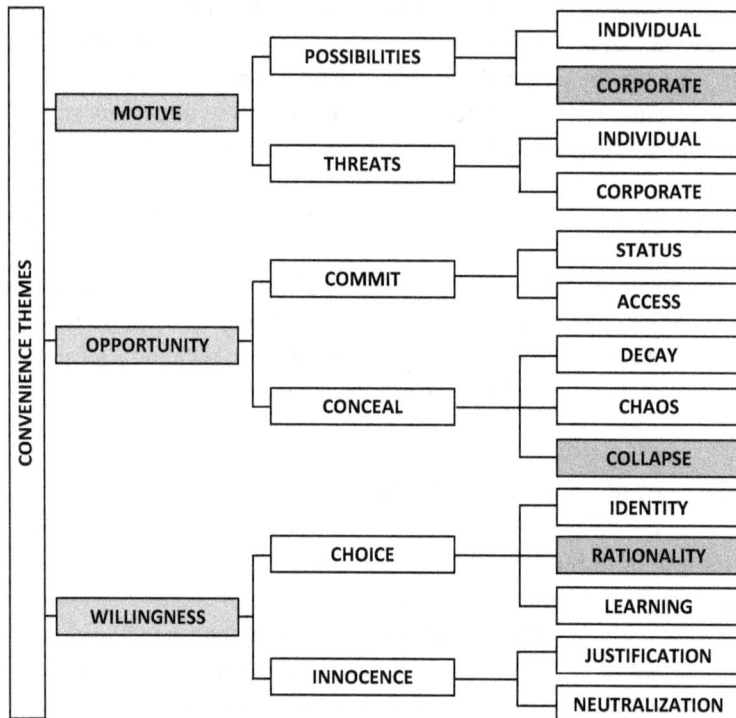

Figure 8.1: Convenience themes for ABB in cables cartel.

However, the criminal market structures did not change. Siemens thus "thrived in the cozy world of national monopolies and cartels, which guaranteed high margins and no worries about rivals" (Berghoff, 2018: 425). While the new management at Siemens attempted trust repair among stakeholders by introducing updates rules and guidelines, Eberl et al. (2015: 1205) found that the new rules were paradoxical in nature and thus difficult to implement in practice:

> Our findings suggest that tightening organizational rules is an appropriate signal of trustworthiness for external stakeholders to demonstrate that the organization seriously intends to prevent integrity violations in the future. However, such rule adjustments were the source of dissatisfaction among employees since the new rules were difficult to implement in practice. We argue that these different impacts of organizational rules result from their inherent paradoxical nature.

Convenient Deviance Willingness

As illustrated in Figure 8.1, it is a rational choice for ABB to participate in the cartel. The rational choice of corporate crime by cartel membership is based on advantages exceeding disadvantages by such membership. The rational choice assumption about offending is based on a normative foundation where advantages and disadvantages are professionally compared (Müller, 2018). When there is no perceived likelihood of detection, then there is no deterrence effect to prevent offences (Comey, 2009). If there is a certain perceived likelihood, then willingness might depend on the perceived consequences. For potential white-collar offenders it can be frightening to think of time in jail or prison. Research has shown that some white-collar offenders suffer from special sensitivity in prison, while others have special resilience in prison (Logan, 2015; Logan et al. 2019), which means that they cope better with incarceration than other inmates. Deterrence comes from whether or not an offender has to go to prison, rather than the severity of sanction in terms of imprisonment length. Generally, the severity of punishment has shown to have no effect on recidivism (Mears and Cochran, 2018). Given the likelihood of lenience in exchange for cartel confessions, the minimal penalties often imposed on companies, and the unlikely prosecution of individual executives, the deterrence effect from potential punishment is low in the rational choice consideration of costs versus benefits (Jaspers, 2020).

Rational choice is concerned with benefits of crime exceeding costs (Pratt and Cullen, 2005), where the perceived likelihood of penalties and incarcerations is a cost element. Another cost element is media exposure, where investigative journalists often are the first to disclose suspected corporate crime and the offenders. Press reporters' detection of misconduct and crime "represented an important ingredient of the nineteenth-century newspaper" (Taylor, 2018: 346), and this is certainly also the case so far in the twenty-first century media.

The economic model of rational self-interest is all about weighing up the pros and cons of alternative courses of organizational action. When the desire increases, then the benefits in the rational benefit-cost comparison increase that in turn influences willingness. The rational choice perspective simply states that when benefits exceed costs, we would all do it. The perspective is explicitly a result of the self-regarding preference assumption, where rationality is restricted to self-interested materialism (Paternoster et al., 2018).

The rational choice perspective suggests that anyone might be an offender when the benefits of a crime exceed expected costs of crime (Pratt and Cullen, 2005). Rational choice assumes that the standard economic model of organizational preferences will determine whether crime is committed. The greater the benefits of crime and the smaller the costs of crime, the more attractive it is to commit criminal acts. The economic model of rational self-interest does not imply that every corporation in the same situation will conclude and act in the same way. There will be different choices in the same situation because rationality is a subjective matter. For example, the objective detection risk will be the same for organizations in exactly the same situation, but the subjective detection risk will vary with executive variations in risk willingness and risk perception. Similarly, the threat of punishment works fewer deterrents on some than on others. The economic perspective is thus concerned with the influence of rational self-interest in explaining corporate criminality (Pillay and Kluvers, 2014). The economic model of rational self-interest is all about weighing up the pros and cons of alternative courses of actions. The model considers incentives and probability of detection (Welsh et al., 2014). This applies to both private and professional life of executives. Human behavior finds motivation in the self-centered quest for satisfaction and avoidance of suffering (Hirschi and Gottfredson, 1987).

Norwegian Cartel Business Partners

As described above, a cartel is an association of independent firms in the same industry that agree to remove competition by sharing markets and other forms of collective misconduct (Bertrand and Lumineua, 2016; Goncharov and Peter, 2019). In Norway, many industries are dominated by cartels. Independent firms may have to join cartels to survive and stay in business (Freiberg, 2020). Examples include division of the cable market in Norway between vendors and division of the construction market between entrepreneurs (Lilleås, 2011).

From time to time, cartels are detected in Norway. In 2021, a cartel with members from the alarm industry was exposed in the media. Alarm companies such as Sector Alarm and Verisure were detected and fined by the Norwegian Competition Authority two years earlier (Krattum, 2019). The authority had evidence that the companies had collaborated on market sharing and not selling home alarms to each other's customers between 2011 and 2017. Verisure disagreed with the authority's assessment. The alarm company received a fine of NOK 766 million but made it clear that the decision would be appealed to the Competition Appeals Board. Sector Alarm, on the other hand, accepted a fine of NOK 467 million (Svendsen and Solheimsnes, 2021).

Norway has six million inhabitants located at the border of Sweden, Finland, and Russia. In 2021, Verisure had 240,000 home alarm customers in Norway. The company changed its name from Securitas Direct to Verisure in 2014 (Rise, 2014). The chief executive Tore Staveland did not accept to pay the fine of NOK 766 million (about USD 80 million). Verisure had 454 employees in 2019 with revenues of NOK 1.3 billion (about USD 140 million). Profits before tax were NOK 350 million (about USD 37 million). The fine of USD 80 million thus represented the equivalent of about two years of profits.

The chief executive officer at Sector Alarm is Jørgen Dahl. He is a billionaire who founded Sector Alarm in 1995. He accepted to pay the fine of NOK 467 million (about USD 50 million). In 2021, Sector Alarm had 175,000 customers. The firm expressed the reason for acceptance of the fine (Brenli, 2020):

> -One and a half year ago, we chose to adopt the fee from the Norwegian Competition Authority. This is because we wanted to put the case behind us and use all our efforts to deliver the best possible service to our customers. We considered ourselves finished with the case and beyond that we have no other comments, says communication manager at Sector Alarm Sissel Eckblad.

Sector Alarm is smaller than Verisure with revenues of NOK 865 million (about USD 90 million) and negative profits in 2019. Normally, the company has annual profits of USD 30 million, which implies that a fine of USD 50 represents the equivalent of a little less than two years of profits.

The Norwegian penal code describes general provisions and corporate punishment. Penal code § 27 defines penalty for corporations:

> When a section of law has been violated by someone who has acted on behalf of the enterprise, the enterprise can be punished. This applies even if no individual has shown guilt or is liable. Enterprise means company, cooperative, association, or other mergers, sole proprietorship, foundation, estate, or public business. The penalty is fine. The enterprise may also be deprived of the right to carry on its business or prohibited from carrying it out in certain forms, and confiscation may be imposed.

Penal code § 28 regulate criteria to be applied to the extent of corporate punishment:
(a) The preventive effect of the punishment. (b) The seriousness of the offense, and whether anyone acting on behalf of the enterprise has shown guilt. (c) Whether the enterprise could have prevented the offense by means of guidelines, instructions, training, supervision, or other measures. (d) Whether the offense was committed to promote the interests of the enterprise. (e) Whether the enterprise has had or could have obtained any benefit from the offense. (f) The financial capacity of the enterprise. (g) Whether other reactions as a result of the

offense are imposed on the enterprise or someone who has acted on its behalf, including whether any individual is punished. (h) Whether an agreement with a foreign state presupposes the use of a corporate penalty.

The section of Norwegian law that is violated by a cartel is § 10 in the law regarding competition among enterprises:

> Any agreement between enterprises, any decision taken by associations of enterprises, and any concerted practice, which has the purpose or effect of preventing, restricting, or distorting competition is prohibited, in particular those (a) to determine directly or indirectly purchase or sale prices or other business terms, (b) to limit or control production, sales, technical development or investments, (c) to divide markets or sources of supply, (d) to apply to trading partners different conditions for equal services and thereby place them less favorable in the competition, (e) to make the closing of contracts conditional on the co-contractors accepting additional services which, by their nature or in accordance with normal business practice, have no connection with the object of the contract.

Corporate punishment thus implies an analysis of the basic circumstances for punishing enterprises. It is based on historical, legal-political, and moral assumptions on which corporate liability rests. Nevertheless, corporate punishment is in a state of tension with the traditional criminal law. This has to do with the fact that criminal law is closely linked to moral notions of blame. Blame and guilt are traditionally linked to human actions and consciousness. These are characteristics that an enterprise lacks. The basic conditions for personal criminal liability therefore do not apply here (Alalehto, 2020). At the same time, practically all business activities are organized as enterprises (Bundy and Pfarrer, 2015). This creates a preventive need for corporate penalties for offenses committed in such activities, which the Norwegian government is reluctant to pursue. As argued by Haines and Macdonald (2021), law has an ambivalent presence in criminological analysis and prosecution of corporate crime.

9 Volkswagen in Germany

Car manufacturer Volkswagen in Germany was unable to meet new, lower emission standards for their diesel cars. To avoid detection of emission standards violation, the car manufacturer installed a defeat device in each of its diesel engines (Jung and Sharon, 2019: 6):

> This software enabled the vehicles to pass emission tests under laboratory conditions while emitting 40 times the level of pollution allowed in the United States during normal use. The software was installed in 11 million diesel vehicles worldwide, including 590,000 in the United States.

The fraud was detected in 2015 by researchers at the University of West Virginia who discovered the defeat device. The chief executive at Volkswagen, Martin Winterkorn, had to resign later that year. Winterkorn's resignation came less than a week after the company admitted that some US diesel cars contained software designed to evade emissions tests.

Criminal Car Market Activities

Van Erp and Lord (2020: 3) commented on corporate crime seriousness in Europe compared to the United States, and they presented the Volkswagen emission scandal as an anecdotal evidence of corporate crime being more serious in the US:

> In 2015, it was revealed how software manipulation and emissions fraud were deeply embedded in one of the most iconic European companies, Volkswagen (VW), as well as in several other European car manufacturers. In addition to confirming concerns about the lenient EU regulation of diesel emissions, the discovery of the fraud in the US painfully illustrated the complete absence of enforcement in the European car manufacturing industry as compared with the US. Moreover, the VW fraud provides a perfect illustration of strain, as Volkswagen did not have the technical ability to manufacture a 'clean' diesel engine that was at the same time attractive enough to survive in a competitive global market.

The US Environmental Protection Agency brought the Volkswagen fraud to light, which led to inquiries in Europe as well. Van Erp and Lord (2020) claimed that there are many more examples of reluctance in Europe to be tough on corporate crime. In particular, they mentioned Irish, Dutch, and UK governments that find companies beneficial to their economy despite criminal activities.

The criminal car market activity included car manufacturers BMW and Daimler in addition to Volkswagen. The European commission charged the three automakers with colluding to limit the introduction of clean emission technology in the preliminary findings of an antitrust investigation. The European commission took out a similar cartel case against MAN, Volvo/Renault, Daimler, Iveco, and DAF some years earlier that ended with penalties totaling three billion Euros (Neslen, 2019).

https://doi.org/10.1515/9783110766950-010

Corporate crime seriousness might be measured by changes in company share price and changes in the demand for cars. While the share price for Volkswagen dropped to almost half of its normal value, it quickly recovered. The demand for cars was not affected, and in 2017, two years after the scandal, Volkswagen was the world's largest automaker (Jung and Sharon, 2019).

Convenient Financial Motive

The financial motive was to avoid loss in revenues and higher innovation and production costs. Both represent threats to Volkswagen's financial performance as indicated in Figure 9.1. Revenue loss would occur when car markets such as the United States denied Volkswagen access because of diesel omissions. Higher innovation and production costs would occur when Volkswagen would have to innovate and rebuild their diesel cars to meet omission standards.

Threats can create moral panic. Moral panic can characterize reactions that do not accurately reflect the actual danger of a threat. During a moral panic, sensitization processes generate an escalation in the individual and organizational disturbance (Kang and Thosuwanchot, 2017).

Chattopadhyay et al. (2001) studied organizational actions in response to threats. They found that threats are associated with urgency, difficulty, and high stakes. Threats involve a negative situation in which loss is likely and over which one has relatively little control.

A possibility implies a positive situation in which gain is likely and over which one has a fair amount of control, while at the same time been characterized by urgency, difficulty, and high stakes (Chattopadhyay et al., 2001).

In conformity with the managerial perspective in business literature which highlights the role of managers as agents in deciding enterprise strategies and operations (Lopez-Rodriguez, 2009), as well as leading the activities required to implement corporate priorities, managers can develop and implement both legal and illegal strategies. Managers' perceptions and interpretations determine their commitment to certain goals over other goals (sub-goals). The goal of business enterprises is to make a profit, where enterprises often have the choice between legal and illegal means. Strong and ambitious goal-orientation in competitive markets can lead to a strategic choice of white-collar crime. We understand profit-driven crime by both legal and criminal business enterprises mainly in economic rather than sociological or criminological terms. The amounts involved can be staggering (Menon and Siew, 2012).

Convenient Organizational Opportunity

Corporate offenders at Volkswagen typically had legitimate access to resources to commit and conceal crime (Williams et al., 2019). A resource is an enabler applied and used to satisfy human and organizational needs. A resource has utility and limited availability. A white-collar offender has usually access to resources that are valuable (application of the resource provides desired outcome), unique (very few have access to the resource), not imitable (resource cannot be copied), not transferrable (resource cannot be released from context), combinable with other resources (results in better outcome), exploitable (possible to apply in criminal activities), and not substitutable (cannot be replaced by a different resource). According to Petrocelli et al. (2003), access to resources equates access to power. Others are losers in the competition for resources (Wheelock et al., 2011). In the conflict perspective suggested by Petrocelli et al. (2003), the upper class in society exercises its power and controls the resources.

Opportunity is dependent on social capital available to the offenders. The structure and quality of social ties in hierarchical and transactional relationships shape opportunity structures. Social capital is the sum of actual or potential resources accruing to the criminal by virtue of his or her position in a hierarchy and in a network. Social capital accumulated by the individual in terms of actual and potential resources, which are accessible because of profession and position, creates a larger space for individual behavior and actions that others can hardly observe. Many initiatives by trusted persons in the elite are unknown and unfamiliar to others in the organization. Therefore, white-collar criminals do not expect consequences for themselves.

Berghoff and Spiekermann (2018: 291) argue that all economic transactions depend on a certain degree of trust, without which transaction costs would simply be too high for economic activity:

> White-collar criminals abuse the good faith of various stakeholders, from customers to the general public, from shareholders to the authorities. Therefore, white-collar crime often coincides with the breach of trust.

Offenders take advantage of their positions of power with almost unlimited authority in the opportunity structure (Kempa, 2010), because they have legitimate and often privileged access to physical and virtual locations in which crime is committed, are totally in charge of resource allocations and transactions, and are successful in concealment based on key resources used to hide their crime. Offenders have an economic motivation and opportunity (Huisman and Van Erp, 2013); linked to an organizational platform and availability, and in a setting of people who do not know, do not care or do not reveal the individual(s) with behavioral traits who commit crime. Opportunity includes people who are loyal to the criminal either as a follower or as a silent partner, for example, when the follower perceives ambitious goals as invariable.

The resource-based perspective postulates that differences in individuals' opportunities find explanation in the extent of resource access and the ability to combine and exploit those resources. Executives and other members of the elite are potential offenders that are able to commit financial crime to the extent that they have convenient access to resources suitable for illegal actions. Access to resources in the organizational dimension makes it more relevant and attractive to explore possibilities and avoid threats using financial crime. The willingness to exploit a resource for fraud and corruption increases when a potential offender has a perception of relative convenience. Criminal acts disappear from easy detection in a multitude of legal transactions in different contexts and different locations performed by different people. The organizational affiliation makes crime look like ordinary business. Offenders conceal economic crime among apparently legal activity. Offenders leverage resources that make it convenient to conceal crime among regular business transactions. In particular, businesses that practice secrecy rather than transparency enable convenient concealment of financial crime (Transparency, 2018). Chasing profits leaves people more creative in finding ways to make more legal as well as illegal profits for themselves and the organization, and people become more creative in concealing crime in various ways (Füss and Hecker, 2008). Offenders carry out crime in such a way that the risk of detection is minimal and even microscopic (Pratt and Cullen, 2005).

As suggested by Berghoff and Spiekermann (2018: 290), sophisticated concealment is an important factor in white-collar crime:

> The privileged position of white-collar criminals is the result of several factors. Their offences are especially difficult to prosecute because the perpetrators use sophisticated means to conceal them. They can also often afford the best lawyers and have the political clout to influence the legislative process to their advantage and, if need be, to bribe prosecutors and judges. Additionally, the class bias of the courts works to their benefit. The law is often seen as not binding, at least not for and by economic elites.

White-collar offenders have legitimate access to premises (Benson and Simpson, 2018; Williams et al., 2019), and they have specialized access in routine activities (Cohen and Felson, 1979). The routine activity perspective suggests three conditions for crime to occur: a motivated offender, an opportunity in terms of a suitable target, and the absence of a capable or moral guardian. The existence or absence of a likely guardian represents an inhibitor or facilitator for crime. The premise of the routine activity perspective is that crime is to a minor extent affected by social causes such as poverty, inequality, and unemployment. Motivated offenders are individuals who are not only capable of committing criminal activity but are willing to do so. Suitable targets are financial sources that offenders consider particularly attractive. Lack of guardians is not only lack of protective rules and regulations, audits and controls, but also lack of mental models in the minds of potential offenders that reduce self-control against attraction from criminal acts.

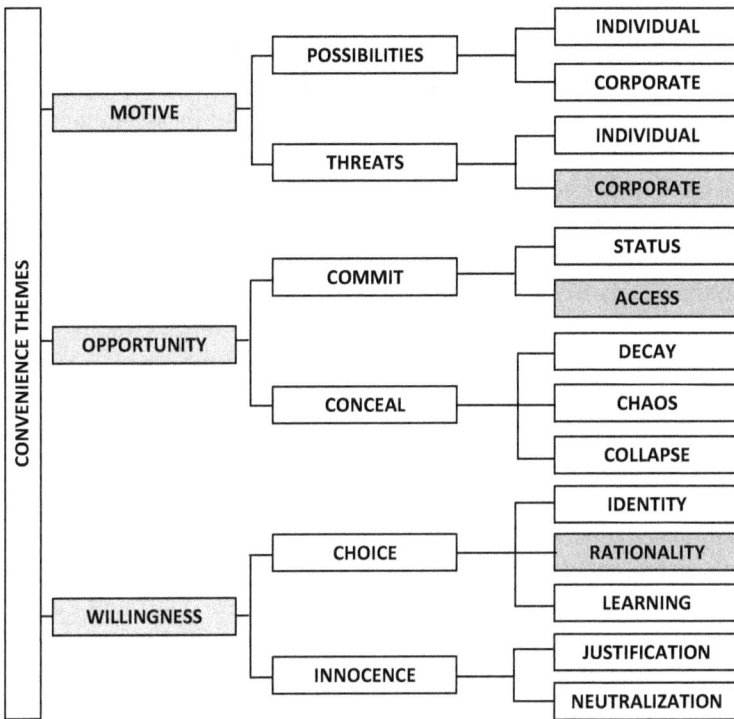

Figure 9.1: Convenience themes for Volkswagen in omission fraud.

Convenient Deviance Willingness

It was a rational choice by Volkswagen executives to install a defeat device in each of its diesel engines. The rational choice assumption about offending is based on a normative foundation where advantages and disadvantages are professionally compared (Müller, 2018). When there is no perceived likelihood of detection, then there is no deterrence effect to prevent offences (Comey, 2009). If there is a certain perceived likelihood, then willingness might depend on the perceived consequences. For potential white-collar offenders it can be frightening to think of time in jail or prison. Research has shown that some white-collar offenders suffer from special sensitivity in prison, while others have special resilience in prison (Logan, 2015; Logan et al. 2019), which means that they cope better with incarceration than other inmates. Deterrence comes from whether or not an offender has to go to prison, rather than the severity of sanction in terms of imprisonment length. Generally, the severity of punishment has shown to have no effect on recidivism (Mears and Cochran, 2018). Given the likelihood of lenience in exchange for corporate crime confessions in Europe, the minimal penalties often imposed on companies, and the unlikely prosecution of individual executives, the deterrence effect from potential punishment is low in the rational choice consideration of costs versus benefits (Jaspers, 2020).

Rational choice is concerned with benefits of crime exceeding costs (Pratt and Cullen, 2005), where the perceived likelihood of penalties and incarcerations is a cost element. Another cost element is media exposure, where investigative journalists often are the first to disclose suspected corporate crime and the offenders. Press reporters' detection of misconduct and crime "represented an important ingredient of the nineteenth-century newspaper" (Taylor, 2018: 346), and this is certainly also the case so far in the twenty-first century media.

The economic model of rational self-interest is all about weighing up the pros and cons of alternative courses of organizational action. When the desire increases, then the benefits in the rational benefit-cost comparison increase that in turn influences willingness. The rational choice perspective simply states that when benefits exceed costs, we would all do it. The perspective is explicitly a result of the self-regarding preference assumption, where rationality is restricted to self-interested materialism (Paternoster et al., 2018).

The rational choice perspective suggests that anyone might be an offender when the benefits of a crime exceed expected costs of crime (Pratt and Cullen, 2005). Rational choice assumes that the standard economic model of organizational preferences will determine whether crime is committed. The greater the benefits of crime and the smaller the costs of crime, the more attractive it is to commit criminal acts. The economic model of rational self-interest does not imply that every corporation in the same situation will conclude and act in the same way. There will be different choices in the same situation because rationality is a subjective matter. For example, the objective detection risk will be the same for organizations in exactly the same situation, but the subjective detection risk will vary with executive variations in risk willingness and risk perception. Similarly, the threat of punishment works fewer deterrents on some than on others. The economic perspective is thus concerned with the influence of rational self-interest in explaining corporate criminality (Pillay and Kluvers, 2014). The economic model of rational self-interest is all about weighing up the pros and cons of alternative courses of actions. The model considers incentives and probability of detection (Welsh et al., 2014). This applies to both private and professional life of executives. Human behavior finds motivation in the self-centered quest for satisfaction and avoidance of suffering (Hirschi and Gottfredson, 1987).

10 Wirecard in Germany

Wirecard was founded in 1999 to handle digital money transactions for pornography and gambling. In 2020, the financial institution went bankrupt (Kagge, 2021). The Wirecard scandal is a series of accounting frauds that resulted in the insolvency of the German payment processor and financial services provider (Storbeck, 2020). Erikstad (2020) suggests that Wirecard may have been drained of funds before bankruptcy. Wirecard failed in 2019 in its attempt to take over Deutsche Bank, which had not made any profits since 2014 (Håland, 2020). Wirecard's chief executive, Markus Braun, was ambitious both on behalf of the company and on behalf of himself (Solgård, 2020). Wirecard auditor Ernst & Young was in trouble for failing to uncover the fraud (Bugge, 2020).

Project Panther Deutsche Bank

Storbeck (2020) wrote about the Wirecard scandal in the UK newspaper Financial Times under the heading "Wirecard: The frantic final months of a fraudulent operation":

> A plan to buy Deutsche Bank is now seen as part of a desperate effort to disguise fraud at the German payments group. The codename was "Project Panther". Markus Braun, the chief executive of German payments group Wirecard had hired McKinsey & Co to help prepare his most audacious idea yet, a plan to take over Deutsche Bank. In a 40-page presentation last November, the consultants insisted the new entity, to be dubbed "Wirebank", would be "thinking and acting like a fintech, at the scale of a global bank". By 2025, it could generate €6bn in additional profit, McKinsey claimed.
>
> While Germany's largest bank sat on €1.4tn in assets, it was a mere €14bn on the stock market, roughly the same as Wirecard. The McKinsey report promised that the combined stock market valuation would double to close to €50n. A deal to acquire Deutsche Bank would have been the crowning achievement for a company which within a few years had become one of the most valuable in the country, winning the label of "Germany's PayPal". An upstart financial technology company would be running Germany's most illustrious bank. A tie-up with Deutsche Bank had another potential attraction: A deal offered the prospect of a miraculous exit from the massive fraud Wirecard had been operating. Around €1.9bn in cash was missing from its accounts and large parts of its Asian operations were actually an elaborate sham. By blending Wirecard's business into Deutsche's vast balance sheet, it might be possible to somehow hide the missing cash and explain it away later in post-merger impairment charges. There was one catch. To even start preparing such a deal in earnest, the company needed to get a clean bill of health from KPMG, which was conducting a special audit of Wirecard's books.

Wirecard had hired audit firm KPMG (2020a, 2020b) to conduct a fraud examination into alleged increase in revenue through fictitious customer relationships and other forms of accounting manipulation. Wirecard's motive to hire KPMG was to get a clean bill of health from fraud examiners according to Storbeck (2020):

https://doi.org/10.1515/9783110766950-011

With the KPMG investigation in full flow, the Wirecard executives behind the fraud saw Project Panther and a deal with Deutsche, which was first reported by Bloomberg, as one possible way to fend off discover, says an adviser to the payments group who was involved in the discussions. But they also worked on a separate plan: a vast cover-up operation in Asia.

KPMG did not provide a clean bill of health, since fraud examiners in their report criticize Wirecard's internal controls and compliance functions. However, fraud examiners did neither confirm nor reject accounting manipulation and other kinds of financial wrongdoing. Therefore, Wirecard management quickly stated that "no evidence was found for the publicly raised allegations of balance sheet manipulation" (Storbeck, 2020). Nevertheless, the company collapsed half a year later.

Chief executive Markus Braun at Wirecard resigned on June 19 and was arrested on June 22, 2020. Jan Marsalek, Wirecard's second-in-command who oversaw operations in Asia escaped arrest and was on the run in August 2020. A key Wirecard business partner died. Thomas Eichelmann was the finance director at Wirecard. Susanne Steidl was the chief product officer. Consultants from McKinsey & Co had helped Wirecard prepare a plan of Project Panther to take over Deutsche Bank. To do so, the value of Wirecard needed to exceed the value of Deutsche Bank. The scheme was detected by investigative journalists at Financial Times (Storbeck, 2020).

Markus Braun denied allegations of fraud and embezzlement. He denied having inflated sales and profits. Nevertheless, he had been eager to carry out Project Panther and make a deal with Deutsche Bank to fend off discovery of potential wrongdoing.

Offender Convenience Themes

At first, the motive was possibilities of creating a market value for Wirecard so high that it exceeded the market value of Deutsche Bank and thereby enabled a possible takeover of Deutsche Bank by Wirecard. It was corporate crime to develop possibilities as illustrated in Figure 10.1. The ambitious business objective probably justified illegal means in the minds of Wirecard executives (Welsh et al., 2019). Both the company and its executives were greedy, where nothing was ever enough (Goldstraw-White, 2012). It was all about making as much profit as possible to improve the market value of the company (Alalehto, 2020).

Next, the motive was possibilities of individual enrichment as exemplified by Jan Marsalek who had transferred funds to Asian countries where he later probably was on the run. Marsalek and other executives at Wirecard were young and ambitious, and they wanted to climb the hierarchy of needs for status and success (Maslow, 1943). Maybe they wanted to realize the American dream of prosperity where material wealth is far more important than anything else in life (Cullen, 2010).

Finally, the motive was threats against individual wealth and success as Wirecard moved towards insolvency and bankruptcy. Concealing funds is about avoidance of loss of self-esteem after organizational failure (Crosina and Pratt, 2019).

Having personal control over funds can reduce and remove strain, pain, and uncertainty (Thaxton and Agnew, 2018). Having funds can also prevent falling too far from positions in the privileged elite (Benson and Chio, 2020).

In the organizational dimension of convenience theory, there are themes related to the convenience of committing crime. Convenience themes address the status of offenders as well as access to resources by offenders as illustrated in Figure 8.1. CEO Markus Brown and other executives at Wirecard were rising stars in German business, where they soon could reach the level of elite members who are too big to fail and too powerful to jail (Kakkar et al., 2020). They used an executive language about their business transactions that auditors from Ernst & Young and examiners from KPMG could not understand (Srivastava and Goldberg, 2017). They applied the blame game by misleading attributions to others in Asia and by scapegoating (Resodihardjo et al., 2015). Executives at Wirecard were entrepreneurial both on the right side and on the wrong side of the law. Entrepreneurs create opportunities where others mainly see problems (McElwee and Smith, 2015). They had legitimate access to premises and systems to be criminal entrepreneurs (Logan et al., 2019). In particular, they had access to strategic resources (Patel and Cooper, 2014).

Scheaf and Wood (2021: 2) found that entrepreneurial fraud has stimulated a wide array of research related to white-collar crime, where they provided the following definition of entrepreneurial fraud:

> Enterprising individuals (alone or in groups) deceiving stakeholders by sharing statements about their identity, individual capabilities, elements of new market offerings, and/or new venture activities that they know to be false in order to obtain something of value.

In the organizational dimension of convenience theory, there are also themes related to the convenience of concealing crime. Convenience themes address decay in terms of disorganized institutional deterioration, chaos in terms of lack of oversight and guardianship, and collapse in terms of criminal market structures as illustrated in Figure 9.1. Institutional deterioration was based on legitimacy (Crosina and Pratt, 2019). Interference and noise in crime signals (Szalma and Hancock, 2013) helped conceal misrepresentation in accounting (Qiu and Slezak, 2019) and prevented effective auditing (Balakrishnan et al., 2019).

There were signs of chaos, such as lack of control in principal-agent relationships (Wall-Parker, 2020), where the board did not know what top management was doing, and top management did not know what local branch managers were doing. Sensemaking of actions was difficult for outsiders (Weick et al., 2005). While there was an instance of whistleblowing related to misconduct in Singapore, costs did exceed benefits for whistleblowers (Tankebe, 2019). In addition to lack of control in principal-agent relationships, problems in sensemaking of actions for outsiders, and costs exceeding benefits for whistleblowers, an ethical climate conflict also contributed to chaos (Potipiroon and Wongpreedee, 2020). While some ignored

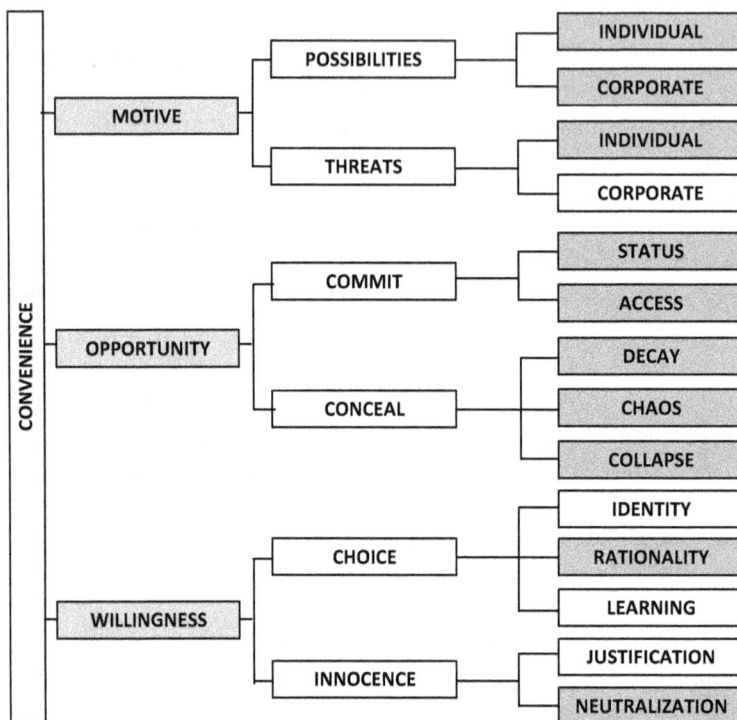

Figure 10.1: Convenience themes in the case of Wirecard.

violations of laws in achieving goals, others wanted to watch compliance, which created an ethical climate conflict. Collapse is also evident as some Wirecard executives involved themselves in markets with crime forces (Freiberg, 2020) and in crime networks (Geest et al., 2017).

In the willingness dimension of convenience theory, there are themes related to the convenience of deviant behavior. Convenience themes address the choice of crime and the feeling of innocence as illustrated in Figure 10.1. The rational choice of accounting manipulation had benefits exceeding costs if Wirecard was successful in taking over Deutsche Bank. The rational choice perspective suggests that crime is a rational choice if benefits exceed costs (Müller, 2018). Wirecard executives were sliding on the slippery slope over on the wrong side of the law (Gamache and McNamara, 2019). Some Wirecard executives lacked self-control (Craig and Piquero, 2016).

Fraud Investigation Outcome

KPMG conducted the investigation on the premises of Wirecard AG, a well as at KPMG's branch offices between October 31, 2019 and April 24, 2020. In addition,

KPMG inspected documents on the premises of the auditor and conducted interviews with Wirecard business partners on their premises in Dubai, the Philippines and, in one case, via video conferencing. KPMG determined the scope and nature of the relevant investigation activities independently and at their discretion in accordance with the examination mandate.

KPMG (2020a: 12) examined the amount and existence of revenues from the TPA business relationships between Cardsystems Middle East, Wirecard UK & Ireland, as well as Wirecard Technologies and the respective relevant TPA partners:

> KPMG can, as a result of the forensic investigation conducted in relation to the investigation period 2016 to 2018, neither make a statement that the revenues exist and are correct in terms of their amount, nor make a statement that the revenues do not exist and are incorrect in terms of their amount. To this extent, there is an obstacle to the investigation.

In our perspective of evaluating the KPMG investigation, the examiners failed in establishing facts concerning the existence or non-existence of revenues. A different approach in terms of knowledge strategy and information strategy might have been successful.

Within a few days of investigation, KPMG realized that Wirecard's core payments processing operations in Europe were not making any money – a fact that Wirecard had never disclosed to investors (Storbeck, 2020):

> All of the profit was generated by the operations overseen by Mr Marsalek, Wirecard's Asia business, where the processing of transactions was outsourced to third-party business partners.

Jan Marsalek claimed that € 1.9 billion in cash was transferred from Singapore to the Philippines and into a bank account in the name of Manila-based lawyer Mark Tolentino. KPMG discovered that two months after the money supposedly was paid into Tolentino's account, Wirecard still did not have a contractual relationship with the new trustee, nor had it conducted background checks on him (Storbeck, 2020).

In their final report, KPMG examiners detailed shortcomings in Wirecard's internal controls and compliance functions and outline severe doubts about the company's accounting practices (Storbeck, 2020), but they did not draw any definitive conclusions. KPMG neither verify the existence of the outsourced business nor the cash in escrow accounts, and they describe "the dogged obstruction by Wirecard and its business partners" (Storbeck, 2020).

The examiners' report presents results of the investigation activities into third party acquiring in regard to 1) existence and revenues from third party acquirers (TPA) business, 2) customer relationships in the TPA business, and 3) descriptions of the TPA business in Wirecard's annual statements:

1. Questionable amount and existence of revenues, in particular with reference to allegedly questionable customer relationships. KPMG (2020a: 13) examiners could not make a statement regarding existence and correctness of numbers:

"This is due to deficiencies in the internal organization and, in particular, to the unwillingness of the Third-Party Acquirers to participate in this special investigation in a comprehensive and transparent manner".

2. Questionable customer relationships. KPMG (2020a: 28) examiners could not verify the existence and correctness of customer names: "According to the information available, the names given in the press were 'account name' designations or aliases under which the revenues of customers referred to a TPA partner were recorded at the time. As we could not be provided with the actual names of the 43 alleged customers (aliases) quoted in the press, KPMG was unable to verify the existence of these customer relationships for the investigation period 2016 to 2018".

3. Questionable descriptions of third-party business in annual statements. KPMG (2020a: 30) provides no clear answer: "The presentation of debtor risk and existing customer risk in the report casts doubt on whether the scope of these risks in relation to the TPA business is sufficiently apparent to addressees of the financial statements. With regard to the debtor risk, the presentation made in the management report could give the impression that the risk from chargebacks is exclusively related to the receivables from the acquiring area. However, according to the information obtained, the chargeback risk in Wirecard's TPA business actually affects a considerable portion of the escrow accounts reported as cash and cash equivalents."

The examiners' report presents results of the investigation activities into digital lending business in regard to 1) amount and composition of the merchant cash advance business, 2) legal permissibility of business activities in Turkey and Brazil, 3) business background of certain lending activities, 4) acts at subsidiaries in Singapore, and 5) payment to middleman in India:

1. Questionable amount and composition of the merchant cash advance business in the context of the company's disclosures. KPMG (2020a: 37) provides no clear answer: "According to an internal memorandum submitted to KPMG, the published information on the volume of merchant cash advance should be used to explain business models. It is said not to be a defined product, but a value-added service, which is in part an integral component of Wirecard's services. This volume is therefore a management estimate based on various assumptions and calculations". Examiners neither questioned the management estimate nor inquired into assumptions and calculations.

2. Questionable legal permissibility of Wirecard's business activities in Turkey and Brazil in connection with the merchant cash advance product. KPMG (2020a: 39) conducted no independent investigation in Turkey but trusted instead a law firm paid for by Wirecard: "In the course of the investigation of the permissibility of the merchant cash advance business in Turkey, KPMG reviewed results summarized in the memorandum of a law firm commissioned by Wirecard. With regard

to the appropriateness of the structure of the merchant cash advance business with international customers ('international merchants'), including Wirecard Bank, KPMG concluded that the transactions with international customers in Turkey were legally permissible". Similar conclusion was drawn for Brazil based on "the information we received" (KPMG, 2020a: 40). The passivity of examiners in obtaining information is striking.

3. Questionable business background of possible unsecured loans granted to a specific company. Again, KPMG (2020a: 42) was unable to reconstruct past events: "In 2018, Wirecard Asia Holding Pte. Ltd, Singapore, granted company 4 several unsecured loans with a total volume of EUR 115 million with a one-year term for the purpose of 'merchant cash advance business'. Since KPMG did not receive any information on the customers of company 4 in the course of the investigation – in particular, not on the customers forwarded by Wirecard to company 4 – KPMG could not determine which companies or persons participated economically and to what extent in the loans granted to company 4 for 'merchant advance purposes'". The passivity of examiners in obtaining information is again striking.

4. Whistleblower alleging that there are indications of fraudulent acts at Wirecard subsidiaries in Singapore. KPMG (2020a: 45) base again their assessment on secondary sources: "In response to the whistleblower's accusations in spring 2018, Wirecard AG engaged Law Firm 1 to conduct a compliance audit and, at a later date, engaged Law Firm 2 to conduct an internal investigation. The background was that the compliance audit of Law Firm 1 has weaknesses. For example, the data basis, in particular consisting of accounting data and e-mail traffic, was not completely saved. The incompleteness of the data basis could not be fully remedied in the course of the investigation by Law Firm 2. EY Audit has supplemented individual results of the compliance audit and the internal investigation of the Law Firms 1 and 2 respectively, with its own auditing activities – including the use of EY FIS. As a result, the investigation activities of Law Firm 2 and the auditing activities of EY Audit under the extended audit procedures were not carried out on a complete data and information basis. Therefore, it cannot be ruled out that the investigation activities of Law Firms 1 and 2 and the auditing activities of EY Audit within the framework of the extended audit procedures would have come to a different conclusion if a complete database had been available. EY Audit has carried out auditing activities on the basis of the available data in relation to the accusations made". While fraud examiners here express that deviance is possible, they made no attempt to interview the whistleblowers or others who could tell where to find evidence.

5. Questionable payment of excessive purchase price to middleman in India. Fraud examiners at KPMG (2020a: 50) admit another failure despite attempted background research: "The auditors were unable to identify the beneficial owner of Fund 1. The background research by KPMG also failed to identify the

beneficial owner of Fund 1. Consequently, the accusation that Fund 1 is an intermediary cannot be conclusively clarified. Since knowledge of the beneficial owner is of essential importance for the question of who benefited from the purchase price, further investigations are not useful at this time as long as the identity has not been clarified. According to the information provided to KPMG, Wirecard AG does not know the beneficial owner of Fund 1".

KPMG (2020a: 59) presents the following text under the heading "Conclusion":

> KPMG issues this report to the best of its knowledge and belief on the basis of the documents submitted to KPMG, information provided and its own investigation activities, and with reference to the Code of Professional Conduct.

This is certainly no conclusion regarding findings. However, as there were no findings and no fraud investigation outcome, the chosen conclusion text illustrates the complete failure of Sven-Olaf Leitz and Alexander Geschonneck at KPMG.

Investigation Report Review

Storbeck (2020) suggests that Wirecard "needed to get a clean bill of health from KPMG" to prepare for a deal "blending Wirecard's business into Deutsche's vast balance sheet". If examiners had delivered a report of investigation according to such client expectations, it would be a commissioned work lacking independence and objectivity. However, the investigative journalist Storbeck (2020) concludes that "the approval from KPMG never came". While there was no approval in the investigation report, there was also no conclusion. Lack of conclusion is surprising, as Wirecard only six months later collapsed into insolvency after it was exposed as one of Germany's biggest postwar accounting frauds. There are thus certainly grounds to suggest that while KPMG examiners did not provide approval, they avoided condemnation of Wirecard board and management by claiming that they were unable to reconstruct critical events.

Wirecard's motive for a clean bill of health from KPMG was also evidenced by the statement of board members to chairman Wulf Matthias that "we told him that he needed the audit to protect himself and his money" (Storbeck, 2020). KPMG was thus far from an ideal initiation situation for the investigation. The ideal situations is a client who has a genuine interest in finding out what happened, how it happened, when it happened, and who did what to make it happen or not happen. The initiation stage for the investigation was dominated by client expectation that fraud examiners would refute with clear evidence what Wirecard was accused of in the media and elsewhere. While influenced by this expectation, KPMG did not meet such an expectation.

Another relevant issue to consider at the initiation stage is the extent to which KPMG's competitor Ernst & Young (EY) might implicitly be criticized if KPMG would find solid evidence of wrongdoing. The global audit business is characterized by shifting roles in fraud examinations, where they investigate each other. Chairman Matthias argued that EY was "evaluating the matters sufficiently". Maybe next time EY will investigate failing audit by KPMG, which might influence KPMG's extent of criticism of EY. The blame game among global audit firms seems restricted by industry loyalty.

According to Storbeck (2020), "40 forensic accountants from KPMG started to dig through Wirecard's books". While the number of examiners might seem impressive, the knowledge strategy is interesting. Probably, not all examiners were forensic accountants. Almost always are lawyers the dominating professionals participating in internal investigations. The relevant knowledge strategy for the challenge of reconstructing activities at Wirecard includes investigative interviewing since key people normally are willing to tell if they trust the interviewers. Since the examination team was dominated by forensic accountants who searched data and transactions, it is not at all obvious that they successfully accessed individuals who had insights into what was going on inside Wirecard globally.

This seemingly lack of relevant information sources is further evidenced by the lack of whistleblowing (KPMG, 2020a: 9):

> At the end of the investigation, we received confirmation that no information had been received through the whistleblower system.

All existing information and information submitted during the examination period to Wirecard's internal whistleblowing system regarding the subject of investigation was to be forwarded to KPMG. It is thus interesting to note that nothing was received through the whistleblowing system. While it is obvious in the aftermath that employees had relevant information to contribute through the whistleblowing system, the reasons for not contributing information might vary among employees. One typical reason is the fair of retaliation and reprisals that have harmed so many whistleblowers in the past. Another typical reason is the lack of trust in those who handled the messages (Mesmer-Magnus and Viswesvaran, 2005; Park et al., 2020; Rehg et al., 2009; Shawver and Clements, 2019).

According to Storbeck (2020), Sven-Olaf Leitz and Alexander Geschonneck, the two veterans KPMG partners running the fraud examination, told CEO Markus Braun and that the documents on the escrow accounts were not good enough. They insisted on seeing original documents, ideally directly obtained from OCBC. Escrow is a legal concept describing a financial instrument whereby an asset or escrow money is held by a third party on behalf of two other parties that are in the process of completing a transaction. OCBC bank is located in Singapore.

Jan Marsalek attempted to manipulate KPMG examiners by arranging a series of meetings in Manila introducing KPMG to the alleged Wirecard trustee for escrow accounts (Storbeck, 2020). KPMG was unconvinced, but did not conduct interviews independent of Marsalek, which fraud examiners should have done. Fraud examiners failed in having separate meetings with important information sources in the Philippines, Dubai, and Singapore. One of the meetings monitored by Marsalek was with Christopher Bauer who ran PayEasy, which processed high-risk transactions for Wirecard – mostly payments for pornography, gambling, and gaming. A few months after the meeting, Bauer was reported dead.

According to Storbeck (2020), KPMG told Wirecard that fraud examiners where thinking of terminating their work because of obstacles to the investigation. But they did not. To preserve fraud examiner integrity, they might have done so. Instead, KPMG extended the deadline for submission of their report.

The first draft of the KPMG report was not accepted by the client. KPMG revised the report of investigation before it was published (Storbeck, 2020). Whether or not the revision represented commissioned work that harmed KPMG's integrity is not obvious.

The investigation was hit by the Corona pandemic on March 12, 2020, when examiners were no longer able to travel. They had to conduct video conferencing with interviewees for the remaining investigation period until submission of their report on April 27. Generally, digital media reduce the quality of information compared to face-to-face interaction.

Fraud examiners admit that they failed in verifying information (KPMG, 2020a: 6):

> The basis of our investigation and evaluation were the documents received and information provided, but it was not possible for us to verify the completeness and authenticity of the documents and documentations provided to us. Consequently, we cannot make any conclusive statement as to whether these documents and information are complete, accurate, and free of contradictions. Nor can we conclusively assess whether all information and evidence relevant to the assessment has been made available to us. In this respect, we also cannot rule out the possibility that we would have come to a different conclusion if we had been aware of additional information or documents.

Investigative interviewing and digital forensics might have helped solve this problem (Goodman-Delahunty and Martschuk, 2020). Collins and Carthy (2018) studied the relationship between rapport and communication during investigative interviews. Attention, positivity, and coordination are important rapport components. Rapport is a close and harmonious relationship in which individuals understand each other and are sympathetic to each other. The purpose of investigative interviewing is to gain information, and persons providing information may not always be motivated to do so, especially if the persons perceive being subject to suspicion or blame for misconduct. The aim is for the examination interviewer and the information source to have a productive relationship that builds on cooperation and respect. An interview takes place because the interviewer assumes that the subject of an interview has information of value to the interviewer.

Digital forensics is the recovery and investigation of material found in digital devices. For example, email accounts and mobile phones tend to have personal and sensitive information that could lead examiners towards conclusions. Search engines might have been applied by fraud examiners on all digital devices available to executives at Wirecard.

A further action to verify information is triangulation where several sources confirm or disconfirm the same piece of information. By combining multiple observers, documents, and theories, examiners can overcome the weakness of single source investigations.

Fraud examiners admit that they did not even try to verify information (KPMG, 2020a: 7):

> KPMG points out that KPMG has not carried out an authenticity check, in particular for documents delivered on or after April 17, 2020.

Anonymous providers of information are an unreliable, yet often important source in fraud investigations. Examiners have to assess the reliability of the information as well as the source, but KPMG (2020a: 9) seemingly ignored that important task in assessing anonymous reports:

> During our special investigation, KPMG was provided with information and documents by third parties, in part anonymously. KPMG examined these pieces of information and documents with regard to their relevance to the areas under investigation and took them into account to the extent they were related to one of the areas under investigation. KPMG included these pieces of information and documents in its investigation to the extent that KPMG in its discretion considered this to be necessary for the purposes of the investigation.

KPMG (2020a: 10) blame Wirecard for their lack of cooperation and thus avoid self-blame for failing:

> Wirecard AG did not supply some of the documents requested by KPMG in the course the investigation (. . .) Wirecard repeatedly postponed individual agreed interview appointments (. . .) The transfer of transaction data at least for the years 2016 and 2017 required the support of the TPA partners, which has so far been lacking.

Self-blame is rare and often non-existent. Nobody will blame oneself for a negative event. Self-blame is attributing a negative event to one's behavior or disposition (Lee and Robinson, 2000).

The failing investigation is confirmed by KPMG (2020a: 12), who label it an obstacle rather than a failure as presented earlier in this chapter:

> KPMG can, as a result of the forensic investigation conducted in relation to the investigation period 2016 to 2018, neither make a statement that the revenues exist and are correct in terms of their amount, nor make a statement that the revenues do not exist and are incorrect in terms of their amount. To this extent, there is an obstacle to the investigation.

Wirecard Bankruptcy Collapse

Chancellor Angela Merkel in Germany had to explain herself about helping Wirecard accused of a billion-dollar fraud. The creditors of Wirecard were left with a loss of three billion Euros. Merkel had to explain how she could vouch for the bankrupt company (Kagge, 2021). The payment company Wirecard, which was hailed as one of Germany's rare technology successes, collapsed into insolvency in the summer of 2020 after revealing that two billion Euros in cash did not exist (Storbeck and Morris, 2021).

A German finance deputy claimed in April 2021 that Wirecard was given no privileged treatment (Chazan, 2021):

> Jörg Kukies, Germany's deputy finance minister denied seeking to protect the disgraced payment company Wirecard as a national champion, insisting that it had never received "privileged treatment" at the hands of his ministry. Kukies' denial was part of a long opening statement at the parliamentary inquiry into one of the biggest frauds in Germany's postwar history. "I personally never acted or intervened in favor of Wirecard", he said. He said that Germany had "learnt the lesson from the Wirecard scandal, initiating sweeping reform of BaFin, the German financial regulator, that would give it "more bite" and poaching the respected head of Swiss regulator Finma, Mark Branson, a its new boss. Members of parliament are investigating why the German authorities failed to prevent the Wirecard debacle and ignored a plethora of warning signs of suspicious activity at the payment provider. Their hearings reach a climax this week with the questioning of Olaf Scholz, the finance minister, and Angela Merkel, Germany's veteran chancellor.

Wirecard auditor Ernst & Young was in trouble for failing to uncover the fraud (Bugge, 2020). German parliament expanded its probe into the firm's audit of Wirecard (Storbeck, 2021b):

> German members of parliament have asked a special investigator to expand probe into EY's audits of Wirecard after his initial report uncovered serious shortcomings. The Big Four firm has been under intense scrutiny since last year's collapse of Wirecard, which was awarded unqualified audits by EY for a decade. Concern has grown in recent days after a report commissioned by a German parliamentary inquiry examining the scandal reached a damning verdict over the quality of EY's work. The report, which was seen by the Financial Times, describes how EY failed to spot fraud risk indicators, did not fully implement professional guidelines and, on key questions, relied on verbal assurances from executives.

Markus Braun, Wirecard's former chief executive officer, gave himself up to German police and testified in the fall of 2020 in front of the Bundestag commission investigating the Wirecard collapse. Jan Marsalek, former chief operating officer, disappeared to Belarus and was on Interpol's most-wanted list (Storbeck, 2021a). As the Wirecard scandal evolved, more elite members in German society got involved. One of them was Alexander Schütz, a Deutsche Bank board member who was accused of insider trading in Wirecard shares (Storbeck and Morris, 2021):

Germany's financial watchdog has filed a criminal complaint against Deutsche Bank supervisory board member Alexander Schütz over alleged insider trading of Wirecard shares. Munich prosecutors told the Financial Times that they received the criminal complaint from BaFin by fax on Monday, adding that they were waiting for details, which the watchdog has sent by post. They will evaluate the matter once all documents have been received. Schütz, a close confidant of former Wirecard chief executive Markus Braun, has already announced that he will step down from Deutsche's board next month.

When Markus Braun testified in front of the parliamentary commission, he did not tell much. He refused to answer whether he had a daughter and what the topic was in his doctoral dissertation. Braun claimed that he was innocent, and that Wirecard had suffered from major fraud by others (Kagge, 2021).

11 Economic Crime Statistics

Public statistics from government agencies do not have corporate crime as a category for their statistical reporting. The only known registration of corporate crime occurred in Norway from 2009 to 2013. During those four years, 39 corporate representatives were convicted to prison for white-collar crime committed on behalf of their organizations. The average age of the convicts was 52 years, and the average age of the offenders when crime occurred was 47 years. The average sentence was 2 years in prison. The average amount of money involved in crime was NOK 195 million (USD 21 million). The average size of the corporation was 379 employees and revenues of NOK 524 million (USD 54 million).

In the same period from 2009 to 2013, 264 occupational white-collar criminals were convicted to prison for financial crime committed no behalf of themselves. The average age of the convicts was 47 years, and the average age of the offenders when crime occurred was 42 years. The average sentence was 2.2 years in prison. The average amount of money involved in crime was NOK 25 million (USD 2,7 million). The average size of the corporation was 84 employees and revenues of NOK 138 million (USD 15 million).

It is interesting to note that occupational criminals are punished slightly more than corporate criminals with a marginal difference of 3 additional months in prison. This slightly more severe punishment is passed by Norwegian courts despite the amount of money involved in crime is far below that of corporate criminals. Corporate criminals commit financial crime for almost eight times more money than occupational criminals. A potential explanation for this discrepancy is that corporate criminals are not the direct beneficiaries of their own wrongdoing. Occupational criminal benefit directly from their wrongdoing. This kind of reasoning finds support in corruption sentencing in Norwegian courts, where bribers are less severely punished compared to bribed individuals.

The metaphor of a tip of the iceberg is often used to illustrate the low detection fraction for corporate crime. It is suggested that less than one out of ten corporate law violations end up in the criminal justice system.

National Crime Statistics

Norwegian police received slightly more than three hundred thousand crime reports in the form of complaints in the year 2000. As indicated in Figure 11.1, there has been a slow decrease in police reports in recent years in Norway. The total number of police reports can be compared to the population of six million inhabitants in the country. Assuming that each individual notifying the police about an incident does it no more than once in a year, we can calculate that every twentieth Norwegian

https://doi.org/10.1515/9783110766950-012

reported a crime incident to the Norwegian police in 2020. Among various crime categories, violence against persons is the largest crime category.

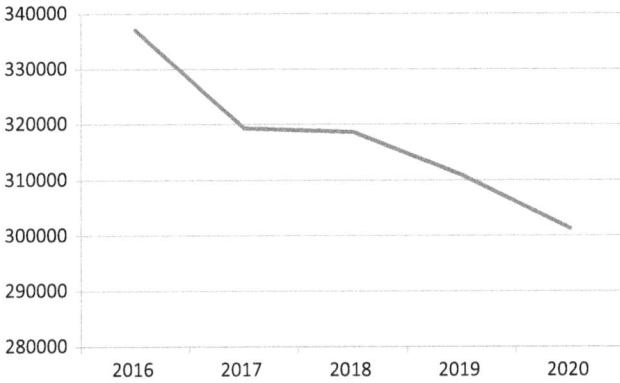

Figure 11.1: All crime cases reported to the police annually.

Figure 11.2 illustrates the number of police reports concerned with economic crime complaints. There were a little less than twenty-five thousand reports regarding economic crime. This means that eight percent of the police reports were concerned with economic crime, while ninety-two percent were concerned with other forms of crime. Both for economic crime and for other forms of crime, it is assumed that the detection rate is low, indicating that the frequency of the various forms of crime is much higher. We return to the issue of detection rate when looking at the specific group of offenders labelled white-collar criminals.

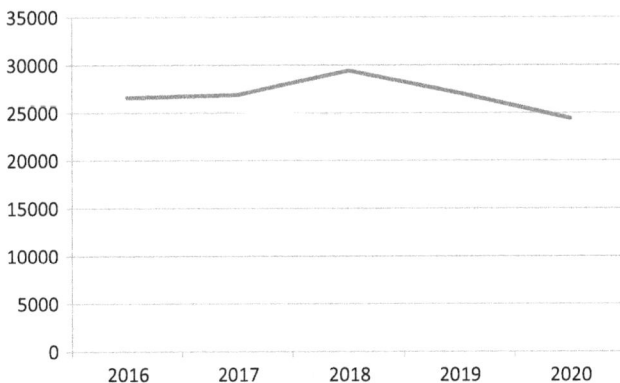

Figure 11.2: Economic crime cases reported to the police annually.

The police claim that they are able to find out what happened or not happened in all reported complaints as indicated in Figure 11.3. The percentage above forty-nine in the figure indicates that the police was unable to solve fifty-one percent of the reported cases.

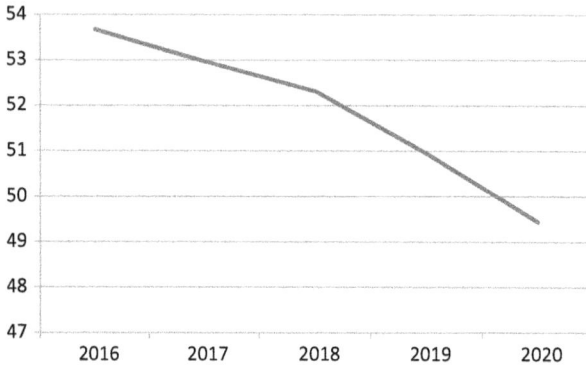

Figure 11.3: Percentage clearance of all crime cases reported to the police.

For the crime category of economic crime, the percentage was lower, as indicated in Figure 11.4. Instead of one out of two cases solved, the police solved only one out of three cases.

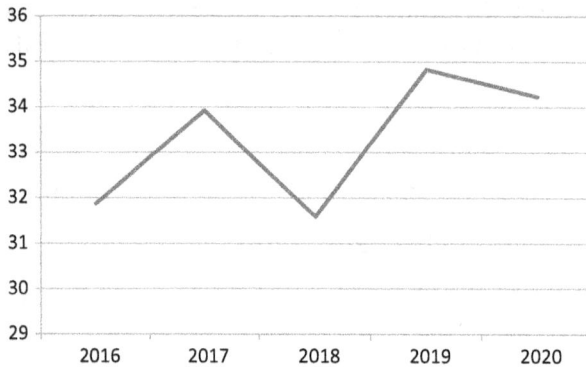

Figure 11.4: Percentage clearance of economic crime cases reported to the police.

The elite within economic crime is labelled white-collar crime. A total of 408 individuals in the privileged elite were convicted in court for economic crime from 2009 to 2015. The annual rate was thus sixty-eight. We do not know how many white-collar offenders are reported to the police every year, since white-collar crime is no category in Norwegian crime statistics. We only know the fraction of white-collar defendants in court who are convicted. While the serious fraud office claims that they get eight or nine out of ten prosecuted defendants convicted to prison in Norwegian courts, police districts seem to have a far lower success rate. Assuming that they only get half of the prosecuted convicted while the other half gets their cases dismissed, then we can double the annual number from 68 individuals to 136 individuals per year. Compared to the thirty-four thousand economic crime suspects, white-collar offenders represent only .004 percent.

However, the detection rate for white-collar offenders might be lower than the detection rate for other economic criminals. Gottschalk and Gunnesdal (2017) found that only one out of eleven white-collar offenders are assumed to be detected.

Macroeconomic Estimations

Corporate crime by white-collar offenders is part of the shadow economy. The shadow economy is defined as market-based production of goods and services, whether legal or illegal, that escapes detection in the official estimates of the gross national product (Evans, 2016; Imamoglu, 2016; Petersen et al., 2010; Schneider et al., 2010). The shadow economy comprises those economic activities and the income derived from them that circumvent or otherwise avoid government regulation, taxation, or observation (Schneider and Williams, 2013). The shadow economy is sometimes labeled the informal economy (Edelbacher et al., 2016).

Just like the magnitude of white-collar crime specifically cannot be observed, the shadow economy is generally not observable, so its magnitude must be estimated (Breusch, 2005). Schneider and Williams (2013) argue that there is no appropriate methodology to assess the scope of the shadow economy. Rather, there are three competing methods of assessment of the size of the shadow economy that are used:

- Direct procedures at a micro level that aim at determining the size of the shadow economy at one particular point in time. An example is survey method.
- Indirect procedures that make use of macroeconomic indicators in order to proxy the development of the shadow economy over time.
- Statistical models that use statistical tools to estimate the shadow economy as an unobserved variable.

The most commonly used method of measurement is based on a combination of the multiple indicators multiple cause (MIMC) procedure and on the currency demand method. The MIMC procedure assumes that the shadow economy remains an unobserved phenomenon, which can be estimated using quantitatively measurable causes of shadow economic activity as well as indicators of illicit activity (Schneider and Williams, 2013: 28):

The causes will include variables such as the tax burden and the intensity of regulation, and the indicators will include variables such as the demand for currency, official national income figure and official working hours data. The econometric models are complex and have to deal with a range of well-known challenges such as endogeneity problems. For example, the size of the tax burden might make it more difficult for the government to raise taxes, so it responds by raising tax rates and therefore the tax burden on the level of official national income.

The MIMIC procedure produces relative estimates of the size and development of the shadow economy. Typically, the shadow economy is estimated at around 14 percent in countries such as Norway. 14 percent of gross national product in Norway represents 420 billion Norwegian kroner (US $53 billion). In comparison, the shadow economy is estimated at 16 percent in Belgium, 14 percent in Sweden, 13 percent in Denmark and Germany, and 8 percent in Austria.

Samfunnsøkonomisk analyse (2017) estimated the size of labor market crime in Norway between 1973 and 2015. Corporate crime is part of labor market crime such as cartel activities, social security fraud for employees, and dumping of wages for workers. Actions related to labor market crime include violations of the working environment act, tax evasion, and social security fraud. Both employers and employees may have incentives to commit such actions. Labor market crime results in the loss of income for law-abiding businesses, deterioration of individual industries, and unfair conditions for law-abiding businesses.

Samfunnsøkonomisk analyse (2017) applied two estimation methods combined to calculate the development of labor market crime. Criminal acts are hidden, and hence are difficult to identify. It is therefore necessary to use special estimation methods, to estimate the scope. In general, these methods can be divided into direct approaches (when one has access to crime data from the control agencies) and indirect approaches (when one does not have such data). However, there will always be considerable uncertainty attached to this type of analysis. In this project, researchers were granted access to rarely available data for revealed tax evasion. Therefore, the research could utilize both direct and indirect approaches. The direct approach gives an estimate of the level of labor marked crime in Norway as a share of GDP, while the indirect gives the development over time. In the direct approach, researchers utilized control data for Norwegian businesses to calculate the value of labor market crime related to taxation and fraud of social security. The size of tax evasion was calculated from predicted probabilities for labor marked crime for all businesses in Norway. Combined with social security fraud figures from the social security agency, it gives an estimate of the level of labor market crime, measured as a share of GDP. Then researchers used an indirect approach by MIMIC to estimate changes in the size of labor market crime over a longer period (1973 to 2015). In this model, researchers used cause and indicator variables, which are assumed to be highly correlated with labor market crime, to say something about the changes of labor market crime over time.

The result was an estimate of labor market crime of NOK 40 billion (USD 4 billion). This estimate is based on indicators. One indicator is the extent of hits versus misses in control activities. If control of a business activity reveals crime, then it is a hit. If the control reveals no crime, it is a miss. If every tenth control reveals a crime, then the magnitude of crime is larger than if every twentieth control reveals a crime.

Crime Expert Elicitation

Tip of the iceberg is a small, noticeable part of a problem, the total size of which is really much greater. Tip of the iceberg is only the beginning and just a small indication of a larger problem. The problem is much bigger than it seems. Tip of the iceberg is a metaphor where floating icebergs have a significant proportion of their mass below the surface of the water. This is likely the case for corporate crime. Tip of the iceberg is the few corporate offenders who are caught, prosecuted, and convicted. The iceberg itself includes the many offenders who are never brought to justice.

One approach to estimate the size of the iceberg is the use of expert elicitation. Expert elicitation refers to a systematic approach to synthesize subjective judgments of experts on a topic where there is uncertainty due to lack of data. (Heyman and Sailors, 2016; Valkenhoef and Tervonen, 2016).

The purpose of eliciting and analyzing expert judgment is to use all available information to make expert judgment inference, which is different from statistical inference. Statistical inference means that conclusions about the population can be established when the sample is randomly drawn for the population. Expert judgment inference means that experts' estimates represent the state of knowledge. It represents previously unknown and undocumented information. The limited ability to infer does not mean that expert judgments are not valid data. Expert judgments are indeed valid data in that it must be carefully gathered, analyzed and interpreted (Meyer and Booker, 2001). When a number of experts are interviewed, their accumulated guestimates tend to converge towards numbers that remain stable when more experts are added. Therefore, approximately ten experts from various backgrounds are often sufficient (Heyman and Sailors, 2016; Slottje et al., 2008; Valkenhoef and Tervonen, 2016).

Expert elicitation seeks to make explicit and utilizable the unpublished knowledge and wisdom in the heads of experts, based on their accumulated experience as well as their interpretation and reflection in a given context.

Expert elicitation is a systematic approach to include expert insights into the subject and also insights into the limitations, strengths and weaknesses of published studies (Slottje et al., 2008: 7):

Usually, the subjective judgment is represented as a "subjective' probability density function (PDF) reflecting the experts' belief regarding the quantity at hand, but it can also be for instance the experts' beliefs regarding the shape of a given exposure response function. An expert elicitation procedure should be developed in such a way that minimizes biases in subjective judgment and errors related to that in the elicited outcomes.

Table 11.1 summarizes all seven approaches that resulted in an overall average of 11.9 billion NOK in white-collar crime damage annually in Norway. It varies from 10.1 billion to 13.4 billion (Gottschalk and Gunnesdal, 2018).

The research applied the following seven approaches to estimate the magnitude of white-collar crime (Gottschalk and Gunnesdal, 2018):
1. Fraction of white-collar criminals that are caught and brought to justice
2. Fraction with probability distribution of white-collar criminals that are caught and brought to justice
3. Fraction of white-collar offender groups that are caught and brought to justice
4. Fraction of white-collar crime categories that are detected and lead to conviction
5. Fraction of white-collar crime victim groups that lead to detection and conviction
6. Fraction of white-collar male and female offenders that are caught and brought to justice
7. Total magnitude of white-collar crime in billions of Norwegian kroner (NOK).

Table 11.1: Estimation based on seven approaches.

ALL APPROACHES COMBINED	
Approach	Expert elicitation
1	13.4 billion
2	12.3 billion
3	12.9 billion
4	11.8 billion
5	10.6 billion
6	12.2 billion
7	10.1 billion
Average	**11.9 billion**

Fifteen experts were interviewed in the research: an investigative journalist in major newspaper, an experienced bankruptcy lawyer, an experienced internal auditor, three tax administration fraud examiners, an investigative bank manager, a police detective, a corruption researcher, a private fraud examiners, a corporate investor, a defense attorney, and a social security fraud investigator.

It is a diverse range of experts, as recommended by Meyer and Booker (2001), so that the problem of estimating the magnitude is likely to be thoroughly considered from many viewpoints. Diversity of participants is one way to minimize the influence of a single individual. Some of these categories, however, are not relevant or feasible. For example, while a victim of white-collar crime has a strong memory of the episode, there is only one episode, from which the victim as a respondent hardly can generalize.

We developed a questionnaire for the experts and applied the survey in two steps. First, an email was sent to experts informing them about the attached questionnaire and telling them that they would be contacted for a phone interview by a researcher a few days later. During the phone interview, experts had the opportunity to ask the researcher for clarification and discuss issues. While they were talking on the telephone, the researcher filled in the questionnaire based on the responses from the expert. The combination of mail and phone as two different communication channels are considered a feasible response mode in line with normative expertise.

12 Corporations in Tax Havens

Tax havens offer convenience for corporate crime. Not only is tax evasion an obvious benefit where corporations can avoid taxes on profits in their domestic markets by transferring profits to tax havens with low or no corporate taxes. Corporations can enjoy secrecy regarding ownership. They can remove traces of corruption by transferring bribes via tax havens, and they can launder money from crime by help of the secrecy in tax havens (Deng et al., 2020; Granda, 2021). In some languages, a tax haven is labeled tax paradise, where a paradise is a place of exceptional happiness and delight (Schmal et al., 2021).

Several examples in this book indicate the extensive use of tax havens. Mannheimer Swartling (2016) describe how the Swedish bank Nordea has its subsidiary in Luxembourg illegally backdating contracts and help clients with tax evasion as leaked from the Panama Papers. The bank first denied its link to the Panamanian law firm Mossack Fonseca, which specializes in establishing corporate mailbox companies in tax havens (Associated Press, 2016). Gunn Wærsted resigned from her group executive position at Nordea and chair at Nordea Luxembourg (Ekeberg, 2016; Grinde, 2016; Kristjansson, 2016; Trumpy, 2016). Several other Scandinavian banks are also helping their corporate clients in tax havens such as Danske Bank in Denmark (Bruun Hjejle, 2018), Swedbank in Sweden (Clifford Chance, 2020), and Norwegian bank DNB helping Icelandic fishing company Samherji bribe Namibian officials through tax havens (Amundsen, 2021; Ekroll et al., 2019; Kibar, 2020a, 2020b; Kleinfeld, 2019; Reuters, 2019; Schultz, 2019; Schultz and Trumpy, 2019a, 2019b). We return to these and other cases of corporate activity in tax havens in this chapter.

Schmal et al. (2021) use the term tax paradise as a synonym for tax haven when they describe corporate activity in tax havens:

> Multinational firms shift billions of income into tax havens to decrease their taxes. Through the use of transfer pricing and tax-optimizing transactions such as intrafirm debt and royalty payments, firms reduce their tax payments. Using tax havens can be legal. However, financial statement users are concerned that tax havens enable firms to obfuscate information. Tax havens are often related to secretive tax planning schemes because these states often lack transparency and information exchange.

A tax haven or paradise is a state or geographical area with autonomy in tax policy, which offers foreign enterprises zero tax terms or very low tax rates, and a legislation that prevents insight from the outside world. Examples of tax havens include the Bahamas, Bermuda, Cayman Islands, Dubai, British Virgin Islands, Guernsey, Hong Kong, Isle of Man, Jersey, Liechtenstein, Luxembourg, Mauritius, Monaco, Panama, Singapore, and Switzerland. Less well known is that countries such as Ireland and the Netherlands have also been mentioned as tax havens, and that the

https://doi.org/10.1515/9783110766950-013

united state of Delaware might be the most secret tax haven in the world (Schjel-derup, 2020).

Swedish Bank Nordea

As presented earlier in this book, Nordea is a bank in Sweden with subsidiaries in other countries, including a subsidiary in Luxembourg. When the Panama Papers revealed money flows to and from tax havens, investigative journalists discovered misconduct in Luxembourg. For example, the bank backdated contracts for custom-ers for tax evasion purposes. Law firm Mannheimer Swartling (2016) conducted a fraud examination and wrote an investigation report on the bank practice of wealth management for its customers. Illegal backdating of contracts and corporate tax evasion was thus revealed by investigative journalists and fraud examiners. The ini-tial corporate account by Nordea was communicated to Associated Press (2016):

> Nordea, the Nordic region's biggest bank, says it doesn't help wealthy customers evade taxes in response to reports linking it to the Panamanian law firm at the center of a media investiga-tion into offshore accounts.

The Panama Papers consisted of 11.5 million leaked documents that detailed finan-cial and attorney-client information for more than 214,000 entities in tax havens. The Panama Papers disclosed involvement by Nordea in tax havens, but the bank first denied responsibility for what customers might do in tax havens. However, a few months later, Mannheimer Swartling (2016) confirmed bank involvement:

> The investigation has found deficiencies in the procedures regarding renewal of Powers of At-torney (POA). In at least seven cases the investigation has shown that backdated documents have been requested or provided during the last six years, which is illegal when it aims at al-tering the truth.

Fraud examiners thus confirmed that the Panama Papers had disclosed Nordea in-volvement in tax havens, and the investigation documents law violations in the Luxembourg branch. Gunn Wærsted resigned from her group executive position in the bank before fraud examiners from law firm Mannheimer Swartling (2016) pre-sented their investigation report. She was responsible for wealth management in-volving tax havens (Associated Press, 2016). She resigned officially to concentrate on a board chair position at another company, so her resignation did not seem linked to the scandal (Ekeberg, 2016; Grinde, 2016; Kristjansson, 2016; Trumpy, 2016).

Fraud examiners found illegal backdating of contracts by Nordea wealth man-agement that was headed by Gunn Wærsted (Kristjánsson, 2016):

> The big bank is one of the many banks that were caught with their pants down in the Panama Papers leak. The bank's internal investigation establishes that offenses were committed in the

Luxembourg branch, as the bank helped customers backdate documents. The bank also provided customers with annual reports that could be used to mislead tax authorities. Wærsted denies knowing about this but defends the practice of creating straw companies in tax havens, as long as they were used for "legitimate tax planning".

Gunn Wærsted was not only head of wealth management at Nordea. She was also chairperson at the Luxembourg branch. Shortly after the scandal became public, Wærsted resigned from her position at the bank (Kaspersen and Eriksen, 2015).

Another bank presented earlier in this book is Danske Bank in Denmark. Wealth management is a profitable service for most global banks where they take care of money values for affluent individuals, families, and firms. It is a banking service which incorporates structuring and placement of wealth to assist in preserving and protecting owner fortunes. Often, wealth management involves secrecy by placement in tax havens. Therefore, suspicions of tax evasion and money laundering are often associated with wealth management. Recent scandals involving Danske Bank in Denmark (Bruun Hjejle, 2018), Swedbank in Sweden (Clifford Chance, 2020), and Nordea bank in Sweden (Mannheimer Swartling, 2016) have provided evidence of criminal market structures in the banking sector. While the cases involving Danske Bank and Swedbank in money laundering were detected and reported by whistleblowers, the case involving Nordea in tax evasion was detected and reported by the Panama Papers.

Icelandic Fishing Samherji

Yet another Scandinavian bank was involved in tax havens. According to Reuters (2019), Samherji transferred more than $70 million through a shell company in the tax haven Marshall Islands from 2011 to 2018. Samherji transferred the money through bank accounts in DNB. The bank's largest shareholder is the Norwegian state, which holds 34% stake in the bank (Ekroll et al., 2019; Kibar, 2020a, 2020b). Starting with DNB in Norway, the broadcasting corporation Al Jazeera investigated allegations and published the report entitled "Anatomy of a bribe: A deep dive into an underworld of corruption – An Al Jazeera investigation into the corrupt power brokers and global business elites defrauding the Namibian people" (Kleinfeld, 2019). The alleged corruption payments from the Icelandic fishing corporation Samherji traveled via the Norwegian bank DNB to state officials in Namibia to obtain fishing rights off the coast of Namibia (Amundsen, 2021; Schultz, 2019; Schultz and Trumpy, 2019a, 2019b).

Samherji is a seafood company in Iceland. The country's largest fishing group was accused of paying bribes to trawl an African country's waters (Samherji, 2019a, 2019b, 2020a, 2020b). Financial Times reported in November 2019 that two ministers in Namibia had resigned and that Samherji's chief executive had temporarily stepped down over allegations the company paid bribes for fishing quotas in the southern African nation's maritime waters (Cotterill, 2019; Samherji, 2019b). The whistleblower at Samherji was Johannes Stefansson who told WikiLeaks and then Al Jazeera.

Johannes Stefansson came to Namibia in Africa in 2011, where he was assigned the task by the Icelandic seafood company Samherji of looking for business opportunities. To complete the mission, he involved himself in questionable payments to politicians and businesspeople in Namibia and Angola. After a while, he developed a bad conscience and felt guilty of wrongdoing. He decided to give notice of the situation. The police arrested the former minister of fisheries in Namibia, Bernhard Esau, and indicted him for corruption and money laundering in November 2019. Stefansson provided information to WikiLeaks and then Al Jazeera, where investigative journalist James Kleinfeld interviewed local sources in Namibia. Kleinfeld (2019) then wrote a report on the "Anatomy of a bribe: A deep dive into an underworld of corruption". Iceland public broadcasting, similar to BBC in the UK, interviewed the whistleblower and cooperated with Al Jazeera. Al Jazeera's investigative unit secretly filmed officials in Namibia demanding cash in exchange for political favors. It was a story of how foreign companies plunder Africa's natural resources. Using confidential documents provided to Al Jazeera by WikiLeaks, "Anatomy of a Bribe" exposes the government ministers and public officials willing to sell off Namibia's assets in return for millions of dollars in bribes. Al Jazeera journalists spent three months undercover posing as foreign investors looking to exploit the lucrative Namibian fishing industry. The country's minister of fisheries demonstrated a willingness to use a front company to accept a $200,000 'donation'. Exclusive testimony from a whistleblower, who worked for Iceland's biggest fishing company, revealed that his employer seemingly instructed him to bribe ministers and even the president in return for fishing rights worth hundreds of millions of dollars.

The prosecuting authority in Namibia claimed in December 2019 that the accused officials in the country had received 103 million Namibian dollars – equivalent to 6 million US dollars – in kickbacks to ensure the Icelandic company access to fishing quotas. According to court documents, a large number of false invoices had been made to hide the payments (Kibar, 2020a).

Samherji in Iceland hired fraud examiners at law firm Wikborg Rein in Norway to investigate of all these allegations. The report of investigation was completed in the summer of 2020.

The broadcasting corporation Al Jazeera investigated allegations and published the report entitled "Anatomy of a bribe: A deep dive into an underworld of corruption", "An Al Jazeera investigation into the corrupt power brokers and global business elites defrauding the Namibian people", and "The storm is brewing – We are preparing ourselves for war" (Kleinfeld, 2019):

Since Al Jazeera first presented the accused parties with evidence of their alleged wrongdoing, the response has been swift and overwhelming: Minister of Fisheries Bernhard Esau and the minister of justice have both resigned from their cabinet positions; James Hatuikulipi has resigned as the chairman of Fishcor and has also resigned from his job as the managing director of Investec Asset Management. In the run-up to elections in Namibia, the #Fishrot affair has caused outrage in the country, leading to protests in the capital, Windhoek, with hundreds of people marching to the Anti-Corruption Commission demanding decisive action against corruption in the country. On the day of the elections on November 27, most of the Namibians implicated in the investigation were arrested on charges of corruption, money laundering and fraud.

All the Namibians featured in the Al Jazeera investigation deny all wrongdoing. Sacky Kadhila told The Namibian newspaper that he knew from the start that our undercover reporters were "fake businessmen". "I played along ... in order to confirm my suspicions," he wrote. He added that he had reported the matter to the president's lawyer, Sisa Namandje, who in turn claimed he had alerted police.

In Iceland, the scandal has led to the suspension of Samherji's longtime CEO.

Al Jazeera is an independent news organization funded in part by the Qatari government. In 2006, Al Jazeera Satellite Network was changed to a public utility and private corporation by a public memorandum and articles of association in accordance with the provisions of Qatar Law and was re-named Al Jazeera Media Network. The investigative journalist who wrote the above report continued his investigations in Namibia where he detected corruption allegations because of a 5G deal with Huawei. Bribes were offered to politicians to ensure Chinese tech giant Huawei would win an exclusive 5G telecommunication network in Namibia (Kleinfeld, 2020).

Norwegian Thule Drilling

Legitimate access to crime resources can be illustrated by the case of a chairman of the board who published his autobiography (Olav, 2014, 2015). The chairman used a tax haven where he had an account when he ran business through another company there (Bjørklund, 2018; Oslo tingrett, 2015). As defined above, a tax haven is a country or place with very low or no rates of taxation for foreign investors, where foreigners enjoy complete secrecy about their investments. Money laundering of proceeds from criminal activity is an attractive opportunity in tax havens. On the legitimate side, the use of tax havens enables transfer-pricing strategies to lower overall tax burdens for multinational corporations. Subsidiaries located in tax havens serve multinationals to avoid taxes by shifting income from high-tax countries to low-tax countries. Firms also use tax havens in strategies that involve intercompany debt or leasing arrangements to shift income across jurisdictions. Tax authorities in various countries attempt to challenge this kind of tax evasion (Dyreng et al., 2019; Guenther et al., 2019).

Some members of the upper echelon in society violate laws whenever they feel necessary. They have access to resources to commit and conceal financial crime while they deny the guilty mind. Autobiographies by convicted white-collar offenders are an interesting source of information to understand motives, opportunities, and willingness for deviant behaviors.

This research applies the theory of convenience to study the autobiography of a convicted chairperson of the board in Norway. While claiming corporate crime for the benefit of the business, he actually carried out occupational crime to benefit himself (Benson and Chio, 2020; Shepherd and Button, 2019). As an entrepreneur, he felt entitled to do whatever he considered necessary. He suffered from narcissistic identification, where there is little difference between personal money and company money.

Hans Eirik Olav was the chairman of the board at the Norwegian offshore corporation Thule Drilling. He received a sentence of four years in prison for embezzlement and bankruptcy fraud (Bjørklund, 2018; Olav, 2014, 205; Oslo tingrett, 2015).

An autobiography can represent an individual's response strategy after a crisis. Bundy and Pfarrer (2015) describe response strategies on a continuum from defensive to accommodative. A defense strategy attempts to avoid social approval loss by eliminating an individual's responsibility for or association with a crisis. Examples range from outright denial of responsibility, via attacking accusers and shifting blame onto other persons, to perceive being a victim of an incident.

An autobiography can be studied by content analysis. Content analysis is any methodology or procedure that works to identify characteristics within texts attempting to make valid inferences (Krippendorff, 1980; Patrucco et al., 2017). Content analysis assumes that language reflects both how people understand their surroundings and their cognitive processes (Gibbs, 2007; McClelland et al., 2010).

Our selected autobiography by a chairman of the board was written before he was sentenced to prison. Olav (2014, 2015) attempted publicly to defend himself before he was sentenced to incarceration for 4 years (Oslo tingrett, 2015). He tried to appeal the verdict from Oslo district court, but his case was neither admitted to an appeal court nor the Supreme Court in Norway. While the district court sentence is 42 pages long, his books have a length of 471 pages and 479 pages respectively. Olav's criminal case was also covered extensively in Norwegian media (e.g., Bjørklund, 2018).

Hans Eirik Olav was convicted of gross infidelity of US$ 6 million and gross money laundering of US$ 1.75 million in the period 2007–2011. The reason was that he had drained the company Thule Drilling – where he was chairman of the board – wrongfully for these funds. He used the firm Strategic Alliances Corporation where he was a co-owner to receive funds that were supposed to be used to complete the work on the oil rig Thule Power in Saudi Arabia. The oil rig work was delayed and had stopped as a result of conflicts, and lack of repayments of loans from Thule to the shipyard QGM in Saudi Arabia, which was to complete the rig. Thule Drilling had a strained liquidity, and shareholders had to invest more money that was mainly to be used to get started and complete the work on the rig Thule Power.

Olav used a number of mechanisms to complete and conceal his fraud against Thule Drilling. In addition to the firm Strategic Alliances Corporation, he also used his firm Juno Finance. A number of banks were involved in his transactions, including Bank Julius Baer & Co Ltd. in Geneva, Switzerland, UBS in Geneva, Switzerland, HSBC in Valletta, Malta, Bank of Valletta in Malta, as well as a bank in Monaco.

Other board members and management at Thule Drilling were not aware that the firms Strategic Alliances Corporation and Juno Finance were partly owned by Olav. They believed large sums were transferred to these firms to solve problems in Saudi Arabia.

Already on the cover of his book entitled "The Grand Self-Deception", Olav (2015) formulates a number of rhetoric and provocative questions: "What if we no longer accept the government's actions that would be deemed morally reprehensible and/or criminal if they were to be done by you and me? What if we showed determination and courage and pushed back against a system that has made us morally impotent? We have to take our freedom back because freedom is unilaterally positive in all interpersonal relationships. Freedom will create a better, more sustainable, and happier society. If we don't do something fundamentally different before it's too late, it will be a betrayal to future generations." Olav labels his book a libertarian manifesto against the deep state.

Olav as a suspect at this stage takes on a role of not just defending himself but also defending society at large. Benson (2013) finds that narcissistic self-confidence when coupled with drive, ambitiousness, and insensitivity to others may enable some people to successfully undertake risky business endeavors that more prudent and introspective individuals would never attempt. An ambitious and convenient mindset may also permit if not drive these individuals in the single-minded pursuit of their goals to engage in financial crime.

Dutch Company Vimpelcom

Gulnara Karimova, the daughter of the Uzbek president, had her own firm Takilant. The Dutch telecommunication company Vimpelcom transferred USD 60 million to her through a tax haven to her firm's account on Gibraltar. VimpelCom admitted corruption in Uzbekistan to gain access to telecom licenses in the country. Vimpelcom had to pay authorities in the United States and the Netherlands fines totaling USD 798 million (Schjelderup, 2020).

The description of VimpelCom's Uzbekistan transactions by Deloitte (2016) was based on statement of facts by United States and Dutch investigating authorities related to the settlement with VimpelCom. The statement of facts can be downloaded from www.justice.gov/usao-sdny/file/826456/download. The statement was incorporated by reference as part of the deferred prosecution agreement between US Department of Justice and VimpelCom, where VimpelCom admitted, accepted, and acknowledged that it was responsible for acts of its officers, directors, employees, and agents.

VimpelCom corruptly entered the Uzbek market in 2005 and 2006 (Deloitte, 2016). In internal VimpelCom documents, foreign officials were identified only as "partner" or "local partner" rather than by name. For example, documents prepared for board meetings concerning partnership agreement with a shell company referred only to a "local partner" who was the 100% owner of the shell company. VimpelCom structured the partnership agreement to hide the bribe payments to foreign officials.

In 2007, VimpelCom arranged to pay foreign officials, through the shell company, an additional $25 million bribe to obtain 3G frequencies in Uzbekistan. The year before, VimpelCom had paid $114 million in bribes for foreign officials' understood influence over decisions made by the Uzbek government. Furthermore, VimpelCom directly or through a subsidiary, entered into fake consulting contracts, where real work did not justify the large consulting fees.

Two executives at VimpelCom closely monitored the approval process and ensured that the shell company was paid quickly. In 2011, the two executives received an email showing that all approvals had been received also for the 4G consulting agreement. The shell company never provided any legitimate consulting services to justify its $30 million fee. In fact, the shell company's consulting reports and presentations, which were prepared in supposed satisfaction of its obligations under the consulting agreement, were not needed by VimpelCom, and the reports were almost entirely plagiarized from Wikipedia entries, other Internet sources, and internal VimpelCom documents.

While Telia admitted to charges and paid $965 million, VimpelCom entered into a deferred prosecution agreement with the US Department of Justice and with the prosecution service in the Netherlands, where the company paid $835 million to the US Securities and Exchange Commission and to the public prosecution service of the Netherlands. According to the statements of facts for the agreement, the bribe related to the acquisition of 3G frequencies in 2007 was falsely recorded in VimpelCom's consolidated books and records as the acquisition of an intangible asset, namely, 3G frequencies, and as consulting expenses.

Tax Haven Convenience

Convenience themes in this book are illustrated again in Figure 12.1, where the theory of convenience distinguishes between three dimensions. First, the financial motive is mainly based on possibilities or threats. Next, the organizational opportunity is mainly to commit or to conceal financial crime. Third, the personal willingness for deviant behavior is mainly based on choice or innocence.

The Scandinavian banks have possibilities to make illegitimate profit in their wealth management service. DNB in Norway, Nordea and Swedbank in Sweden, and Danske Bank in Denmark can profit from wealthy clients who prefer secrecy in tax havens (Bruun Hjejle, 2018; Clifford Chance, 2020; Kleinfeld, 2019, 2020; Mannheimer Swartling, 2016). Therefore, the financial motive of banks is possibilities at the corporate level as indicated in Figure 12.1.

Similarly, for the fishing corporation Samherji in Iceland, there were possibilities for obtaining fishing rights along the coast of Namibia (Kleinfeld, 2019, 2020; Reuters, 2019). By bribing Namibian officials, the company could successfully start profitable fishing. The bribes were channeled through tax havens to remove traces of corruption.

The motive for Thule Drilling was a threat of bankruptcy (Olav, 2014, 2015; Oslo tingrett, 2015). First, tax havens were used to transfer money to various parties to save the company. Next, when the bankruptcy threat became real, the chairman of the board made transactions through tax havens to make sure that he himself would not suffer from the emerging bankruptcy. Convenience themes were thus both corporate and individual threats as illustrated in Figure 12.1.

The final example in this chapter is the Dutch telecommunication company Vimpelcom, which bribed the daughter of the president in Uzbekistan to obtain mobile phone licenses in the country (Deloitte, 2016; Schjelderup, 2020). As for the banks and Samherji, the financial motive was possibilities at the corporate level. While the bribe was a substantial amount of money, it was nevertheless microscopical compared to the profits expected from mobile network operations in Uzbekistan.

The organizational opportunity to commit and conceal corporate crime is the next dimension of convenience theory. Access to tax havens might be based on the status of the individual (Kakkar et al., 2020) such as Olav as the chair of the board at Thule, or it might be based on access (Benson and Simpson, 2018) through business relationships between companies such as banks with Samherji and Vimpelcom. The secrecy of tax havens represent an efficient opportunity to conceal wrongdoing since tax havens can be characterized by moral collapse (Shadnam and Lawrence, 2011) in transparency and in guardianship against misconduct. Therefore, three convenience themes are emphasized in Figure 12.1: status, access, and collapse.

In the willingness dimension of convenience theory, both Samherji and Vimpelcom seem to fit the convenience theme of choice as a rational decision (Kamerdze et al., 2014). Samherji bribed Namibian officials to obtain profitable fishing rights, while Vimpelcom bribed the president's daughter to obtain profitable licenses for mobile phone in Uzbekistan. The banks will probably claim innocence by arguing that they do not know what their clients do in tax havens. They will justify their wealth management actions by arguing that it is up to clients what they do with

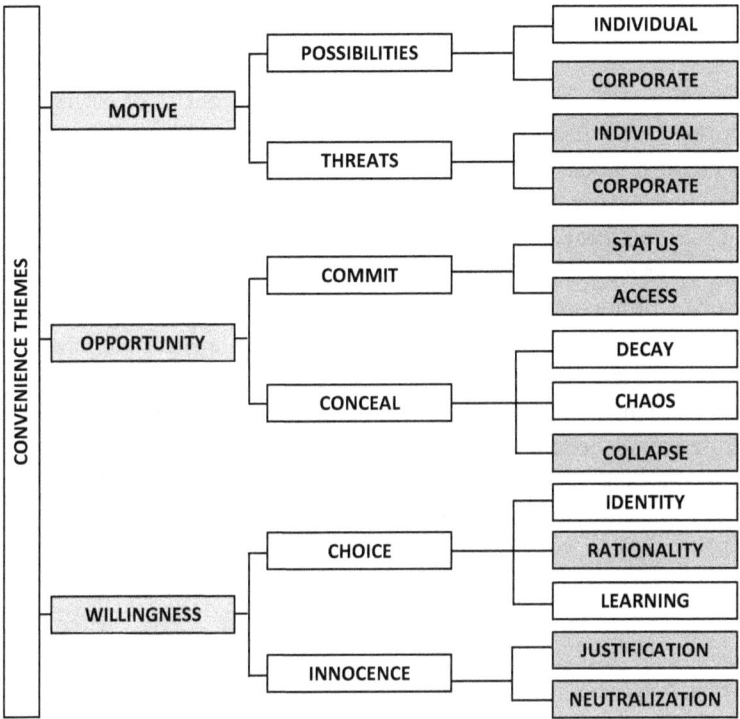

Figure 12.1: Convenience themes for corporations in tax havens.

their money and what motives the clients have for their transactions. The act of wrongdoing might be morally justifiable (Schnatterly et al., 2018) based on strong peer pressure (Gao and Zhang, 2019). Similarly, along the innocence perspective, Olav at Thule might neutralize potential guilt feelings by arguing that it was business for a higher loyalty (Schoultz and Flyghed, 2016, 2020a, 2020b, 2021).

13 Crime Service Professionals

Bottom-up approaches exist to compensate for the lack of control of trusted offenders in corporate crime. It is matter of people in the organization who prevent potential white-collar offenders from committing financial crime and who detect white-collar offenders having committed financial crime. A different approach in the same line of reasoning is the outside-in approach where outsiders rather than insiders prevent and detect white-collar wrongdoing in the organization. The outside-in approach involves professional service providers such as law firms, accounting firms, auditing firms, real estate agencies, and banks with their lawyers, accountants, auditors, real estate agents, and bank clerks.

Often, the convenience of white-collar crime is dependent on the cooperation with external professionals who may turn a blind eye to potential law violations by and together with their clients. Instead of turning a blind eye, they might indeed help their clients with compliance to avoid misconduct and crime. This chapter discusses the outside-in perspective of corporate control of white-collar offenses as it influences crime convenience.

Law Firm Client Barriers

A law firm is in the business of applying legal knowledge to client opportunities and threats (Gottschalk, 2014). Lawyers and their clients enjoy the attorney-client privilege in many jurisdictions such as the United States and Norway. Attorney-client privilege is the name given to the common law concept of legal professional privilege (Oh, 2004). The privilege is the lawyer's as well as the client's right to refuse to disclose and to prevent any other person from disclosing confidential communications between the client and the attorney. For a potential white-collar offender as the client of a law firm, the privilege represents a convenient opportunity for financial crime (Økokrim, 2021: 6):

> It can be difficult to know whether a lawyer knowingly and intentionally assists criminals, or whether he or she is being exploited. At several law firms, there seems to be a lack of understanding of, and knowledge of, money laundering regulations. There is also a big difference in how the regulations are interpreted, and what routines exist to comply with the money laundering act. For example, there is a different understanding of where the line between the money laundering act and the duty of confidentiality lies.

In an outside-in perspective, knowledgeable lawyers and law firms based on integrity and accountability can prevent potential offenses in client organizations, and they can report instances legitimized by the money laundering act in violation of the duty of confidentiality. However, many lawyers and law firms ted to slide on the

https://doi.org/10.1515/9783110766950-014

slippery slope over to the wrong side of the law when there is a profitable client (Økokrim, 2021: 6):

> Among the lawyers who can be linked to crime, few have convictions, even though they have been registered as suspects or charged in several serious cases. There are several lawyers who are charged or suspected of financial crime. In many cases, they are involved in tax evasion, fraud, bankruptcy, accounting crime, financial infidelity /embezzlement or money laundering. A lawyer who has now lost his license has been charged with gross embezzlement of more than NOK 90 million belonging to the lawyer's clients. The embezzlement took place in connection with the settlement of real estate transactions.

Økokrim quoted here is the Norwegian national authority for investigation and prosecution of economic and environmental crime. The public agency is a specialist skills function for the police and the prosecuting functions in the criminal justice system. Økokrim was established in 1989 and is both a police investigative agency as well as a public prosecutors' office. Økokrim (2021: 6) found that secret client accounts can facilitate financial crime:

> Lawyers also facilitate financial crime by using client accounts. The client account is used, among other things, to avoid creditor debt, fraud and money laundering. In one case, a client account was used in a fraud case in such a way that bank loans granted to two companies were paid into a client account. The person who later was convicted of fraud was then given access to the funds in this account. The person in question was the real general manager, but without formal roles and should thus not be able to dispose of the company's funds.

In another case investigated and prosecuted by Økokrim, a lawyer acted as the formal owner of a property through his own company. The prosecuting authority believed that in reality it was one of the lawyer's clients who was the real owner, and that the lawyer was listed as the lawyer to prevent creditors from getting the property as settlement for outstanding debts. Both the district court and the court of appeal agreed with the prosecution's point of view.

A lawyer received millions of Norwegian kroner in a client account which was used, among others, for property purchases. The money originated at actors belonging to a family well known to the police and registered in police systems. Økokrim suspected that the client account was used to launder proceeds from criminal activity via the real estate market.

Lawyers who offer real estate transactions may be well-equipped to prevent and detect white-collar crime in an outside-in perspective. If not reporting to the police, they may contact the client organization for confirmation or disconfirmation of transaction legality.

Lawyers who offer client accounts may prevent creditor evasion by denying access to a company by people and firms who might want to place their assets in the company rather than repay debt. In practice, the lawyer avoids acting as a straw man and avoids being considered a pro forma owner. The lawyer denies access to persons and firms who want to evade values. Økokrim concluded regarding law firms and lawyers that it is highly likely that some lawyers function as facilitators for white-collar crime. Highly likelihood in their assessment is a probability above 90%. The typical lawyer helping facilitate white-collar crime works as partner in a small law firm.

Furthermore, Økokrim (2021) found that it was a recurring pattern that lawyers who have lost their legal license to practice as attorneys tend to resume their criminal activity when they get the license back. It was also a recurring pattern that lawyers who had lost their license found other ways to use their competence to commit, or facilitate, crime. It was therefore likely that lawyers who lose their legal license will resume their criminal activity if they get it back, and that lawyers who do not get their license back will find other ways to use their competence to commit, or facilitate, crime. Økokrim here used the term likely, which is a probability of 60% to 90%. In our perspective of outside-in, law-abiding, often larger law firms, can help expose criminal, often smaller law firms, which have been deprived of their legal license permanently or temporarily.

Certified Accountant Control

Certified accountants are sometimes asked to create legitimacy for a client company. Accountants can be asked to facilitate money laundering, fictitious invoicing, tax evasion, work-related crime, payment of bribes, as well as disguise of real rights holders and the origin of the funds through complicated corporate structures domestically and globally (Qiu and Slezak, 2019). In a rich country such as Norway, where the state subsidies a number of business sectors, accounting misrepresentation can conveniently lead to subsidies from the government. In many countries, it may be so important to have a bottom line in accounting that satisfies investors and others that crime emerges as potentially acceptable.

Misreporting in accounting is often a convenient way of concealing illegal transactions (Qiu and Slezak, 2019). Lack of transparency makes concealment in accounting convenient (Davidson et al., 2019; Goncharov and Peter, 2019). Managers can withhold bad news by accounting misrepresentation (Bao et al., 2019), since financial statements are a substantive component of a firm's communications with its stakeholders (Gupta et al., 2020). Balakrishnan et al. (2019) found that reduced corporate transparency in accounting is associated with increased corporate tax aggressiveness. Accounting fraud in terms of account manipulation is lacking transparency (Toolami et al., 2019).

Since accounting is no machine that can provide correct answers regarding the financial health of a company, since accounting information has limited representational properties, and since accounting cannot fully inform decision-makers (O'Leary and Smith, 2020), determination of final accounting figures are often left to the discretion of financial managers.

Incentive systems such as bonus arrangements can lead to white-collar crime such as corruption to meet sales targets or other targets on which bonus payments depend. Alternatively, the offender can pretend having met targets by manipulating accounting (Nichol, 2019: 329):

> Bonus contracts have come under a great deal of criticism in the past few years for creating incentives that encourage managers to manipulate accounting information in order to maximize their pay. Such manipulation can range from subtle earnings manipulation to outright fraud.

Økokrim (2021: 8) found that deviant executives who commit criminal activities, for example for fraud, often attempt to use accountants to manipulate accounts, for example to do the following:

> A criminal group uses the same accountant in several cases. This accountant changes the accounts so that the liquidity ratio and profitability look better than they actually are. The manipulated accounts are then used to raise loans on an incorrect basis. Later the company goes bankrupt. The accountant is not listed at the financial supervisory authority of Norway.

> Another way accountants can assist offenders is in the event of inadequate follow-up. Such a case was discovered during an investigation. Here it became clear that the external accountant was not critical enough of the documentation handed over, in addition to being creative in keeping accounts. This made the criminal offenses possible. In another case, the accountant neglected his responsibility to prepare documentation for several of the transactions in the company, as well as establish routines for correct accounting.

Among potential offenders, Økokrim (2021) found that some accountants have a reputation of not asking too many questions, or accepting whatever answers they get, and they are therefore popular. It can be difficult to know if such offenses are being committed deliberately. Økokrim (2021) also found evidence of cases where persons who were trained accountants allowed the legitimacy this gives to be exploited by culprits. This happened, for example, through fake invoicing, which is a widespread mode within work-related invoicing as well as in corruption, where the bribed submits a non-real invoice for consulting services. Again, it can be difficult to know whether the accountants in question were unaware of criminal relationships, or an accomplice.

The association of certified accountants might introduce more strict reviews of their members. For example, a few accounting firms seem only to offer their services to criminal actors where they provide crime-as-a-service. One such accounting firm had specialized in assisting business owners draining companies for assets and then files for bankruptcy causing losses to debtors. Another accounting firm had specialized in avoidance of taxes.

Økokrim's (2021) assessment was that accounting firms that only provide services to criminal actors with crime-as-a-service, highly likely (above 90% probability) work as facilitators of financial crime. It seems to be a conscious strategy of labor market offenders to ask accounting firms to produce fake time sheets and invoices to enable payment of salaries in cash where withholding tax is not necessary.

Økokrim (2021) found several cases of accountants who had lost their license but continued to act as accountants anyway. In one case, an accountant without license helped by creative accounting sot that the main person could empty the company of several million. Others did set up their own business and rent out their services from there. Such deviance should not be too difficult to detect and report by the association of certified accountants.

Auditor Denial of Acceptance

Like certified accountants, certified auditors can give the company legitimacy and can be used to facilitate or commit various forms of financial crime. Økokrim (2021) found that auditors often have chosen to resign from their role at those companies where they have not received sufficient answers to questions. Some auditors are suspected of approving accounts without special control, or they even more actively assist criminals. These auditors are often associated with companies that operate in the gray zone for what is legal. Some auditors accept reporting and being loyal to deviant management (Hurley et al., 2019). In our outside-in perspective, the ideal contribution from auditors would be to deny acceptance of accounts where their queries are not satisfactorily answered and report their findings to the board of directors as well as externally to public authorities.

Concealing illegal transactions may result from the failure of auditors to do their job. Alon et al. (2019) argue that accounting and auditing functions have undergone a legitimacy crisis in recent years. Auditors are supposed to serve as gatekeepers to protect shareholders and other stakeholders, but deviant corporate management tend to hire and control auditors instead of letting auditors report to the board of directors or the supervisory board (Hurley et al., 2019). Skeptical auditors tend to be replaced by less skeptical auditors. Reporting fraud to public authorities will also harm auditors (Mohliver, 2019: 316):

> As organizations, audit firms are often severely penalized for client malfeasance. Yet the individual auditors working for these firms are susceptible to "motivated blindness" stemming from conflicts of interest that bias their moral judgment toward choices that help their clients.

The lack of detection by auditors can also be explained by standardization. Herron and Cornell (2021) found that audit work is standardized which harms auditors creativity, thereby preventing recognition of and responses to fraud cues. Standardization harms an improvisational style of thinking, tolerance for unpredictability, and uncertainty, and open-mindedness that is associated with responses to perceived fraud risk cues.

Shadnam and Lawrence (2011) found that morale collapse increases the tendency to financial crime. In fact, repetition of criminal actions might institutionalize such actions. Dion (2008) found that the larger the corporation, the less deterrence effect from laws on financial crime, which may have to do with increased convenience in concealing crime.

A chief financial officer (CFO) in Norway became divorced and his financial motive became stronger. The growing motive caused him to search for opportunity expansion in the organization. One of his actions was to take control over the auditing process, where he succeeded in controlling that what the auditor presented to the chief executive officer (CEO) and the board of directors. He was thus able to make the organizational opportunity larger. As he noticed that he succeeded in organizational opportunity expansion, his willingness for deviant behavior became higher than it was before.

Hestnes (2017) asked the question in his study of the CFO case: Why did the auditor fail in detecting embezzlement at the company? Normally in a Norwegian context, the auditor is to report annually to the board in the business where the auditor has reviewed accounts. Since the cooperation between the auditor and the CFO went so smoothly, the CEO did not invite the auditor anymore to board meetings. This is where the fourth opportunity expansion occurred. The CFO became the actual person to report external audit results to the board. Mohliver (2019) found that auditor bias towards accepting deviant financial reports increased when there is ambiguity about the appropriateness of a course of action. Financial misreporting that is viewed favorably by the client organization can be recommended by external auditors on the grounds that such reporting is already adopted among companies served by the same auditing firm.

A mechanism for outside-in effects on executive compliance is the threat for both accountants and auditors to be fined and potentially sent to prison. A financial scandal in Norway in a company named Finance Credit caused prison sentences not only for two executives at Finance Credit but also for two auditors from audit firm KPMG. The auditors were incarcerated because they had helped the white-collar offenders create a non-transparent and complicated corporate structure enabling the offenders to make it look like all subsidiaries were financially sound. A similar case in Norway was the auditor for Sponsor Service who was reluctant to criticize and question some of the numbers in the accounts. This auditor ended up in prison as well.

Økokrim's (2021) overall assessment regarding auditors was that auditors associate with crime mainly as passive participants. It was considered highly likely that those companies where white-collar crime occur, that both accounting and auditing suffered from shortcomings. The challenge for the criminal justice system is to determine to what extent such professional service providers facilitate crime.

The financial supervisory authority of Norway has revoked the approval as state-authorized public accountants for, among other things, failure to obtain documentation, lack of documentation of performed audits, for not having acted neutrally by having changed the accounts of clients at their requests, and inadequate assessments when entering into client relationships.

Real Estate Agent Reporting

Økokrim (2021: 12) found that real estate agents are often used as facilitators for money laundering via real estate, including through the use of client accounts as well as illegal borrowing and refinancing, where business enterprises in the real estate market commit financial crime:

> In at least one case, a real estate agent, in collaboration with a bank employee, forged documents for borrowers so that they got a higher mortgage than what they would otherwise get. So far, twenty cases have been uncovered, and findings have been made that indicate money laundering in some of these. Several of the loans are also in default. Two of the real estate agents are linked to the use of drugs and the removal of money from the sale of drugs. One of the two real estate agents also has large cash deposits, as well as deposits and payments to and from own accounts with internet-based gaming companies. The person in question has also set up a real estate company. The bank official has reacted to a number of valuations made by the broker and believes these are too high. Because of their role as real estate agents, they are both in a position to launder money through the real estate market.

A different modus is when the real estate agent facilitates a disproportionately high price assessment of homes. This means that the homeowner can get a higher refinanced mortgage, possibly a higher home loan, than the value of the home indicates. In such a case, the homeowner has then used the borrowed money to buy more homes, and then repeat the process several times (Økokrim, 2021: 12):

> In one case, the culprits probably tried to launder money by hiding real rights holders. The apartment was bought on the open market by a private company where the real estate agent in question stated to be the 100 percent owner. Settlement for payment should come from a separate financial company that should not have a mortgage on the property. The broker was chairman of the board, but not the owner. The real owner was another company well documented in police systems for, among other things, financial crime and money laundering. It was also a subsidiary of this company that was responsible for payment of settlement, not the financial firm specified in the agreement.

Real estate agents were involved in fraud schemes by the convicted white-collar offender Christer Tromsdal in Norway (Hultgreen, 2012). The total number of accomplices in his network was 15 persons. They worked in different organizations, including real estate firms, and they had established a criminal network. Christer Tromsdal has been sentenced for financial crime several times. In June 2015, he was sentenced to six years in prison. Anthony Bratli, a property appraiser, and Terje Hvidsten, a real estate agent, were both at the same time sentenced to four and a half years in prison. At about the same time, Arne Aarsæther, an attorney, was sentenced to four months in prison for handling illegal proceeds for Tromsdal (Borgarting, 2015; Oslo tingrett, 2015). Christer Tromsdal made frequent media appearances (Kleppe, 2015; Meldalen, 2015).

White-collar offender Christer Tromsdal was running the company Aker Brygge Invest. In our perspective of outside-in, a total of fifteen criminal professionals in various roles might have blown the whistle on him. Even far more people knew about his fraud scheme of property bankruptcy where investors and banks lost money. Real estate agents and other professionals supporting and facilitating the fraud scheme ended up in prison. The fraud was detected by the police as Tromsdal contacted the police to offer his services as a police informant (Dahle, 2011; Hultgreen et al., 2019; NTB, 2015).

Økokrim's (2021) experience with crime service professionals such as real estate brokers is that real estate firms facilitate money laundering via the real estate market using a client account. In the case above concerning the broker who was chairman of the board, but not the owner, more than one million US dollars was transferred from an account in the Middle East to the client account. One of the main shareholders in the real estate firm had access rights to dispose of the money. The broker was later convicted of fraud and violation of narcotics legislation.

Økokrim (2021: 13) wrote in their overall assessment of crime service by professionals at real estate firms:

> It is very likely that several real estate agents are committing systematic and organized financial crime or facilitating this. It will mainly be in the form of money laundering via real estate or by enabling higher mortgages or home loans by using forged documents. It is likely that real estate agents will be exploited for money laundering by hiding real rights holders from the agent.

While Norway has a very long coastline, the attractive real estates for vacation houses and summer guests are located south of the capital of Oslo. In particular, the island of Tjøme is popular. The theme of environmentally harmful construction and expansion of summerhouses serves as an example in relation to convenience theory. The motive is often to climb Maslow's (1943) hierarchy of needs, the opportunity is typically access to resources (Huisman and Erp, 2013), and the willingness for deviant behavior is dependent on neutralization techniques (Sykes and Matza, 1957), lack of self-control (Craig and Piquero, 2016) and other factors. Real estate agents ignored the lack of permits when they were involved in transactions between old mansion owners and new mansion owners. Even when an architect and two municipal case workers were convicted in court for corruption, real estate agents continued helping the rich and mighty people from the capital of Oslo. Økokrim considered prosecuting some of the mansion owners for harming the environment by building enormous mansions along the shoreline that was reserved for wildlife and public access (Feratovic, 2021; Holmøy, 2021).

Financial Services Detection

The final group of crime service professionals reviewed by Økokrim (2021: 14) was bank and finance clerks:

> In banking and finance, special arrangements for granting loans on the wrong basis are a widespread problem. This occurs in both small and large banking enterprises. Loans are granted on incorrect grounds either through unfaithful employees and/or through the use of forged documents.

In our perspective of combatting white-collar crime through outside-in measures, a bank that discovers attempt at bank fraud should not only consider reporting it to the police but also to the supervisory committee and the compliance officer in the company where someone made the fraudulent attempt. Since police agencies sometimes lack both competence and capacity to investigate, a more preventive measure would be to let the offender organization know of the attempt.

Some white-collar offenders are able to recruit a bank insider for larger fraud transactions. For example, a construction company owned by Norwegians in Dubai needed funding. A woman whose regular position was being a nurse in hospital took on the role of being the rich widow after a deceased entrepreneur. The fake widow told the bank to transfer some of her assets from Norway to Dubai. The internal bank clerk approved the transfer. After the transfer of ten million dollars had taken place, bank management called the real rich widow about the transactions. The real rich widow responded that she had not noticed a reduction on her bank account of ten million dollars (Berge, 2011).

According to Økokrim (2021), some bank employees have committed embezzlement by virtue of their positions. Some employees in banking firms have direct links to criminal actors and environments. For example, a bank executive was invited to a party at a Hells Angels estate. He was offered services by a sex worker, that he accepted. Afterwards, pictures of the act were presented to him with a request for a substantial bank loan. He forged documents so that a bank loan was granted to the blackmailer.

Økokrim (2021: 14) found that several employees in banks who are involved in arranging for granting of loans on a misleading and manipulated basis were linked to known criminal actors:

> These have close ties to or are in the same circle of friends as key players in organized crime. A named bank employee in a prominent position must in several cases have granted a loan and given favorable loan terms to criminal actors, as well as persons who are not creditworthy due to bankruptcies. One of the criminal actors associated with the bank employee appears as a central figure in a criminal network. Another bank employee in a prominent position is assumed to be involved in committing fraud in collaboration with known criminal actors.

Banks and other financial institutions help white-collar offenders into tax havens. Tax havens offer convenience for corporate crime. Not only is tax evasion an obvious benefit where corporations can avoid taxes on profits in their domestic markets by transferring profits to tax havens with low or no corporate taxes. Corporations can enjoy secrecy regarding ownership. They can remove traces of corruption by transferring bribes via tax havens, and they can launder money from crime by help of the secrecy in tax havens (Deng et al., 2020; Granda, 2021). In some languages, a tax haven is labeled tax paradise, where a paradise is a place of exceptional happiness and delight (Schmal et al., 2021).

Mannheimer Swartling (2016) described how the Swedish bank Nordea had its subsidiary in Luxembourg illegally backdating contracts and help clients with tax evasion as leaked from the Panama Papers. The bank first denied its link to the Panamanian law firm Mossack Fonseca, which specializes in establishing corporate mailbox companies in tax havens (Associated Press, 2016). Gunn Wærsted resigned from her group executive position at Nordea and chair at Nordea Luxembourg (Trumpy, 2016). Several other Scandinavian banks are also helping their corporate clients in tax havens such as Danske Bank in Denmark (Bruun Hjejle, 2018), Swedbank in Sweden (Clifford Chance, 2020), and Norwegian bank DNB helped Icelandic fishing company Samherji bribe Namibian officials through tax havens (Kibar, 2020a, 2020b; Kleinfeld, 2019).

Schmal et al. (2021) use the term tax paradise as a synonym for tax haven when they describe corporate activity in tax havens:

> Multinational firms shift billions of income into tax havens to decrease their taxes. Through the use of transfer pricing and tax-optimizing transactions such as intrafirm debt and royalty payments, firms reduce their tax payments. Using tax havens can be legal. However, financial statement users are concerned that tax havens enable firms to obfuscate information. Tax havens are often related to secretive tax planning schemes because these states often lack transparency and information exchange.

A tax haven or paradise is a state or geographical area with autonomy in tax policy, which offers foreign enterprises zero tax terms or very low tax rates, and a legislation that prevents insight from the outside world. Examples of tax havens include the Bahamas, Bermuda, Cayman Islands, Dubai, British Virgin Islands, Guernsey, Hong Kong, Isle of Man, Jersey, Liechtenstein, Luxembourg, Mauritius, Monaco, Panama, Singapore, and Switzerland. Less well known is that countries such as Ireland and the Netherlands have also been mentioned as tax havens, and that the united state of Delaware might be the most secret tax haven in the world (Schjelderup, 2020).

Legitimate access to crime resources at a bank can be illustrated by the case of a chairman of the board who published his autobiography (Olav, 2014, 2015). The chairman used a tax haven where he had an account when he ran business through another company there (Bjørklund, 2018).

Unfortunately, the report by the Norwegian national authority for investigation and prosecution of economic and environmental crime (Økokrim, 2021) did not address the role of banks in enabling white-collar offenders transfer corruption funds and launder money in tax havens. It seems that Økokrim was reluctant to label bank activities as corporate crime or helping white-collar offenders as crime service professionals. Fortunately, the OECD (2021) was willing to label banks professional enablers of crime in tax havens as described in the following.

Professional Tax Crime Enablers

The organization for economic co-operation and development, OECD (2021), states that white-collar crime like tax evasion, bribery, and corruption are often concealed through complex legal structures and financial transactions facilitated by lawyers, accountants, financial institutions, and other professional enablers of such kinds of crime. These various forms of crime opportunity have significant impacts on government revenue, public confidence, and economic growth. The OECD (2021) report delineates a range of strategies and actions for countries to take to tackle professional intermediaries who enable tax evasion and other forms of financial crime on behalf of their criminal clients. The report highlights the damaging role played by these intermediaries and the importance of concerted domestic and international action in clamping down on the enablers of crime, and includes recommended counter-strategies for deterring, disrupting, investigating and prosecuting the professionals who enable tax evasion as white-collar crime.

OECD (2021: 10) described crime service providers as professional enablers:

> In general, professional enablers of tax crime and other financial crimes are intermediaries with specialized knowledge who play a specific role to facilitate the commission of a tax offence (and possibly other related financial crimes) by others. Professional enablers of tax crime and other financial crimes can include for example: tax professionals, lawyers and legal advisors, accountants, financial advisors, banks and financial institutions, company formation agents, registered agents, notaries, business trustees, trust and corporate service providers, and other promoters of tax evasion schemes.

According to OECD (2021), a professional enabler is typically an individual or entity with professional expertise to perform a specific service to aid their customer in carrying out a tax offence or other financial crime. Most countries do not have a specific definition of a professional enabler. However, the common attributes of a professional enabler include:

- Professional qualifications or training;
- Expertise in taxation, legal or financial processes;
- Experience in setting up tax structures, or structures with cross-border elements; and

- Experience setting up opaque structures for avoiding investigative scrutiny into the clients' tax and economic activities.

Professionals offer various legitimate business services to clients such as legal and accounting advice (OECD, 2021: 11):

> They may also be experts on finding legal loopholes giving room for the creation of "tax-avoidance" strategies. These strategies operate in the so-called "grey areas of the law", allowing professionals to use the inadequacies or ambiguities of a jurisdiction's legal framework to maximize the tax outcomes for their client. The possibility of using "grey areas of the law", while not technically illegal, should be limited by jurisdictions through the enhancement of their tax legislation and by fostering international co-operation.

In the outside-in perspective, OECD (2021: 27) argued that tax authorities can encounter professional enablers across a number of different functions, from those business areas involved in promoting voluntary compliance to those undertaking audits or investigations, through those leading on enforcement activity such as civil penalties and criminal prosecution:

> Lawyers, tax advisors, notaries and accountants are valued gatekeepers to a sound legal and financial system. Their unique sets of skills, together with the professional privileges awarded to them by statutes, put them in a special place within societies. They are experts who are in a position of trust and enjoy certain rights that are not shared by other professions. Jurisdictions should ensure that advisors perform their tasks in accordance with the law, and penalize those few who use their skills, expertise and privileges to design structures with the purpose of breaking the law. This requires that countries have in place a legal framework to support criminal investigators and the justice system in addressing and punishing professional enablers that engage in and facilitate the commission of such crimes.

Among the OECD (2021) suggestions is to target the actions of intermediaries before they become professional enablers. Once professional enablers such as banks have activities, mechanisms to deter and intercept it are necessary. Regulators and professional bodies have to stand up to the challenge of controlling banks across jurisdictions. There is a need for mechanisms of voluntary as well as mandatory reporting of wrongdoing.

The title of the OECD (2021) report is "ending the shell game" and "cracking down on the professionals who enable tax and white collar crimes". Ending the shell game addresses shell companies that are registered in the name of other legal persons in tax havens. Shell companies assist in opening of bank accounts in names that obscure the ownership, both domestic and abroad. Shell companies hold safe custody of incriminating data. Shell companies hold unaccounted funds in offshore jurisdictions, which are the proceeds of crime in overseas jurisdictions.

OECD (2021: 9) made the following recommendations for counter-strategies to combat professional enablers:

- Awareness: Ensure tax crime investigators are equipped with the understanding, intelligence, and analytics skills to identify the types of professional enablers operating in their jurisdiction, and to understand the risks posed by the ways that professional enablers devise, market, implement, and conceal tax crime and other financial crime.
- Legislation: Ensure the law provides investigators and prosecutors with sufficient authority to identify, prosecute, and sanction professional enablers, so as to deter and penalize those found to be professional enablers of tax crime.
- Deterrence and disruption: Ensure there is a coherent and multi-disciplinary strategy for preventing and disrupting the behavior of professional enablers, including engaging in communication, leveraging the role of supervisory bodies and industry sectors, incentivizing early disclosure and whistleblowing and taking a strong approach to enforcement in practice.
- Co-operation: Ensuring relevant authorities are proactively maximizing the availability of information, intelligence, and investigatory powers held by other domestic and international agencies to tackle professional enablers that are sophisticated and operating cross-border.
- Implementation: Appoint a lead person and agency in the jurisdiction with responsibility for overseeing the implementation of the professional enabler's strategy; including to undertake a review of its effectiveness over time and devise further changes as necessary.

The report by OECD (2021) emphasized that the majority of professionals are law-abiding and play an important role in assisting businesses and individuals to understand and comply with the law and helping the financial system run smoothly. Such law-abiding professionals are to be differentiated from a small set of professionals who use their skills and knowledge of the law to actively promote, market, and facilitate the commission of crime by their clients. The report was to support policy makers and law enforcement authorities to address the actions of that small set of lawyers, tax advisors, notaries, financial institutions, and other intermediaries that are professional enablers, with the intent of facilitating wrong-doing by their clients.

Employees in Health Care Crime

White-collar crime in the health care sector is growing as individual patients as well as public agencies spend a growing amount of money on health care for themselves and for the population. An example is the pharmaceutical industry, which hands out prizes and awards to medical doctors at hospitals. The awards, prizes, and funding for research do frequently resemble regular bribes. In our perspective of outside-in, pharmaceutical officials not involved in bribing should notify hospitals about corrupt medical doctors.

Mulinari et al. (2021) studied responsive regulation to offset pharmaceutical industry illicit behavior in areas such as drug marketing based on self-regulation backed up with threats of government sanctions. The researchers argue for a more probing, critical and government-led regulatory approach instead of the self-regulatory approach. They found extensive abusive business practices, corporate non-compliance, and impression management. They used Astellas wrongdoing regarding off-label promotion of a prostate cancer drug as an example (Mulinari et al. 2021: 71):

> While initially denying wrongdoings, Astellas has fully accepted the findings and rulings, and global company executives have referred to the situation as a "corporate crisis". The company's official explanation for wrongdoings is one of "significant cultural and compliance failings created and caused by the actions and behaviors of some of its very senior managers" in Europe.

Økokrim (2021: 15) found that the criminal activity in the health sector in Norway is particularly evident in the issuance of fictitious medical statements that provide a basis for social security benefits, illegal issuance and sale of prescription medicine, as well as fraud of the reimbursement schemes to the health administration:

> There are several of the actors who have dealt with this type of criminal activity over several years; some have close relationships with known criminal actors and groups. The intention behind the criminal activity of employees in the health service appears to be only profit-motivated. The police have information that indicates that several doctors sell or write sick leave sheet for a fee, as well as write expert reports to help people get disability benefits and compensation from insurance companies. There are concrete examples of doctors who have made large cash deposits into their own personal bank accounts over several years, as well as received suspicious transfers from private individuals. In one case, it is a matter of millions. The money is assumed to be payments received for sick leave messages. The same doctors are in police systems identified with a number of other serious offenses.

Overall, Økokrim (2021) found it highly likely that many doctors will be paid to write fake sick leave reports and, in that way, acquire illegal income, which leads to social benefits being paid on the wrong basis.

Professional Crime Supporters

Attorneys at law firms can either take on the role of enablers of or the role of barriers to white-collar crime by their clients (Gottschalk, 2014). Certified accountants at accounting firms can either ignore crime signals or detect and report suspicions when they register transactions for their clients (Qiu and Slezak, 2019). Auditors at audit firms can either ignore crime signals or detect and report suspicions when they review accounting statements from their clients (Herron and Cornell, 2021). Real estate agents can either ignore crime signals or detect and report suspicions of money laundering or fraud when they meet buyers and sellers of real estate (Festovic, 2021). Professionals at financial services institutions can either take on the role of enablers of or the role of barriers to illegitimate loans or investments by their clients (Kleinfeld, 2019). Professional intermediaries can either take on the role of enablers of or the role of barriers to transfer of funds to and from tax havens for their clients (OECD, 2021). The pharmaceutical industry, hospitals and other actors within health care either be silently accepted for their occasional wrongdoing or doctors, nurses, and others can blow the whistle whenever they notice wrongdoing (Mulinari et al., 2021).

Surprisingly often in detected white-collar crime cases, there were professional crime supporters who enabled, facilitated, or ignored deviant behavior by white-collar offenders. In the following, empirical evidence of professional crime supporters are collected from investigation reports by fraud examiners. Corporate investigators are in the business of reconstruct past events and sequences of events when there is suspicion of wrongdoing in organizations. They are hired by organizations to reconstruct past events and sequences of events in the client organizations. Investigation reports are the property of client organizations since they have paid for the work by the fraud examiners. Very seldom, the investigation reports become publicly available since client organizations have a variety of reasons for their secrecy (Gottschalk and Tcherni-Buzzeo, 2017).

Table 13.1 list investigation reports by fraud examiners from recent years that were possible to find for this research. The year of each white-collar crime investigation is listed in the first column. They range from 2018 to 2021. The second column lists organizations where potential wrongdoing occurred. The third column lists the home country of the client organization. The fourth column lists fraud examination firms that where hired by the client organizations in the second column. Most of the investigators in the fourth column are located at low firms. The fifth column lists individuals who were suspected of wrongdoing, and the sixth column lists the suspected wrongdoing. The final column is our major interest in terms of professional crime supporters identified as actors who helped suspected white-collar crime become more convenient:

1. A local audit firm in Estonia ignored lack of money laundering procedures at the local branch office of Danske Bank. CEO Thomas Borgen at Danske Bank had to leave his position (Milne and Binham, 2018) after the bank disclosed the report from Bruun Hjejle (2018). Borgen was charged with white-collar crime by Danish prosecution authorities (Milne, 2019a), and the body of Danske Bank's former Estonian chief executive was found (Milne, 2019b).

2. Banks in Latvia were at the receiving end of funds illegally transferred from Moldova. Politician Ilan Shor left the country when the report from Kroll (2018) was published. The New York Times reported in October 2015 that Moldova "was rocked this year by the discovery that $1 billion had fraudulently siphoned from Moldova's banking system over a period of years, a huge amount for an impoverished country whose entire economic output is only about $8 billion a year" (Nechepurenko, 2015).

Table 13.1: Investigation reports indicating professional crime supporters.

Year	Organization	Country	Investigator	Suspect	Wrongdoing	Professional
2018	Danske Bank	Denmark	Bruun Hjejle (2018)	CEO	Money laundering	Local audit firm
2018	Moldova Banks	Moldova	Kroll (2018)	Chair	Bank fraud	Latvian banks
2019	Oceanteam	Norway	Sands (2019)	CEO	Embezzlement	Legal incentive plan
2019	Social Security	Denmark	PwC (2019)	Manager	Embezzlement	Family members
2020	Banedanmark	Denmark	Kammeradvokaten (2020a)	Managers	Corruption	Vendor representative
2020	Danske Bank	Denmark	Plesner (2020)	Executives	Client fraud	Software company
2020	Military Property	Denmark	Kammeradvokaten (2020b)	Manager	Corruption	Vendor representative
2020	Mercy Corps	Congo	Smith (2020)	Manager	Corruption	Vendor representative
2020	Swedbank	Sweden	Clifford Chance (2020)	CEO	Money laundering	Local audit firm
2020	Berkley University	United States	State Auditor (2020)	Coach	Corruption	External consultant
2020	Wells Fargo	United States	Waters (2020)	CEO	client fraud	Financial regulators
2020	Wirecard Banking	Germany	KPMG (2020a)	CEO	Embezzlement	Audit firm
2021	Apollo Global	United States	Dechert (2021)	CEO	Insider investments	External consultant
2021	Biathlon Union	Austria	Commission (2021)	President	Corruption	National biathlon
2021	Nasdaq Clearing	Sweden	Finansinspektionen (2021)	Investor	Manipulation	Investment banker

3. A consulting firm in the Netherlands designed an incentive plan for executives at Oceanteam enabling them to withdraw money to cover personal expenses. After the release of the Sands (2019) report, executives at Oceanteam wanted to avoid disclosure of it, even to the company's own shareholders (Strandli, 2019). A letter sent to all shareholders of Oceanteam on March 30, 2020, illustrated the dispute,

dissatisfaction, and reluctance to distribute the private policing report, as the let-ter emphasized the lack of trust that major shareholders and the company placed in the Sands (2019) report.

4. Family members helped create accounts where embezzled money could be laundered (PwC, 2019). BBC (2020) reported the following year: "A Danish court is due to deliver its verdict in the case of a woman accused of stealing 117 million Danish kroner (£13m; $17m) of government funding. Britta Nielsen worked at Denmark's social services board for 40 years, distributing funding to people in need".

5. Vendor representative offered favors and gifts to employees who happened to select that vendor. Investigative journalist at a Danish newspaper learned about potential fraud at Banedanmark, a governmental body under the ministry of transportation and housing in Denmark. The state-owned company is respon-sible for tracks, signals, and safety systems for the railroad traffic. They renovate the rail network and build new lines. They monitor rail traffic and steer trains in and out of stations and across the entire rail network. The Danish newspaper Ber-lingske reported in 2020 that they had started their inquiries in 2018 and that Banedanmark had reported suspects to the police two years later (Jessen and Jung, 2020): "Banedanmark suspects employees of bribery and illegal circum-stances. Banedanmark has reported an employee and a contractor to the police for potential bribery. This is happening on the basis of a request for access to documents by Berlingske in 2018. The minister takes the matter very seriously". Banedanmark hired Danish law firm Kammeradvokaten (2020a) to investigate al-legations against 23 named individuals who were former and current employees at the state-owned company. The individuals were suspected of bribery, abuse of office, and theft.

6. A software company developed a system where money on old client accounts were confiscated by the bank (Plesner, 2020). Danske Bank admitted in September 2020 that they had known for years about the bank's practice of collecting outdated and excessive debt from customers. Denmark's financial watchdog Finanstilsynet (2020) launched the previous month an inquiry into how Danske Bank had wrongly collected debt from up to 106,000 customers since 2004. The bank blamed IT system errors (Reuters, 2020).

7. Vendor representative offered favors and gifts to an employee who happened to select that vendor (Kammeradvokaten, 2020b). Dennis Bechmann Engmann, who was previously head of the building department at Karup Airport, was sen-tenced by the court in Viborg to two years in prison. The verdict was the end of the case of bribery in the Ministry of Defense's property management agency (Julsgaard, 2020). In 2015 and 2016, Dennis Bechmann Engmann made exten-sive renovations of his house in Møldrup and an extension of the building at a total value of 1.7 million kroner (about USD 240,000). The building work was

completed free of charge by one of the vendors who did construction work for the Ministry of Defense's property management agency.

8. Local service providers offered foreign aid officials bribes when they selected those providers (Smith, 2020). Mercy Corps is a charity. The international non-government organization (NGO) experienced a scam in the Democratic Republic of Congo (DRC). The scam involved corrupt aid workers, business owners, and community leaders (Kleinfeld, 2020): "Together they zeroed in on the humanitarian sector's flagship rapid response programmes – the main mechanism for helping displaced people in Congo, where hundreds of millions of dollars of foreign aid are spent every year".

9. A local audit firm in Estonia ignored lack of money laundering procedures at the local branch office of Swedbank. Swedbank carried out bank transactions of more than 37 billion Euros (about US$40 billion) with a high risk for money laundering over a five-year period according to private policing in terms of an internal investigation by fraud examiners from law firm Clifford Chance (2020). The investigation report suggests that the Swedish bank actively targeted high-risk individuals in the Baltic region and points to failings from both top management and the board (Milne, 2020).

10. An external consultant who ran a California-based edge college and career network helped rich parents bribe athlete coaches at prestigious universities. The University of California was investigated by the auditor of the state of California. The California state auditor found that qualified students faced an inconsistent and unfair admissions system that had been improperly influence by relationships and monetary donations (State Auditor, 2020). Several rich and mighty people were involved in the corruption scandal (Puente, 2020; Taylor, 2020).

11. Financial regulators were reluctant to intervene when bank clients were fraudulently assigned cards and accounts at their expense (Shichor and Heeren, 2021). Waters (2020) at the U.S. House of Representatives investigated Wells Fargo in the United States. Examiners draw conclusions stating that Wells Fargo's board and management prioritized financial and other considerations above fixing the deviant issues identified, Wells Fargo's board did not hold senior management accountable for repeated deviance, and management gave inaccurate and misleading testimony (Rothacker, 2016; Shearman Sterling, 2017; Wieczner, 2017).

12. Audit firm confirmed that money had disappeared but was reluctant to trace it. The background for the investigation of Wirecard by KPMG (2020a) was to examine the validity of various accusations that were presented in the press and on the internet (Chazan and Storbeck, 2020a, 2020b). Among these allegations, it was suggested that Wirecard has, among other things, recorded higher revenues through fictitious customer relationships, suspicious loan relationships through what is called merchant cash advance, over reporting of profits in the Singapore branch and in the United Arab Emirates, and a suspicious transaction by a company in India (McCrum, 2019). The allegations were concerned with

deficiencies in the accounts and mysterious collaborations with third-party companies in countries such as Singapore, the United Arab Emirates, and India (McCrum, 2020).

13. Financial advisor helped design fraud scheme for insider investments. The media reported in 2020 that "the billionaire who stood by Jeffrey Epstein", "Dechert's Leon Black investigation: things you may have missed", "what a sad tale of sycophants: Wall Street is not buying Leon Black's Epstein story", "Jeffrey Epstein's deep ties to top Wall Street figures", "billionaire Leon Black is leaving Apollo following scrutiny over ties to Jeffrey Epstein", and "billionaire Leon Black, revealed to pay Jeffrey Epstein $158, is stepping down" (Gara and Voytko, 2021). These headlines emerged as law firm Dechert (2021) concluded an investigation on behalf of Apollo Global Management' board. Jeffrey Epstein committed suicide in jail in August 2019 after conviction as a sex offender abusing underage female prostitutes (Sampson, 2020). The suspected fraud was concerned with Black's involvement with Epstein.

14. A national biathlon union invited the president to experience favors and adventures that emerged as bribes (Commission, 2021). Anders Besseberg was president of the International Biathlon Union (IBU) from 1992 until he was laid off in 2018 on the basis of accusations of wrongdoing (Ellingworth and Dunbar, 2018). During those years, the sport of biathlon evolved from being a sport for people who were particularly interested to becoming one of the most popular winter sports on television. Besseberg is considered the architect of the various successful forms of competition in biathlon such as hunting start, joint start, and mixed relays. He lifted the sport of biathlon to new heights during his period as president. By being in the position of president over such a long time, he became a powerful individual with great influence internationally. There were no restrictions on being the union president and how many periods he could be in such a central position without being replaced. Besseberg has been a central figure in shaping the business, culture, ethics, structure, and compliance of right and wrong at IBU as an organization. The suspected fraud was concerned with the president receiving favors and bribes from Russian biathlon union officials.

15. Investment banker ignored red light signals for risky gambling in different energy prices. Finansinspektionen (2021) found deviations at the company so serious that they fined the company $36 million. Nasdaq Clearing appealed the fine as the company disagreed with several of the fundamental assessments that underpinned the decision as well as its conclusions.

Conclusion

As documented in a number of case studies in this book, recidivism seems to be of a substantial magnitude in corporate crime. Corporations tend to repeat white-collar crime in various forms as long as they find it convenient. A minor fine from time to time and dismissal of some executives as scapegoats do not prevent corporations from committing and concealing new offenses as long as there is a convenient financial motive, a convenient organizational opportunity, and a convenient willingness for deviant behavior. Businesses and their executives tend to be recidivists who get away with light punishment (Haines and Macdonald, 2021; Sutherland, 1983). Generally, the severity of punishment has shown to have no effect on recidivism (Mears and Cochran, 2018).

Rational choice among convicted corporations is a matter of recidivism, i.e., what subjectively perceived benefits and costs are after punishment. Repeating white-collar crime might be a rational choice since the collateral effects of being sentenced a second time can be much lower than the first time. On the other hand, the opportunity can be drastically reduced the second time. If someone has been incarcerated, the prison experience can either support the special resilience hypothesis or the special sensitivity hypothesis (Logan, 2015; Logan et al., 2019), which strongly influences perceived costs of recidivism at the individual level.

Recidivism is a research topic within criminology (Chen et al., 2007; Skardhamar and Telle, 2012), and recidivism in corporate and occupational economic crime is no exception (Barnard, 2008; Henning, 2005; Murphy and Harris, 2007; Listwan et al., 2010; Piquero and Weisburd, 2009; Podgor, 2007; Slawotsky, 2015).

According to Collins et al. (2017), recidivism is the behavior of a person or persons repeating an illegal act after having experienced negative penal consequences of a previous offence. In our perspective concerned with white-collar offenders, convicted criminals need to return to elite positions before they have an opportunity for recidivism (Henning, 2015: 1):

> There was virtually no chance he would be trusted again, so there is no likelihood of recidivism; nor did he pose any future physical danger to society.

Among all those white-collar offenders who return to trusted positions with access to resources to commit and conceal misconduct and crime, recidivism is indeed possible. Slawotsky (2015: 280) found that:

> Some financial institutions have become serial lawbreakers, violating not only civil, but also criminal laws. Many of the institutions are subject to multiple investigations, and some of them previously assured prosecutors and regulators that criminal activity would not be repeated after they were involved in what was widely considered a historic settlement. Financial corporations' systemic violation of the law reveals that financial institutional misconduct is widespread, deeply embedded, and broad based.

https://doi.org/10.1515/9783110766950-015

Harbinson et al. (2019) suggest that elite members with narcissistic and neurotic traits are more likely to recidivate. They report that an appreciable proportion of the people convicted of white-collar offenses (about 30%) recidivated and some did repeatedly. Those who were recidivists could be distinguished from non-recidivists on the basis of certain personal and social characteristics.

In the Norwegian sample of white-collar convicts presented by Gottschalk (2019), seven percent reoffended, faced prosecution, and returned to prison. About seven percent was also the case for a comparison group who did not commit economic crime. According to Gottschalk and Gunnesdal (2018), the detection rate for white-collar offenders in Norway is one out of eleven criminals. The actual recidivism is thus much higher than seven percent.

In a sample of white-collar offenders in the United States, Listwan et al. (2010) found that half of the individuals in the sample suffered rearrests. However, new arrests of the individuals often occurred because of a variety of charges such as system violations that include offenses such as failure to appear and failure to adhere to conditions. Nevertheless, there was a substantial fraction of recidivism in terms of repeated and detected financial crime by white-collar offenders.

The recidivism exemplified from Norway and the United States is interesting, because the suspected misconduct or crime investigated by fraud examiners is not necessarily the first time or the last time for offenders. While convicted companies suffer financial loss in the form of fines by the state, individual offenders suffer incarceration after failing defense in court. The implication for private policing is that fraud examiners might expand their perspective historically and into the future. They do sometimes the latter by recommending measures that serve to prevent future occurrences. For example, sanctioning deviant individuals including shaming (Murphy and Harris, 2007) has a deterrent effect, while a material appreciation to whistleblowers has a detecting effect. Ethical guidelines and formal auditing routines, however, have probably little or no effect.

This book has applied convenience orientation as an emerging theoretical perspective on corporate crime (Gottschalk, 2019, 2020). Convenience theory was demonstrated in several case studies. As an emerging perspective, future research might strengthen the idea of convenience through a fresh look at the theoretical structure that is to support empirical work on corporate crime.

Bibliography

Agence France (2014). Telenor involved in Uzbek corruption case: report, *Agence France-Presse*, https://infoweb.newsbank.com/apps/news/document-view?p=AWNB&t=&sort=YMD_date%3AD&maxresults=20&f=advanced&val-base-0=telenor&fld-base-0=alltext&bln-base-1=and&val-base-1=VimpelCom&fld-base-1=alltext&bln-base-2=and&val-base-2=2014&fld-base-2=YMD_date&bln-base-3=and&val-base-3=corruption&fld-base-3=alltext&docref=news/151A057C74610AD8.

Agnew, R. (2014). Social concern and crime: Moving beyond the assumption of simple self-interest, *Criminology*, 52 (1), 1–32.

Aguilera, R.V., Judge, W.Q. and Terjesen, S.A. (2018). Corporate governance deviance, *Academy of Management Review*, 43 (1), 87–109.

Akers, R.L. (1985). *Deviant Behavior: A Social Learning Approach*, 3rd edition, Belmont, CA: Wadsworth.

Alalehto, T. (2018). The logic of agency or the logic of structure in the concept of white collar crime: A review, *Crime, Law and Social Change*, 69, 385–399.

Alalehto, T. (2020). Corporate crime: A logical misconception, but with one analytical point, *Journal of Financial Crime*, 28 (1), 112–119.

Albrecht, S. (1996). *Crisis Management for Corporate Self-Defense: How to Protect Your Organization in a Crisis– How to Stop a Crisis before it starts*. New York, NY: American Management Association.

Albrecht, C.C., Albrecht, W.S. and Dunn, J.G. (2001). Can auditors detect fraud: A review of the research evidence. *Journal of Forensic Accounting*, II, 1–12.

Alcadipani, R. and Medeiros, C.R.O. (2020). When corporations cause harm: A critical view of corporate social irresponsibility and corporate crimes, *Journal of Business Ethics*, 167, 285–297.

Almond, P. and Van Erp, J. (2020). Regulation and governance versus criminology: Disciplinary divides, intersections, and opportunities, *Regulation & Governance*, 14, 167–183.

Alon, A., Mennicken, A. and Samsonova-Taddei, A. (2019). Dynamics and limits of regulatory privatization: Reorganizing audit oversight in Russia, *Organization Studies*, 40 (8), 1217–1240.

Alvarez, J.F.A., Pustina, A. and Hällgren, M. (2011). Escalating commitment in the death zone: New insights from the 1996 Mount Everest disaster. *International Journal of Project Management*, 29, 971–985.

Alvesalo-Kuusi, A. and Barak, G. (2020). Confronting some of the difficulties of developing a «law and order» of white collar and corporate crime, *Journal of White Collar and Corporate Crime*, 1 (2), 1–2.

Amundsen, B. (2021). Politiet overlater etterforskning av økonomisk kriminalitet til de mistenkte (The police leave investigation of economic crime to the suspects), web-based research journal *Forskning*, www.forskning.no, published April 19.

Arjoon, S. (2008). Slippery when wet: The real risk in business, *Journal of Markets & Morality*, Spring, 11 (1), 77–91.

Arlen, J. (2020). The potential promise and perils of introducing deferred prosecution agreements outside the U.S., in: Søreide, T. and Makinwa, A. (editors), *Negotiated Settlements in Bribery Cases*, chapter 8, pages 156–199, Edwardd Elgar publishing, UK: Cheltenham.

Arlen, J. and Buell, S.W. (2020). The law of corporate investigations and the global expansion of corporate criminal enforcement, *Southern Calfornia Law Review*, 93 (4), 697–761.

Arrigo, B.A. and Bernard, T.J. (1997). Postmodern criminology in relation to radical and conflict criminology, *Critical Criminology*, 8 (2), 39–60.

https://doi.org/10.1515/9783110766950-016

Artello, K. and Albanese, J.S. (2021). Culture of corruption: Prosecutions, persistence, and desistence, *Public Integrity*, pages 1–21, published online doi 10.1080/ 10999922.2021.1881300.

Ashforth, B.E., Gioia, D.A., Robinson, S.L. and Trevino, L.K. (2008). Re-reviewing organizational corruption, *Academy of Management Review*, 33 (3), 670–684.

Associated Press (2016). The latest: Ex-PM for Georgia said to have 'nothing to hide', *The Associated Press*, April 4, https://infoweb.newsbank.com/apps/news/document-view?p=AWNB&t=&sort=YMD_date%3AD&page=8&maxresults=20&f=advanced&val-base-0= nordea&fld-base-0=alltext&bln-base-1=and&val-base-1=panama%20papers&fld-base-1=all text&bln-base-3=and&val-base-3=2016&fld-base-3=YMD_date&docref=news/ 15C0ADA08E6FFBE0.

Balakrishnan, K., Blouin, J.L. and Guay, W.R. (2019). Tax aggressiveness and corporate transparency, *The Accounting Review*, 94 (1), 45–69.

Bandura, A. (1999). Moral disengagement in the perpetration of inhumanities, *Personality and Social Psychology Review*, 3 (3), 193–209.

Bao, D., Kim, Y., Mian, G.M. and Su, L. (2019). Do managers disclose or withhold bad news? Evidence from short interest, *The Accounting Review*, 94 (3), 1–26.

Barak, G. (2007). Doing newsmaking criminology from within the academy, *Theoretical Criminology*, 11 (2), 191–207.

Barnard, J.W. (2008). Securities fraud, recidivism, and deterrence, *Penn State Law Review*, 113 (1), 189–228.

Barton, H. (2004). Cultural reformation: a case for intervention within the police service, *International Journal of Human Resources Development and Management*, 4 (2), 191–199.

BBC (2020). Britta Nielsen: Danish social worker accused of stealing millions, *British Broadcasting Corporation*, www.bbc.com, published February 18.

Beam, A. (2008) The new tricky dick. *Boston Globe*, June 5 http://archive.boston.com/news /politics/2008/articles/2009/06/05/cheney_the_new_tricky_dick/ Retrieved December 19, 2019.

Becker, H.S. (1963). *Outsiders: Studies in the Sociology of Deviance*, New York, NY: The Free Press.

Bell, E., Bryman, A. and Harley, B. (2018). *Business Research Methods*, 2nd edition, New York, NY: Oxford University Press.

Bendiktsson, M.O. (2010). The deviant organization and the bad apple CEO: Ideology and accountability in media coverage of corporate scandals, *Social Forces*, 88 (5), 2189–2216.

Benson, M.L. (1985). Denying the guilty mind: Accounting for involvement in a white-collar crime, *Criminology*, 23 (4), 583–607.

Benson, M.L. (2013). Editor's introduction – White-collar crime: Bringing the offender back in, *Journal of Contemporary Criminal Justice*, 29 (3), 324–330.

Benson, M.L. (2019). The neutralization of corporate crime: Organizational and state-facilitated denials of corporate harm and wrongdoing, *Journal of White Collar and Corporate Crime*, https://ascdwcc.org/journal-of-white-collar-and-corporate-crime/, published April 2.

Benson, M.L. (2020). Theoretical and empirical advances in the study and control of white-collar offenders, *Justice Evaluation Journal*, published online doi 10.1080/24751979.2020.1808855.

Benson, M.L. and Chio, H.L. (2020). Who commits occupational crimes, in: Rorie, M. (editor), *The Handbook of White-Collar Crime*, Hoboken, NJ: John Wiley & Sons, chapter 7, pages 97–112.

Benson, M.L. and Simpson, S.S. (2018). *White-Collar Crime: An Opportunity Perspective*, Third Edition, New York, NY: Routledge.

Bentzrød, S.B. (2021). Sentrale ledere dømt for bedrageri. Kan ramme veiprosjekter i Norge (Key executives convicted of fraud. Can affect road projects in Norway), daily Norwegian newspaper *Aftenposten*, Monday, May 10, page 18.

Benson, M.L., Feldmeyer, B., Gabbidon, S.L. and Chio, H.L. (2021). Race, ethnicity, and social change: The democratization of middle-class crime, *Criminology*, 59 (1), 10–41.

Berg, B.L. (2007). *Qualitative Research Methods for the Social Sciences*, Boston, MA: Pearson Education.

Berge, I. (2011). Utga seg for å være Spetalens lillebror (Pretended to be Spetalen's younger brother), web-based Norwegian newspaper *Nettavisen*, www.nettavisen.no, published March 30.

Berghoff, H. (2018). "Organised irresponsibility?" The Siemens corruption scandal of the 1990s and 2000s, *Business History*, 60 (3), 423–445.

Berghoff, H. and Spiekermann, U. (2018). Shady business: On the history of white-collar crime, *Business History*, 60 (3), 289–304.

Bernard, H.R. (2002). *Research Methods in Anthropology: Qualitative and Quantitative Approaches*, Walnut Creek, CA: Alta Mira Press.

Bernat, I. and Whyte, D. (2020). State-corporate crimes, in: Rorie, M.L. (editor), *The Handbook of White-Collar Crime*, Hoboken, NJ: Wiley & Sons, chapter 9, pages 191–208.

Berry, L.L., Seiders, K. and Grewal, D. (2002). Understanding service convenience, *Journal of Marketing*, 66, 1–17.

Bertrand, O. and Lumineau, F. (2016). Partners in crime: The effects of diversity on the longevity of cartels, *Academy of Management Journal*, 59 (3), 983–1008.

Bigley, G.A. and Wiersma, M.F. (2002). New CEOs and corporate strategic refocusing: How experience as heir apparent influences the use of power, *Administrative Science Quarterly*, 47, 707–727.

Bittle, S. and Hébert, J. (2020). Controlling corporate crimes in times of de-regulation and re-regulation, in: Rorie, M.L. (editor), *The Handbook of White-Collar Crime*, Hoboken, NJ: Wiley & Sons, chapter 30, pages 484–501.

Biyalogorsky, E., Boulding, W. and Staelin, R. (2006). Stuck in the past: Why managers persist with new product failures, *Journal of Marketing*, 70 (2), 108–121.

Bjørklund, I. (2018). Må betale over 137 mill i erstatning (Must pay over 137 million in compensation), daily Norwegian business newspaper *Dagens Næringsliv*, www.dn.no, published January 19.

Blickle, G., Schlegel, A., Fassbender, P. og Klein, U. (2006). Some personality correlates of business white-collar crime, *Applied Psychology: An International Review*, 55 (2), 220–233.

Borgarting (2015). Court of appeals case number 14-181913AST-BORG/02, *Borgarting lagmannsrett (Borgarting Court of Appeals)*, July 8.

Bosse, D.A. and Phillips, R.A. (2016). Agency theory and bounded self-interest, *Academy of Management Review*, 41 (2), 276–297.

Braaten, C.N. and Vaughn, M.S. (2019). Convenience theory of cryptocurrency crime: A content analysis of U.S. federal court decisions, *Deviant Behavior*, published online https://doi.org/10.1080/01639625.2019.1706706.

Bradshaw, E.A. (2015). "Obviously, we're all oil industry": The criminogenic structure of the offshore oil industry, *Theoretical Criminology*, 19 (3), 376–395.

Braithwaite, J. (2020). Regulatory mix, collective efficacy, and crimes of the powerful, *Journal of White Collar and Corporate Crime*, 1 (1), 62–71.

Brandvol, I. (2016). AF-gruppen dumpet kloakk på nye E6 (The AF group dumped sewage on the new E6 road), daily Norwegian newspaper *VG*, www.vg.no, published December 17.

Brenli, E. (2020). Jørgen Dahl og Sector Alarm vedtok bot på 425 millioner i fjor. Nå har "alarmkameraten" Verisure også fått sin straff (Jørgen Dahl and Sector Alarm accepted a fine of 425 million last year. Now the "alarm comrade" Verisure has also received their punishment), web-based local newspaper *iFinnmark*, www.ifinnmark.no, published November 25.

Breusch, T. (2005) *Estimating the underground economy using MIMIC models*, paper provided by EconWPA in its series Econometrics with number 0507003, http://econwpa.repec.org /eps/em/papers/0507/0507003.pdf.

Brightman, H.J. (2009). *Today's White-Collar Crime: Legal, Investigative, and Theoretical Perspectives*, Routledge, Taylor & Francis Group, NY: New York.

Brockner, J., Rubin, J. Z. and Lang, E. (1981). Face-saving and entrapment, *Journal of Experimental Psychology*, 17, 68–79.

Brooks, G. and Button, M. (2011). The police and fraud investigation and the case for a nationalized solution in the United Kingdom, *The Police Journal*, 84, 305–319.

Bruun Hjejle (2018). *Report on the Non-Resident Portfolio at Danske Bank's Estonian branch*, law firm Bruun Hjejle, Copenhagen, Denmark, 87 pages.

Bucy, P.H., Formby, E.P., Raspanti, M.S. and Rooney, K.E. (2008). Why do they do it? The motives, mores, and character of white collar criminals, *St. John's Law Review*, 82, 401–571.

Budo, M.N. (2021). Corporate crime and the use of science in the case of asbestos: Producing harm through discursive shields, *Journal of White Collar and Corporate Crime*, 2 (2), 81–96.

Bugge, W. (2020). Wirecard-revisor i trøbbel for å ikke ha avdekket milliardsvindelen (Wirecard auditor in trouble for failing to uncover billionaire fraud), daily Norwegian business newspaper *Dagens Næringsliv*, www.dn.no, published June 26.

Bundy, J. and Pfarrer, M.D. (2015). A burden of responsibility: The role of social approval at the onset of a crisis, *Academy of Management Review*, 40 (3), 345–369.

Burns, R.G. and Meitl, M.B. (2020). Prosecution, defense, and sentencing of white-collar crime, in: Rorie, M.L. (editor), *The Handbook of White-Collar Crime*, Hoboken, NJ: Wiley & Sons, chapter 18, pages 279–296.

Burns, R.G. and Orrick, L. (2002). Assessing newspaper coverage of corporate violence: The dance hall fire in Gotenborg, *Critical Criminology*, 11, 137–150.

Button, M. and Gee, J. (2013). *Countering Fraud for Competitive Advantage – The Professional Approach to Reducing the Last Great Hidden Cost*, Chichester, UK: John Wiley & Sons.

Button, M., Frimpong, K., Smith, G. and Johnston, L. (2007a). Professionalizing counter fraud specialists in the UK: assessing progress and recommendations for reform, *Crime Prevention and Community Safety*, 9, 92–101.

Button, M., Johnston, L., Frimpong, K. and Smith, G. (2007b). New directions in policing fraud: The emergence of the counter fraud specialists in the United Kingdom, *International Journal of the Sociology of Law*, 35, 192–208.

Böhm, M.L. (2020). Criminal business relationships between commodity regions and industrialized countries: The hard road from raw material to new technology, *Journal of White Collar and Corporate Crime*, 1 (1), 34–49.

Campbell, F. (1997). Journalistic construction of news: Information gathering, *New Library World*, 98 (2), 60–64.

Campbell, J.L. and Göritz, A.S. (2014). Culture corrupts! A qualitative study of organizational culture in corrupt organizations, *Journal of Business Ethics*, 120 (3): 291–311.

Carrington, T. and Catasus, B. (2007). Auditing stories about discomfort: Becoming comfortable with comfort theory, *European Accounting Review*, 16 (1), 35–58.

Chan, F. and Gibbs, C. (2020). Integrated theories of white-collar and corporate crime, in: Rorie, M.L. (editor), *The Handbook of White-Collar Crime*, Hoboken, NJ: Wiley & Sons, chapter 13, pages 191–208.

Chang, J.J., Lu, H.C. and M. Chen (2005). Organized crime or individual crime? Endogenous size of a criminal organization and the optimal law enforcement, *Economic Inquiry*, 43 (3), 661–675.

Chatterjee, A. and Pollock, T.G. (2017). Master of puppets: How narcissistic CEOs construct their professional worlds, *Academy of Management Review*, 42 (4), 703–725.

Chattopadhyay, P., Glick, W.H. and Huber, G.P. (2001). Organizational actions in response to threats and opportunities, *Academy of Management Journal*, 44 (5), 937–955.

Chazan, G. (2021). Wirecard given no 'privileged treatment' says German finance deputy, *Financial Times*, www.ft.com, published April 21.

Chazan, G. and Storbeck, O. (2020a). Wirecard: the scandal spreads to German politics, *Financial Times*, www.ft.com, published September 29.

Chazan, G. and Storbeck, O. (2020b). Wirecard's Markus Brown says regulators not to blame in scandal, *Financial Times*, www.ft.com, published November 20.

Chen, Y. and Moosmayer, D.C. (2020). When guilt is not enough: Interdependent self-construal as moderator of the relationship between guilt and ethical consumption in a Confucian context, *Journal of Business Ethics*, 161, 551–572.

Chen, J. and Nadkarni, S. (2017). It's about time! CEOs' temporal dispositions, temporal leadership, and corporate entrepreneurship, *Administrative Science Quarterly*, 62 (1), 31–66.

Chen, M.K. and Shapiro, J.M. (2007). Do harsher prison conditions reduce recidivism? A discontinuity-based approach, *American Law and Economics Review*, 9 (1), 1–29.

Chrisman, J.J., Chua, J.H., Kellermanns, F.W. and Chang, E.P.C. (2007). Are family managers agents or stewards? An exploratory study in privately held family firms, *Journal of Business Research*, 60 (10), 1030–1038.

Cianci, A.M., Clor-Proell, S.M. and Kaplan, S.E. (2019). How do investors respond to restatements? Repairing trust through managerial reputation and the announcement of corrective actions, *Journal of Business Ethics*, 158, 297–312.

Clifford Chance (2020). *Report of Investigation on Swedbank*, law firm Clifford Chance, Washington, DC, USA, 218 pages.

Cohen, S. (2001). *States of Denial: Knowing about Atrocities and Suffering*, Cambridge, UK: Polity Press.

Cohen, M.A. (2020). Punishing corporations, in: Rorie, M.L. (editor), *The Handbook of White-Collar Crime*, Hoboken, NJ: Wiley & Sons, chapter 20, pages 314–333.

Cohen, L.E. and Felson, M. (1979). Social change and crime rate trends: A routine activity approach. *American Sociological Review*, 44, 588–608.

Collier, J.E. and Kimes, S.E. (2012). Only if it is convenient: Understanding how convenience Influences self-service technology evaluation, *Journal of Service Research*, 16 (1), 39–51.

Collins, K. and Carthy, N. (2019). No rapport, no comment: The relationship between rapport and communication during investigative interviews with suspects, *Journal of Investigative Psychology and Offender Profiling*, 16 (1), 18–31.

Collins, S.E., Lonczak, H.S. and Clifasefi, S.L. (2017). Seattle's law enforcement assisted diversion (LEAD): Program effects on recidivism outcomes, *Evaluation and Program Planning*, 64, 49–56.

Comey, J.B. (2009). Go directly to prison: White collar sentencing after the Sarbanes-Oxley act, *Harvard Law Review*, 122, 1728–1749.

Commission (2021). *Final Report of the IBU External Review Commission*, IBU External Review Commission: Jonathan Taylor, Vincent Defrasne, Christian Dorda, Tanja Haug, Anja Martin, and Lauren Pagé, January 28, 220 pages.

Corcoran, J. (2019). Danske Bank to exit Russia amid money laundering scandal, *The Moscow Times*, www.themoscowtimes.com, published August 2.

Cotterill, J. (2019). Two Namibian ministers resign in Icelandic fishing scandal, *Financial Times*, www.ft.com, published November 14.

Craig, J.M. and Piquero, N.L. (2016). The effects of low self-control and desire-for-control on white-collar offending: A replication, *Deviant Behavior*, 37 (11), 1308–1324.

Craig, J.M. and Piquero, N.L. (2017). Sensational offending: An application of sensation seeking to white-collar and conventional crimes, *Crime & Delinquency*, 63 (11), 1363–1382.

Cropanzano, R. and Mitchell, M.S. (2005). Social exchange theory: An interdisciplinary review, *Journal of Management*, 31 (6), 874–900.

Crosina, E. and Pratt, M.G. (2019). Toward a model of organizational mourning: The case of former Lehman Brothers bankers, *Academy of Management Journal*, 62 (1), 66–98.

Cullen, F.T. (2010). Cloward, Richard A., and Lloyd E. Ohlin: Delinquency and opportunity, in: Cullen, F.T. and Wilcox, P. (editors), *Encyclopedia of Criminological Theory*, Volume 1, Los Angeles, CA: Sage Publications, pages 170–174.

Cullen, F.T., Link, B.G. and Polanzi, C.W. (1982). The seriousness of crime revisited, *Criminology*, 20 (1), 83–102.

Cullen, F.T., Cavender, G., Maakestad, W.J. and Benson, M.L. (2006). *Corporate Crime Under Attack – The Fight to Criminalize Business Violence*, Second Edition, Southington, CT: Anderson Publishing.

Cullen, F.T., Chouhy, C. and Jonson, C.L. (2020). Public opinion about white-collar crime, in: Rorie, M.L. (editor), *The Handbook of White-Collar Crime*, Hoboken, NJ: Wiley & Sons, chapter 14, pages 211–228.

Dahle, D.Y. (2011). Christer Tromsdal var politiagent (Christer Tromsdal was police agent), daily Norwegian newspaper *Aftenposten*, publisched October 19.

Davidson, R.H., Dey, A. and Smith, A.J. (2019). CEO materialism and corporate social responsibility, *The Accounting Review*, 94 (1), 101–126.

Davies, J. (2020). Corporate harm and embedded labour exploitation in agri-food supply networks, *European Journal of Criminology*, 17 (1), 70–85.

Dearden, T.E. (2016). Trust: The unwritten cost of white-collar crime, *Journal of Financial Crime*, 23 (1), 87–101.

Dearden, T.E. (2017). An assessment of adults' views on white-collar crime, *Journal of Financial Crime*, 24 (2), 309–21.

Dearden, T.E. (2019). How modern psychology can help us understand white-collar criminals, *Journal of Financial Crime*, 26 (1), 61–73.

Dearden, T.E. and Gottschalk, P. (2020). Gender and white-collar crime: Convenience in target selection, *Deviant Behavior*, published online doi 10.1080/01639625.2020.1756428.

Dechert. (2021). *Investigation of Epstein/Black Relationship and Any Relationship between Epstein and Apollo Global Management*, law firm Dechert, report of investigation, New York, 21 pages.

DeFrank, T. (2009). Former vice president Dick Cheney 'a strong believer' in waterboarding. *Daily News* (June 1), https://www.nydailynews.com/news/world/vice-president-dick-cheney-strong-believer-waterboarding-article-1.374025.

Deloitte (2011). *Investigation Report. Olympus Corporation. Third Party Committee*. Kainaka, T., Nakagome, H., Arita, T., Sudo, O., Katayama, E. and Takiguchi, K., https://www.olympus-global.com/en/common/pdf/if111206corpe_2.pdf, published December 6.

Deloitte (2015). *Investigation report. Summary version*. Independent Investigation Committee for Toshiba Corporation. 90 pages, July 20. Ueda, K., Matui, H. Ito, T. and Yamada, K., http://www.toshiba.co.jp/about/ir/en/news/20150725_1.pdf.

Deloitte (2016). *Review – Ownership VimpelCom Telenor ASA*, signed investigator Anne Helsingeng (partner, attorney-at-law) and Ingebret G. Hisdal (partner, certified public accountant), audit firm Deloitte, Oslo, Norway.

Deloitte (2017). *Investigation Report*, Independent Investigation Committee, by global auditing firm Deloitte, published June 10, Ito, T., Sato, K. and Nishimura, K., https://www.fujifilmholdings.com/en/pdf/investors/finance/materials/ff_irdata_investigation_001e.pdf.

Demaline, C.J. (2021). Image repair during a U.S. Securities and Exchange Commission investigation, *The Journal of Corporate Accounting & Finance*, published online doi.org/10.1002/jcaf.22500.

Deng, Z., Yan, J. and Sun, P. (2020). Political status and tax haven investment of emerging market firms: Evidence from China, *Journal of Business Ethics*, 165, 469–488.

Deseret News (2001). Enron's CEO resigns, *Deseret News*, August 11, https://infoweb.newsbank. com/apps/news/document-view?p=AWNB&t=&sort=YMD_date%3AA&page=8&maxresults= 20&f=advanced&val-base-0=enron&fld-base-0=alltext&bln-base-2=and&val-base-2=accoun ting&fld-base-2=alltext&bln-base-3=and&val-base-3=2001&fld-base-3=YMD_date&docref= news/0F369D49A9F0C1F4.

Dewan, Y. and Jensen, M. (2020). Catching the big fish: The role of scandals in making status a liability, *Academy of Management Journal*, 63 (5), 1652–1678.

Dhami, M.K. (2007). White-collar prisoners' perceptions of audience reaction, *Deviant Behavior*, 28, 57–77.

Dilchert, S., Ones, D.S., Davis, R.D. and Rostow, C.D. (2007). Cognitive ability predicts objectively measured counterproductive work behaviors, *Journal of Applied Psychology*, 92, 616–627.

Dion, M. (2008). Ethical leadership and crime prevention in the organizational setting, *Journal of Financial Crime*, 15 (3), 308–319.

Dodge, M. (2009). *Women and white-collar crime*, Saddle River, NJ: Prentice Hall.

Dodge, M. (2020). Who commits corporate crime? in: Rorie, M. (editor), *The Handbook of White-Collar Crime*, Hoboken, NJ: John Wiley & Sons, chapter 8, pages 113–126.

Donk, D.P. and Molloy, E. (2008). From organizing as projects, to projects as organizations, *International Journal of Project Management*, 26, 129–137.

Downing, S.T., Kang, J.S., and Markman, G.D. (2019). What you don't see can hurt you: Awareness cues to profile indirect competitors, *Academy of Management Journal*, 62 (6), 1872–1900.

Dyreng, S.D., Hanlon, M. and Maydew, E.L. (2019). When does tax avoidance result in tax uncertainty? *The Accounting Review*, 94 (2), 179–203.

Eberl, P., Geiger, D. and Assländer, M.S. (2015). Repairing trust in an organization after integrity violations. The ambivalence of organizational rule adjustments, *Organization Studies*, 36 (9), 1205–35.

Eberly, M.B., Holley, F.C., Johnson, M.D. and Mitchell, T.R. (2011). Beyond internal and external: a dyadic theory of relational attributions, *Academy of Management Review*, 36 (4), 731–753.

Edelbacher, M., Dobovsek, B. and Kratcoski, P.C. (2016). The Relationship of the Informal Economy to Corruption, Fraud, and Organized Crime, in: Edelbacher, M., Kratcoski, P.C. and Dobovsek, B. (editors), *Corruption, Fraud, Organized Crime, and the Shadow Economy*, CRC Press, Taylor & Francis, FL: Boca Raton.

Edelhertz, H. (1970). *The Nature, Impact and Prosecution of White-Collar Crime*, Washington, D.C.: Nattional Institute of Law Enforcement and Criminal Justice, Law Enforcement Administration, U.S. Department of Justice.

Ekeberg, E. (2016). Skuffet over Telenor-toppen (Disappointed over the Telenor top), daily Norwegian newspaper *Klassekampen*, Thursday, July 28, pages 6–7.

Ekeberg, E. (2016). Kritisk til granskinger (Critical to investigations), daily Norwegian newspaper *Klassekampen*, www.klassekampen.no, published May 27.

Ekroll, H.C., Breian, Å. and NTB. (2019). Økokrim starter etterforskning av DNB i forbindelse med islandsk fiskerisak (Økokrim is launching an investigation into DNB related to the Icelandic fisheries case), daily Norwegian newspaper *Aftenposten*, www.aftenposten, published November 29.

Elisha, O.S., Johnson, U.J., Olugbemi, K.O., Olugbemi, M.D. and Emefiele, C.C. (2020). Forensic accounting and fraud detection in Nigerian universities, *Journal of Accounting and Financial Management*, 6 (4), 1–12.

Ellingworth, J. and Dunbar, G. (2018). Biathlon president steps down after police raid in Austria, *AP News*, www.apnews.com, published April 12.

Engdahl, O. (2015). White-collar crime and first-time adult-onset offending: Explorations in the concept of negative life events as turning points, *International Journal of Law, Crime and Justice*, 43 (1), 1–16.

Evans, M. (2016). Social Capital and the Shadow Economy, *Journal of Economic Issues*, L (1), 43–58.

Erikstad, T. (2020). Wirecard kan ha blitt tappet for midler før konkurs (Wirecard may have been drained of funds before bankruptcy), daily Norwegian business newspaper *Dagens Næringsliv*, www.dn.no, published August 11.

Farquhar, J.D. and Rowley, J. (2009). Convenience: a services perspective, *Marketing Theory*, 9 (4), 425–438.

Feratovic, L. (2021). Færder kommune avdekket flere ulovligheter på Pernille Sørensen og Dagfinn Lyngbøs hytteeiendom (Færder municipality detected more illegalities on the summerhouse property of Pernille Sørensen and Dagfinn Lyngbø), daily Norwegian business newspaper *Dagens Næringsliv*, www.dn.no, published January 11.

Finansinspektionen (2021). *Warning and administrative fine – Finansinspektionen's decision (to be announced 27 January 2021 at 8:00)*, Swedish financial supervisory authority, Stockholm, Sweden, January 27, 46 pages.

Finanstilsynet (2020). *Anmodning om redegørelse om Danske Bank A/S' gældsinddrivelsessystem (Request for account concerning Danske Bank Inc.'s debt collection system)*, Finanstilsynet (The Danish Financial Supervisory Authority), Copenhagen, Denmark, 3 pages.

Fischel, D.R. and Sykes, A.O. (1996). Corporate crime, *The Journal of Legal Studies*, 25 (2), 319–349.

Fisse, B. and Braithwaite, J. (1988). The allocation of responsibility for corporate crime: Individualism, collectivism and accountability, *Sydney Law Review*, 11, 468–513.

Fitzgibbon, W. and Lea, J. (2018). Privatization and coercion: The question of legitimacy, *Theoretical Criminology*, 22 (4), 545–562.

Fleming, P. and Zyglidopoulos, S.C. (2008). The escalation of deception in organizations, *Journal of Business Ethics*, 81 (4), 837–850.

Forti, G. and Visconti, A. (2020). From economic crime to corporate violence: The multifaceted harms of corporate crime, in: Rorie, M.L. (editor), *The Handbook of White-Collar Crime*, Hoboken, NJ: John Wiley & Sons, chapter 5, pages 64–80.

Fowler, T. (2014). BP's new tactic in oil spill claims: Go after the 'special master', *The Wall Street Journal*, http://www.wsj.com, published January 27.

Francis, A. and Ryder, N. (2020). Preventing and intervening in white collar crimes: The role of regulatory agencies, in: Rorie, M.L. (editor), *The Handbook of White-Collar Crime*, Hoboken, NJ: Wiley & Sons, chapter 17, pages 263–278.

Freeh, L.J. (2013). *Independent External Investigation of the Deepwater Horizon Court Supervised Settlement Program, Report of Special Master Louis J. Freeh*, www.laed.uscourts.gov, published September 6.

Freiberg, A. (2020). Researching white-collar crime: An Australian perspective, in: Rorie, M.L. (editor), *The Handbook of White-Collar Crime*, Hoboken, NJ: Wiley & Sons, chapter 26, pages 418–436.

Friedrich, C. (2021). *Corporate Misconduct and the Impact of Market Forces, Regulatory Change, and Auditor-Provided Services*, Doctoral dissertation, Technical University of Darmstadt, Germany.

Friedrichs, D.O., Schoultz, I. and Jordanoska, A. (2018). Edwin H. Sutherland, Routledge Key Thinkers in Criminology, Routledge, UK: London.

Füss, R. and Hecker, A. (2008). Profiling white-collar crime. Evidence from German-speaking countries, *Corporate Ownership & Control*, 5 (4), 149–161.

Galvin, M.A. and Simpson, S.S. (2020). Prosecuting and sentencing white-collar crime in US federal courts: Revisiting the Yale findings, in: Rorie, M.L. (editor), *The Handbook of White-Collar Crime*, Hoboken, NJ: Wiley & Sons, chapter 24, pages 381–397.

Galvin, B.M., Lange, D. and Ashforth, B.E. (2015). Narcissistic organizational identification: Seeing oneself as central to the organization's identity, *Academy of Management Review*, 40 (2), 163–181.

Galvin, M.A., Loughran, T.A., Simpson, S.S.and Cohen, M.A. (2018). Victim compensation policy and white-collar crime: Public preferences in a national willingness-to-pay survey, *Criminology & Public Policy*, 17, 553–594.

Gamache, D.L. and McNamara, G. (2019). Responding to bad press: How CEO temporal focus influences the sensitivity to negative media coverage of acquisitions, *Academy of Management Journal*, 62 (3), 918–943.

Gangloff, K.A., Connelly, B.L. and Shook, C.L. (2016). Of scapegoats and signals: Investor reactions to CEO succession in the aftermath of wrongdoing, *Journal of Management*, 42, 1614–1634.

Gao, P. and Zhang, G. (2019). Accounting manipulation, peer pressure, and internal control, *The Accounting Review*, 94 (1), 127–151.

Gao, J., Greenberg, R. and Wong-On-Wing, B. (2015). Whistleblowing intentions of lower-level employees: The effect of reporting channel, bystanders, and wrongdoing, *Journal of Business Ethics*, 126 (1), 85–99.

Gara, A. and Voytko, L. (2021). Billionaire Leon Black, revealed to pay Jeffrey Epstein $158 million, is stepping down, *Forbes*, www.forbes.com, published January 25.

Gedde-Dahl, S., Magnussen, A.E. and Hafstad, A. (2007). Peab får bot på 15 millioner (Peab will be fined 15 million), Norwegian daily newspaper *Aftenposten*, www.aftenposten.no, published February 22.

Geest, V.R., Weisburd, D. and Blokland, A.A.J. (2017). Developmental trajectories of offenders convicted of fraud: A follow-up to age 50 in a Dutch conviction cohort, *European Journal of Criminology*, 14 (5), 543–565.

Ghannam, S., Bugeja, M., Matolcsy, Z.P. and Spiropoulos, H. (2019). Are qualified and experienced outside directors willing to join fraudulent firms and if so, why? *The Accounting Review*, 94 (2), 205–227.

Gibbs, C. and Boratto, R. (2017). Environmental Crime, in: *Oxford Encyclopedia of Criminology and Criminal Justice*, Henry N. Pontell (editor), published online oxfordre.com/criminology.

Gilmour, P.M. (2020). Exploring the barriers to policing financial crime in England and Wales, *Policing: A Journal of Policy and Practice*, published online doi 10.1093/police/paaa081.

Goffman, E. (1971). *Relations in Public; Microstudies of the Public Order*. New York: Basic Books.

Goldstraw-White, J. (2012). *White-Collar Crime: Accounts of Offending Behavior*, London, UK: Palgrave Macmillan.

Gomulya, D. and Mishina, Y. (2017). Signaler credibility, signal susceptibility, and relative reliance on signals: How stakeholders change their evaluative processes after violation of expectations and rehabilitative efforts, *Academy of Management Journal*, 60 (2), 554–583.

Goncharov, I. and Peter, C.D. (2019). Does reporting transparency affect industry coordination? Evidence from the duration of international cartels, *The Accounting Review*, 94 (3), 149–175.

Goodman-Delahunty, J. and Martschuk, N. (2020). Securing reliable information in investigative interviews: Coercive and noncoercive strategies preceding turning points, *Police Practice and Research*, 21 (2), 152–171.

Goossen, M., Seva, I.J. and Larsson, D. (2016). Basic human values and white-collar crime: Findings from Europe, *European Journal of Criminology*, 13 (4), 434–452.

Gormley, T.P. (2009). *Administrative and Criminal Penalties for Illegal Pollution under Pollution Control Act*, International Law Office, www.internationallawoffice.com, published September 14.

Gottfredson, M.R. and Hirschi, T. (1990). *A general theory of crime*, Stanford University Press, Stanford, CA.

Gottschalk, P. (2014). *Financial Crime and Knowledge Workers – An Empirical Study of Defense Lawyers and White-Collar Criminals*, New York, NY: Palgrave Macmillan.

Gottschalk, P. (2019). *Convenience Triangle in White-Collar Crime – Case Studies of Fraud Examinations*, Edward Elgar Publishing, Cheltenham, UK.

Gottschalk, P. (2020). *The Convenience of White-Collar Crime in Business*, Cham, Switzerland: Springer Nature.

Gottschalk, P. and Benson, M.L. (2020). The evolution of corporate accounts of scandals from exposure to investigation, *British Journal of Criminology*, 60, 949–969.

Gottschalk, P. and Gunnesdal, L. (2018). *White-Collar Crime in the Shadow Economy: Lack of Detection, Investigation, and Conviction compared to Social Security Fraud*, Palgrave Pivot, Palgrave Macmillan, London, UK: Springer Publishing.

Gottschalk, P. and Tcherni-Buzzeo, M. (2017). Reasons for gaps in crime reporting: The case of white-collar criminals investigated by private fraud examiners in Norway, *Deviant Behavior*, 38 (3), 267–281.

Granda, M.L. (2021). Tax haven ownership and business groups: Tax avoidance incentives in Ecuadorian firms, *Journal of Business Research*, 130, 698–708.

Greer, C. and McLaughlin, E. (2017). Theorizing institutional scandal and the regulatory state, *Theoretical Criminology*, 21 (2), 112–132.

Greife, M.J. and Maume, M.O. (2020). Do companies pay the price for environmental crimes? Consequences of criminal penalties on corporate offenders, *Crime, Law and Social Change*, 73, 337–356.

Grinde, E. (2016). Mælands vurderinger (Mæland's assessments), daily Norwegian newspaper *Dagens Næringsliv*, Thursday, July 26, page 2.

Guenther, D.A., Wilson, R.J. and Wu, K. (2019). Tax uncertainty and incremental tax avoidance, *The Accounting Review*, 94 (2), 229–247.

Gulating. (2013). Court case LG-2011-60302 – LG-2012-23847, *Gulating lagmannsrett (Gulating court of appeals)*, Bergen, Norway, March 8.

Gulating. (2015). Court case 14-039291ASD-GULA/AVD1, *Gulating lagmannsrett (Gulating court of appeals)*, Bergen, Norway, February 16.

Gupta, V.K., Mortal, S., Chakrabarty, B., Guo, X. and Turban, D.B. (2020). CFO gender and financial statement irregularities, *Academy of Management Journal*, 63 (3), 802–831.

Haines, F. (2014). Corporate fraud as misplaced confidence? Exploring ambiguity in the accuracy of accounts and the materiality of money, *Theoretical Criminology*, 18 (1), 20–37.

Haines, F. and Macdonald, K. (2021). Grappling with injustice: Corporate crime, multinational business and interrogation of law in context, *Theoretical Criminology*, 25 (2), 284–303.

Hamdani, A. and Klement, A. (2008). Corporate crime and deterrence, *Stanford Law Review*, 61 (2), 271–310.

Hamilton, S. and Micklethwait, A. (2006). *Greed and Corporate Failure: The Lessons from Recent Disasters*, Basingstoke, UK: Palgrave Macmillan.

Hamish, M. (2016). SFO closes Fuji Xerox probe, *The Press*, December 24, https://infoweb.news bank.com/apps/news/document-view?p=AWNB&t=&sort=YMD_date%3AD&maxresults= 20&f=advanced&val-base-0=fuji%20xerox&fld-base-0=alltext&bln-base-2=and&val-base-2= new%20zealand&fld-base-2=alltext&bln-base-3=and&val-base-3=2016&fld-base-3=YMD_da te&docref=news/16175F5693A0BFF0.

Hansen, L.L. (2009). Corporate financial crime: Social diagnosis and treatment, *Journal of Financial Crime*, 16 (1), 28–40.

Hansen, L.L. (2020). Review of the book "Convenience Triangle in White-Collar Crime: Case Studies of Fraud Examinations", *ChoiceConnect*, vol. 57, no. 5, Middletown, CT: Association of College and Research Libraries.

Harbinson, E., Benson, M.L. and Latessa, E.J. (2019). Assessing risk among white-collar offenders under federal supervision in the community, *Criminal Justice and Behavior*, 46 (2), 261–279.

Hatch, M.J. (1997). *Organizational Theory – Modern, Symbolic, and Postmodern Perspectives*, Oxford University Press.

Hausman, W.J. (2018). Howard Hopson's billion dollar fraud: The rise and fall of associated gas & electric company, *Business History*, 60 (3), 381–398.

Hearit, K.M. (2006). *Crisis Management by Apology: Corporate Responses to Allegations of Wrongdoing*. Mahwah, N.J.: Lawrence Erlbaum Associates.

Hecklen, A., Ussing, J. and Sommer, M. (2020). 'Beskidte milliarder': Sånn blev hvidvasksag til Danske Banks største krise Se tidslinjen over hvidvaskskandalen I Danske Bank ('Dirty billions': This is how money laundering became Danske Bank's biggest crisis), *Danmarks Radio* (Denmark public broadcasting), www.dr.dk., published September 21.

Henderson, J. (2016). Neil Whittaker exits as local Fuji Xerox MD in shock departure, *ARN Net*, published May 18, https://www.arnnet.com.au/article/600045/shock-departure-neil-whittaker-exits-local-fuji-xerox-md/, retrieved October 29, 2018.

Henning, P.J. (2015). *Is deterrence relevant in sentencing white-collar criminals?* Law Faculty Research Publications, Wayne State University, 1-1-2015, 61 *Wayne Law Reviiew* 27, 1–34.

Herron, E.T. and Cornell, R.M. (2021). Creativity amidst standardization: Is creativity related to auditors' recognition of and responses to fraud risk cues? *Journal of Business Research*, 132, 314–326.

Hestnes, M. (2017). *Hvorfor avdekket ikke revisor underslaget i Hadeland og Ringerike Bredbånd? (Why did the auditor not detect the embezzlement at Hadeland and Ringerike Broadband?)*, Master of Science thesis, BI Norwegian Business School, Oslo, Norway.

Heyman, J. and Sailors, J. (2016). A respondent-friendly method of ranking long lists, *International Journal of Market Research*, 58 (5), 693–710.

Higgins, E.T. (1997). Beyond pleasure and pain, *American Psychologist*, 52, 1280–1300.

Hirschi, T. and Gottfredson, M. (1987). Causes of white-collar crime, *Criminology*, 25 (4), 949–974.

Hjort (2016). *Rapport til styret i DNB (Report to the Board at DNB)*, law firm Hjort, Oslo, Norway, 18 pages.

Hoffmann, J.P. (2002). A contextual analysis of differential association, social control, and strain theories of delinquency, *Social Forces*, 81 (3), 753–785.

Holmøy, E. (2021). Hermine Midelfart og hennes mann vil også søke om ettergodkjenning: Villig til å rive noe (Hermine Midelfart and her husband will also apply for post-approval: Willing to tear something down), local daily newspaper *Tønsbergs Blad*, Wednesday, June 30, page 4.

Holt, R. and Cornelissen, J. (2014). Sensemaking revisited, *Management Learning*, 45 (5), 525–539.

Hovland, K.M. and Gauthier-Villars, D. (2015). VimpelCom bribery investigations spark Telenor review, *The Wall Street Journal*, www.wsj.com, published November 5.

Hovland, K.M., Høgseth, M.H. and Lorentzen, M. (2019). Regjeringen vil ikke lenger selge seg ned i Telenor (The government will no longer sell down at Telenor), web-based Norwegian business newspaper *E24*, www.e24.no, published November 22.

Högseth, M.H. (2019). Thomas Borgen siktet i hvitvaskingssaken (Thomas Borgen charged in the money laundering case), webbased Norwegian newspaper *E24*, www.e24.no, published May 7.

Hsieh, H. and Shannon, S.E. (2005). Three approaches to qualitative content analysis, *Qualitative Health Research*, 15 (9), 1277–1288.

Huang, L. and Knight, A.P. (2017). Resources and relationships in entrepreneurship: An exchange theory of the development and effects of the entrepreneur-investor relationship, *Academy of Management Review*, 42 (1), 80–102.

Huang, J., Diehl, M.R. and Paterlini, S. (2020). The influence of corporate elites on women on supervisory boards: Female directors' inclusion in Germany, *Journal of Business Ethics*, 165, 347–364.

Huisman, W. (2010). *Business as Usual? Corporate Involvement in International Crimes*, The Hague, Netherlands: Eleven International Publishing.

Huisman, W. (2020). Blurred lines: Collusions between legitimate and illegitimate organizations, in: Rorie, M.L. (editor), *The Handbook of White-Collar Crime*, Hoboken, NJ: Wiley & Sons, chapter 10, pages 139–158.

Huisman, W. and Van Erp, J. (2013). Opportunities for environmental crime, *British Journal of Criminology*, 53, 1178–1200.

Hultgreen, G. (2012). Seks års fengsel for Christer Tromsdal (Six years prison for Christer Tromsdal), daily Norwegian newspaper *Dagbladet*, published November 2.

Hultgreen, G., Mogen, T. and Meldalen, S.G. (2019). -En Donald Duck-historie (-A Donald Duck story), daily Norwegian newspaper *Dagbladet*, www.dagbladet.no, published October 8.

Hurley, P.J., Mayhew, B.W. and Obermire, K.M. (2019). Realigning auditors' accountability: Experimental evidence, *The Accounting Review*, 94 (3), 233–250.

Hustadnes, H. (2015). –Brekke må gå før sommeren (-Brekke must leave before the summer), daily Norwegian newspaper *Dagbladet*, Friday, December 11, page 10.

Hällgren, M. (2007). Beyond the point of no return: On the management of deviations, *International Journal of Project Management*, 25, 773–780.

Høgseth, M.H. (2019). Thomas Borgen siktet i hvitvaskingssaken (Thomas Borgen charged in the money laundering case), *E24*, www.e24.no, published May 7, retrieved July 2, 2019.

Håland, S. (2020). De elendige: Hva feiler det tyske banker? (The miserable: What is wrong with German banks?), daily Norwegian business newspaper *Dagens Næringsliv*, www.dn.no, published July 27.

Idris, G. (2019). Ministry of Petroleum: Ibe Kachikwu's impressive turnaround at a glance, *New Telegraph*, www.newtelegraphng.com, published June 11.

Imamoglu, H. (2016). Re-estimation of the size of underground economy in European countries: MIMIC approach, *International Journal of Economic Perspectives*, 10 (1), 171–193.

Inagati, K. (2015). Toshiba scraps dividend after finding accounting irregularities, *Financial Times*, May 8, https://infoweb.newsbank.com/apps/news/document-view?p=AWNB&t=&sort=YMD _date%3AD&page=43&maxresults=20&f=advanced&val-base-0=toshiba&fld-base-0=all text&bln-base-1=and&val-base-1=accounting%20scandal&fld-base-1=alltext&bln-base-2= and&val-base-2=2015&fld-base-2=YMD_date&docref=news/1553B56CCE48DC40.

Isenring, G.L. (2008). Perception of seriousness and concern about white-collar crime: Some results of an opinion survey among Swiss banks, *European Journal of Criminal Policy and Research*, 14 (4), 371–389.

Jaspers, J.D. (2020). Leniency in exchange for cartel confessions, *European Journal of Criminology*, 17 (1), 106–124.

Jenkins, S. and Delbridge, R. (2017). Trusted to deceive: A case study of 'strategic deception' and the normalization of lying at work, *Organization Studies*, 38, 53–76.

Jenner Block (2010). *In regard Lehman Brothers Holdings Inc. to United States Bankruptcy Court in Southern District of New York*, law firm Jenner & Block, A.R. Valukas, https://jenner.com/ lehman/VOLUME%203.pdf.

Jenner Block (2014). *Report to the Board of Directors of General Motors Company regarding ignition switch recalls*, law firm Jenner & Block, A.R. Valukas, http://www.beasleyallen.com/webfiles/valukas-report-on-gm-redacted.pdf.

Jennings, J. (2019). The role of sell-side analysts after accusations of managerial misconduct, *The Accounting Review*, 94 (1), 183–203.

Jessen, C.K. and Jung, E. (2020). Banedanmark mistænker medarbeidere for bestikkelse og ulovlige forhold (Banedenmark suspects Employees for Bribe and illegal circumstances), Danish daily newspaper *Berlingske*, www.berlingske.dk, published March 7.

Johannessen, S.Ø. and Christensen, J. (2020). Swedbank vil ikke betale sluttpakke til toppsjef som matte gå av etter hvitvaskingsskandale (Swedbank will not pay final package to top executive who had to leave after money laundering scandal), daily Norwegian business newspaper *Dagens Næringsliv*, www.dn.no, published March 23.

Jonnergård, K., Stafsudd, A. and Elg, U. (2010). Performance evaluations as gender barriers in professional organizations: A study of auditing firms, *Gender, Work and Organization*, 17 /6), 721–747.

Jordanoska, A. (2018). The social ecology of white-collar crime: Applying situational action theory to white-collar offending, *Deviant Behavior*, 39 (11), 1427–1449.

Jordanoska, A. and Lord, N. (2020). Scripting the mechanics of the benchmark manipulation corporate scandals: The 'guardian' paradox, *European Journal of Criminology*, 17 (1), 9–30.

Josephson, M. (1962). *The Robber Barons: The Classic Account of the Influential Capitalists who Transformed America's Future*, Harcourt, FL: Orlando.

Julsgaard, R.E. (2020). Svindel i Forsvarsministeriets ejendomsstyrelse: Tidligere leder idømt to års fængsel (Fraud in the Ministry of Defense's property management: Former leader sentenced to two years in prison), Danish local TV station *TV Midtvest*, www.tvmidtvest.dk, published December 2.

Jung, J.C. and Sharon, E. (2019). The Volkswagen emissions scandal and its aftermath, *Global Business & Organizational Excellence*, 38 (4), 6–15.

Kagge, G. (2021). Merkel må forklare seg om hjelp til selskap anklaget for milliardsvindel (Merkel must explain herself about help to companies accused of billion fraud), daily Norwegian newspaper *Aftenposten*, Thursday, April 22, page 24.

Kakkar, H., Sivanathan, N., and Globel, M.S. (2020). Fall from grace: The role of dominance and prestige in punishment of high-status actors, *Academy of Management Journal*, 63 (2), 530–553.

Kamerdze, S., Loughran, T., Paternoster, R. and Sohoni, T. (2014). The role of affect in intended rule breaking: Extending the rational choice perspective, *Journal of Research in Crime and Delinquency*, 51 (5), 620–654.

Kammeradvokaten. (2020a). *Undersøgelse af forholdet mellem visse ansatte hos Banedanmark og private virksomheder (Investigation of the relationship between certain employees at Banedanmark and private companies)*, law firm Poul Schmith Kammeradvokaten, Copenhagen, Denmark, October 5, 191 pages.

Kammeradvokaten (2020b). *Advokatundersøgelse af det økonomiske kontrolmiljø i forsvarsministeriets ejendomsstyrelse (Lawyer investigation of the economic control regime in the ministry of defense's property management)*, law firm Poul Schmith Kammeradvokaten, Copenhagen, Denmark, October 6, 270 pages.

Kang, E. and Thosuwanchot, N. (2017). An application of Durkheim's four categories of suicide to organizational crimes, *Deviant Behavior*, 38 (5), 493–513.

Kaptein, M. and Helvoort, M. (2019). A model of neutralization techniques, *Deviant Behavior*, 40 (10), 1260–1285.

Karim, K.E. and Siegel, P.H. (1998). A signal detection theory approach to analyzing the efficiency and effectiveness of auditing to detect management fraud, *Managerial Auditing Journal*, 13 (6), 367–375.

Kaspersen, L. and Eriksen, M.R. (2015). Går av som Nordea-sjef (Resigns as Nordea chief), daily Norwegian business newspaper *Dagens Næringsliv*, www.dn.no, published December 17.

Katz, J.P. (1999). The new global leaders: Richard Branson, Percy Barnevik, David Simon and the remaking of international business, *Academy of Management Executive*, 13 (3), 119–120.

Kawasaki, T. (2020). Review of comparative studies on white-collar and corporate crime, in: Rorie, M.L. (editor), *The Handbook of White-Collar Crime*, Hoboken, NJ: Wiley & Sons, chapter 27, pages 437–447.

Keil, M., Mann, J. and Rai, A. (2000). Why software projects escalate: An empirical analysis and test of four theoretical models, *MIS Quarterly*, 24 (4), 631–664.

Kempa, M. (2010). Combating white-collar crime in Canada: Serving victim needs and market integrity, *Journal of Financial Crime*, 17 (2), 251–264.

Ken, I. and León, K.S. (2021). Necropolitical governance and state-corporate harms: Covid-19 and the U.S. pork packing industry, *Journal of White Collar and Corporate Crime*, published online doi 10.1177/2631309X211011037, pages 1–14.

Kennedy, J.P. (2020). Organizational and macro-level corporate crime theories, in: Rorie, M.L. (editor), *The Handbook of White-Collar Crime*, Hoboken, NJ: Wiley & Sons, chapter 12, pages 175–190.

Khanna, V., Kim, E.H. and Lu, Y. (2015). CEO connectedness and corporate fraud, *The Journal of Finance*, 70, 1203–1252.

Kibar, O. (2020a). Varsleren (The whistleblower), daily Norwegian business newspaper *Dagens Næringsliv*, Saturday, August 8, pages 32–37.

Kibar, O. (2020b). Både ryddet opp for og gransket fiskerikjempe (Both cleaned up and investigated fishing giant), daily Norwegian business newspaper *Dagens Næringsliv*, Tuesday, September 1, pages 18–19.

Kireenko, A.P., Nevzorova, E.N. and Fedotov, D.Y. (2019). Sector-specific characteristics of tax crime in Russia, *Journal of Tax Reform*, 5 (3), 249–264.

Kleinfeld, J. (2019). Anatomy of a Bribe: A deep dive into an underworld of corruption, news organization *Al Jazeera*, www.aljazeera.com, published December 1.

Kleinfeld, J. (2020). Corruption allegations in Namibian 5G deal with Huawei, news organization *Al Jazeera*, www.aljazeera.com, published July 15.

Kleppe, M.K. (2015). Tromsdal: -Der er han skurken som lurte de gamle menneskene (There is the crock who cheated the old people), daily Norwegian business newspaper *Dagens Næringsliv*, published January 8.

Klevstrand, A. (2021). Tidligere Danske Bank-toppsjef Thomas Borgen er ikke lenger siktet i hvitvaskingssak (Former Danske Bank CEO Thomas Borgen is no longer charged in a money laundering case), daily Norwegian business newspaper *Dagens Næringsliv*, www.dn.no, published April 29.

Knottnerus, J.D., Ulsperger, J.S., Cummins, S. and Osteen, E. (2006). Exposing Enron: Media representations of ritualized deviance in corporate culture, *Crime Media Culture*, 2 (2), 177–195.

Knudssøn, K. and Bakke, S. (2009). A spreading of toxic gags, *The Guardian*, www.theguardian.com, published October 26.

Kolthoff, E. (2020). Criminological responses to corruption, in *Handbook on Corruption, Ethics and Integrity in Public Administration*, edited by Graycar, A., Cheltenham, UK: Edward Elgar Publishing, chapter 30, 434–448.

Kostova, T., Roth, K. and Dacin, M.T. (2008). Institutional theory in the study of multinational corporations: A critique and new directions, *Academy of Management Review*, 33 (4), 994–1006.

König, A., Graf-Vlachy, L., Bundy, J. and Little, L.M. (2020). A blessing and a curse: How CEOs' trait empathy affects their management of organizational crisis, *Academy of Management Review*, 45 (1), 130–153.

KPMG (2017). *The Corporation of the Town of Pelham: Forensic Review of Certain Concerns Regarding the East Fonthill Development Project*, KPMG Forensic, https://www.pelham.ca/Mod ules/News/index.aspx?feedId=850db966-1f09-4a4f-9332-0b1683c5c473,5a220134-e962 -4e40-93c0-cad29d1038f0&newsId=79946e04-c2a6-4488-bc6c-26cb8c13748d.

KPMG (2020a). *Report Concerning the Independent Special Investigation at Wirecard AG*, April 27, audit firm KPMG, Munich, Germany, 74 pages.

KPMG (2020b). *Bericht über die unabhängige Sonderuntersuchung, Wirecard AG, München*, 27. April, 74 pages.

Krattum, H.F. (2019). Varsler kjempebot til Verisure og Sector Alarm (Alerts giant fine to Verisure and Sector Alarm), Norwegian public broadcasting *NRK*, www.nrk.no, published June 17.

Kraus, N., Malmfors, T., and Slovic, P. (1992). Intuitive toxicology: Expert and lay judgment of chemical risks, *Risk Analysis*, 12, 215–232.

Krippendorff, K. (1980). *Content Analysis: An Introduction to its Methodology*, Beverly Hills, CA: Sage.

Kristjánsson, M. (2016). Wærsted, daily Norwegian newspaper *Klassekampen*, www.klassekampen, no, published July 28.

Kroll. (2018). *Project Tenor II – Detailed Report, Report Prepared for The National Bank of Moldova*, investigation firm Kroll, 25 Farringdon Street, London, UK, 154 pages.

Landre, E. (2006). Millionbøter fra Økokrim (Millions in fines from the Norwegian national authority for investigation and prosecution of economic and environmental crime), Norwegian web-based newspaper *Nettavisen*, www.nettavisen.no, published June 30.

Langton, L. and Piquero, N.L. (2007). Can general strain theory explain white-collar crime? A preliminary investigation of the relationship between strain and select white-collar offenses, *Journal of Criminal Justice*, 35, 1–15.

Lawler, E.J. and Hipp, L. (2010). Corruption as social exchange, *Advances in Group Processes*, 27, 269–296.

Leasure, P. and Zhang, G. (2018). "That's how they taught us to do it": Learned deviance and inadequate deterrents in retail banking, *Deviant Behavior*, 39 (5), 603–616.

Lee, F. and Robinson, R.J. (2000). An attributional analysis of social accounts: Implications of playing the blame game, *Journal of Applied Social Psychology*, 30 (9), 1853–1879.

Lehman, D.W., Cooil, B. and Ramanujam, R. (2020). The effects of rule complexity on organizational noncompliance and remediation: Evidence from restaurant health inspections, *Journal of Management*, 46 (8), 1436–1468.

Leigh, A.C., Foote, D.A., Clark, W.R. and Lewis, J.L. (2010). Equity sensitivity: A triadic measure and outcome/input perspectives, *Journal of Managerial Issues*, 22 (3), 286–305.

Leonard, W.N. and Weber, M.G. (1970). Automakers and dealers: A study of criminogenic market forces, *Law & Society Review*, 4 (3), 407–424.

Levi, M. and Jones, S. (1985). Public and police perceptions for crime seriousness in England and Wales, *British Journal of Criminology*, 35 (3), 234–250.

Lilleås, H.S. (2011). -Mafiavirksomhet (Mafia activity), Norwegian web-based newspaper *Nettavisen*, www.nettavisen.no, published January 26.

Linstead, S. (2014). Theorizing and researching the dark side of organization, *Organization Studies*, 35 (2), 165–188.

Listwan, S.J., Piquero, N.L. and Voorhis, P. (2010). Recidivism among a white-collar sample: Does personality matter? *Australian & New Zealand Journal of Criminology*, 43 (1), 156–174.

Locatelli, G., Mariani, G., Sainati, T. and Greco, M. (2017). Corruption in public projects and megaprojects: There is an elephant in the room! *International Journal of Project Management*, 35 (3), 252–268.

Locke, E.A. and Latham, G.P. (2013). Goal setting theory: The current state, in: Locke, E.A. and Latham, G.P. (editors), *New Developments in Goal Setting and Task Performance*, New York, NY: Routledge, 623–630.

Locke, S.L. and Blomquist, G.C. (2016). The cost of convenience: Estimating the impact of communication antennas on residential property values, *Land Economics*, 92 (1), 131–147.

Logan, M.W. (2015). *Coping with Imprisonment: Testing the Special Sensitivity Hypothesis for White-Collar Offenders*. A dissertation to the Graduate School of the University of Cincinnati in partial fulfillment of the requirements for the degree of Doctor of Philosophy in the Department of Criminal Justice, Cincinnati, Ohio.

Logan, M.W., Morgan, M.A., Benson, M.L. and Cullen, F.T. (2019). Coping with imprisonment: Testing the special sensitivity hypothesis for white-collar offenders, *Justice Quarterly*, 36 (2), 225–254.

Lopez-Rodriguez, S. (2009). Environmental engagement, organizational capability and firm performance, *Corporate Governance*, 9 (4), 400–408.

Lord, N., Van Wingerde, K. and Campbell, L. (2018). Organising the monies of corporate financial crimes via organizational structures: Ostensible legitimacy, effective anonymity, and third-party facilitation, *Administrative Sciences*, 8 /17), 1–17.

Lønnebotn, L. (2021). Venninnen om Lan Marie Berg: -Lei meg når jeg ser hvor mye dritt hun må tåle (The friend about Lan Marie Berg: -I'm sad when I see how much shit she has to endure), web-based Norwegian newspaper *E24*, http://www.e24.no, published June 19.

Lynch, M.J. (2020). Green criminology and environmental crime: Criminology that matters in the age of global ecological collapse, *Journal of White Collar and Corporate Crime*, 1 (1), 50–61.

Mai, H.T.X. and Olsen, S.O. (2016). Consumer participation in self-production: The role of control mechanisms, convenience orientation, and moral obligation, *Journal of Marketing Theory and Practice*, 24 (2), 209–223.

Makortoff, K. (2019). Swedbank chief sacked amid money laundering scandal, *The Guardian*, www.theguardian.com, published March 28.

Maksimentsev, M. and Maksimentseva, N. (2020). The global impact of exercising extraterritorial jurisdiction over transnational corporate environmental crimes in extractive industries, *Law of Ukraine: Legal Journal*, 1-2020, 278–295.

Mannheimer Swartling (2016). *Report on Investigation of Nordea Private Banking in Relation to Offshore Structures*, law firm Mannheimer Swartling, Stockholm, Sweden, 42 pages.

Martinsen, Ø.L., Furnham, A. and Hærem, T. (2016). An integrated perspective on insight, *Journal of Experimental Psychology*, 145 (10), 1319–1332.

Maruna, S. and Copes, H. (2005). What have we learned from five decades of neutralization research? *Crime and Justice*, 32, 221–320.

Maslow, A.H. (1943). A theory of human motivation, *Psychological Review*, 50 (4), 370–396.

McClanahan, B. and South, N. (2020). 'All knowledge begins with the senses': Towards a sensory criminology, *British Journal of Criminology*, 60, 3–23.

McClelland, P.L., Liang, X. and Barker, V.L. (2010). CEO commitment to the status quo: Replication and extension using content analysis, *Journal of Management*, 36 (5), 1251–1277.

McCrum, D. (2019). Wirecard's suspect accounting practices revealed, *Financial Times*, www.ft.com, published October 15.

McCrum, D. (2020). Wirecard: the timeline, *Financial Times*, www.ft.com, published June 25.

McElwee, G. and Smith, R. (2015). Towards a Nuanced Typology of Illegal Entrepreneurship: A Theoretical and Conceptual Overview, in: McElwee, G. and Smith, R. (editors), *Exploring Criminal and Illegal Enterprise: New Perspectives on Research, Policy & Practice: Contemporary Issues in Entrepreneurship Research Volume 5*, Emerald, Bingley.

McGrath, J. (2020). 'Walk softly and carry no stick': Culture, opportunity and irresponsible risk-taking in the Irish banking sector, *European Journal of Criminology*, 17 (1), 86–105.

McKinley, J. (2015). Settlement in suit against ex-lawmaker, *The New York Times*, Friday, February 6, page A20.

Mears, D.P. and Cochran, J.C. (2018). Progressively tougher sanctioning and recidivism: Assessing the effects of different types of sanctions, *Journal of Research in Crime and Delinquency*, 55 (2), 194–241.

Meldalen, S.G. (2015). –Når noen hører ordet «stråmann», høres det skummelt ut (When someone hears the word «straw man», it sounds scary), daily Norwegian newspaper *Dagbladet*, published January 8.

Menon, S. and Siew, T.G. (2012). Key challenges in tackling economic and cybercrimes – Creating a multilateral platform for international co-operation, *Journal of Money Laundering Control*, 15 (3), 243–256.

Mesmer-Magnus, J.R. and Viswesvaran, C. (2005). Whistleblowing in an organization: An examination of correlates of whistleblowing intentions, actions, and retaliation, *Journal of Business Ethics*, 62 (3), 266–297.

Meyer, M.A. and Booker, J.M. (2001). Eliciting and analyzing expert judgment: A practical guide, SIAM Books, ASA-SIAM Series on Statistics and Applied Probability, Society for Industrial and Applied Mathematics (SIAM), Pennsylvania: Philadelphia.

Michalak, R. and Ashkanasy, N.M. (2013). Emotions and deviance, in: Elias, S.M. (editor), *Deviant and Criminal Behavior in the Workplace*, New York, NY: NYU Press.

Michel, C. (2016). Violent street crime versus harmful white-collar crime: A comparison of perceived seriousness and punitiveness, *Critical Criminology*, 24, 127–143.

Milne, R. (2019a). Prosecutors charge ex-Danske Bank chief in money laundering probe, *Financial Times*, www.ft.com, published May 7.

Milne, R. (2019b). Body of Danske Bank's former Estonian chief found, *Financial Times*, www.ft.com, published September 25.

Milne, R. (2020). Swedbank failing on E37bn of transactions revealed in report, *Financial Times*, www.ft.com, published March 23.

Milne, R. and Binham, C. (2018). Danske Bank chief Thomas Borgen quits over money laundering scandal, *Financial Times*, www.ft.com, published September 19.

Mohliver, A. (2019). How misconduct spreads: Auditors' role in the diffusion of stock-option backdating, *Administrative Science Quarterly*, 64 (2), 310–336.

Moore, C. (2015). Moral disengagement, *Current Opinion in Psychology*, 6, 199–204.

Moscow Times (2017). Danske Bank under investigation for Russian fraud, *Moscow Times*, October 16, https://infoweb.newsbank.com/apps/news/document-view?p=AWNB&t=&sort=YMD_date%3AD&maxresults=20&f=advanced&val-base-0=danske%20bank&fld-base-0=alltext&bln-base-1=and&val-base-1=money%20laundering&fld-base-1=alltext&bln-base-2=and&val-base-2=Estonian%20branch&fld-base-2=alltext&bln-base-3=and&val-base-3=2017&fld-base-3=YMD_date&docref=news/1679489633293E88.

Mulinari, S., Davis, C. and Ozieranski, P. (2021). Failure of responsive regulation? Pharmaceutical marketing, corporate impression management and off-label promotion of enzalutamide in Europe, *Journal of White Collar and Corporate Crime*, 2 (2), 69–80.

Murphy, P. (2010). The intricability of reputation: Media coverage as a complex system in the case of Martha Stewart, *Journal of Public Relations Research*, 22 (2), 208–237.

Murphy, P.R. and Dacin, M.T (2011). Psychological pathways to fraud: Understanding and preventing fraud in organizations, *Journal of Business Ethics*, 101, 601–618.

Murphy, K. and Harris, N. (2007). Shaming, shame and recidivism: A test of reintegrative shaming theory in the white-collar crime context, *British Journal of Criminology*, 47 (6), 900–917.

Müller, S.M. (2018). Corporate behavior and ecological disaster: Dow Chemical and the Great Lakes mercury crisis, 1970-1972, *Business History*, 60 (3), 399–422.

Nakamoto, M. (2011). Olympus turns focus on Japan's governance, *Financial Times*, November 8, https://infoweb.newsbank.com/apps/news/document-view?p=AWNB&t=&sort=YMD_date% 3AD&maxresults=20&f=advanced&val-base-0=tobashi&fld-base-0=alltext&bln-base-1= and&val-base-1=olympus&fld-base-1=alltext&bln-base-2=and&val-base-2=fraud&fld-base-2= alltext&bln-base-3=and&val-base-3=2011&fld-base-3=YMD_date&docref=news/ 13AE854CE15B17D0.

Naumovska, I., Wernicke, G. and Zajac, E.J. (2020). Last to come and last to go? The complex role of gender and ethnicity in the reputational penalties for directors linked to corporate fraud, *Academy of Management Journal*, 63 (3), 881–902.

Naylor, R.T. (2003). Towards a general theory of profit-driven crimes, *British Journal of Criminology*, 43, 81–101.

Neate, R. (2012). Michael Woodford: the man who blew whistle on £1bn fraud, *The Guardian*, www. theguardian.com, published November 23.

Nechepurenko, I. (2015). Moldova parliament dismisses government amid bank scandal, *The New York Times*, www.nytimes.com, published October 29.

Neslen, A. (2019). BMW, Daimler and VW charged with collusion over emissions, *The Guardian*, www.theguardian.com, published April 5.

Newsbank. (2018). *Newsbank* partners with 9.000 publishers worldwide, www.newsbank.com.

Nichol, J.E. (2019). The effects of contract framing on misconduct and entitlement, *The Accounting Review*, 94 (3), 329–344.

Nielsen, R.P. (2003). Corruption networks and implications for ethical corruption reform, *Journal of Business Ethics*, 42 (2), 125–149.

Nordhordland. (2010). Court case 09-098460MED-NOHO, *Nordhordland tingrett (Nordhordland district court)*, Bergen, Norway, March 26.

Norli, K. (2012). Giske til unnsetning for Baksaas i India (Giske to the rescue of Baksaas in India), web-based Norwegian newspaper *E24*, www.e24.no, published April 9.

Norum, H. (2021). Får krass kritikk og gebyr på 400 millioner kroner (Gets harsh criticism and a fee of NOK 400 million), Norwegian public broadcasting *NRK*, www.nrk.no, published May 3.

NRK. (2015). Dirty cargo, Norwegian public broadcasting *NRK*, https://tv.nrk.no/OAUA11005108, published December 9.

NTB (2015). Økokrim ber om seks års fengsel for Tromsdal (Økokrim asks for six years prison for Tromsdal), daily Norwegian newspaper *Klassekampen*, published March 20.

OECD (2021). *Ending the Shell Game: Checking down on the Professionals who enable Tax and White Collar Crimes*, OECD Publishing, Organization for Economic Co-operation and Development, Paris, 57 pages.

Oh, J.J. (2004). How (Un)ethical Are You? Letters to the Editor, *Harvard Business Review*, March, 122.

Olav, H.E. (2014). *Det store selvbedraget: Hvordan statsmakt ødelegger menneskeverd og velferd (The grand self-deception: How state power harms human dignity and welfare)*, Kolofon publishing, Oslo, Norway.

Olav, H.E. (2015). *The Grand Self-Deception: A Libertarian Manifesto Against the Deep State – The Failed Welfare-Taxation Model of Norway*, Kindle Edition, printed in Great Britain by Amazon.

O'Leary, S. and Smith, D. (2020). Moments of resistance: An internally persuasive view of performance and impact reports in non-governmental organizations, *Accounting, Organization and Society*, 85, 1–21.

Oliveira, C.R. and Silveira, R.A. (2020). An essay of corporate crimes in the post-colonial perspective: Challenging traditional literature, *Journal of Contemporary Administration*, 25 (4), 1–17.

Oliver, L. (2010). Trafigura investigators honored with Daniel Pearl Award. *Journalism*, www.journalism.co.uk, published April 26.

Onaran, Y. (2008). Lehman stock falls hard despite CEO's confidence, *The Virginian Pilot*, March 18, https://infoweb.newsbank.com/apps/news/document-view?p=AWNB&t=&sort=YMD_date%3AD&page=46&maxresults=20&f=advanced&val-base-0=lehman%20brothers%20bankruptcy&fld-base-0=alltext&bln-base-1=and&val-base-1=bankruptcy&fld-base-1=alltext&bln-base-2=and&val-base-2=Fuld&fld-base-2=alltext&bln-base-3=and&val-base-3=2008&fld-base-3=YMD_date&docref=news/11F82EF876C656C0.

Onna, J.H.R. and Denkers, A.J.M. (2019). Social bonds and white-collar crime: A two-study assessment of informal social controls in white-collar offenders, *Deviant Behavior*, 40 (10), 1206–1225.

Oslo tingrett (2015). Verdict 14-067448MED-OTIR/06, judge Bjørn Feyling, *Oslo tingrett* (Oslo district court), January 12.

Osoria, J.A. (2021). The Covid-19 pandemic in Puerto Rico: Exceptionality, corruption and state-corporate crimes, *State Crime Journal*, 10 (1), 104–125.

Park, H., Bjørkelo, B. and Blenkinsopp, J. (2020). External whistleblowers' experiences of workplace bullying by superiors and colleagues, *Journal of Business Ethics*, 161, 591–601.

Patel, P.C. and Cooper, D. (2014). Structural power equality between family and nonfamily TMT members and the performance of family firms, *Academy of Management Journal*, 57 (6), 1624–1649.

Paternoster, R., Jaynes, C.M. and Wilson, T. (2018). Rational choice theory and interest in the "fortune of others", *Journal of Research in Crime and Delinquency*, 54 (6), 847–868.

Patrucco, A.S., Luzzini, D. and Ronchi, S. (2017). Research perspectives on public procurement: Content analysis of 14 years of publications in the Journal of Public Procurement, *Journal of Public Procurement*, 16 (2), 229–269.

Patterson, S. (2021). Co-opted cooperators: Corporate internal investigations and Brady v. Maryland, *Columbia Business Law Review*, 1, 417–471.

Payne, B.K., Dabney, D.A. and Ekhomu, J.L. (2011). Sentencing disparity among upper and lower class and health care professional convicted of misconduct, *Criminal Justice Policy Review*, 24, 353–369.

Pedersen, N. (2017). "Professoren" sin kamp for å reinvaska seg ("The professor's" struggle to clean himself), public Norwegian broadcasting *NRK*, www.nrk.no, published August 19.

Peeters, M., Denkers, A. and Huisman, W. (2020). Rule violations by SMEs: The influence of conduct within the industry, company culture and personal motives, *European Journal of Criminology*, 17 (1), 50–69.

Petersen, H.G., Thiessen, U. and Wohlleben, P. (2010). Shadow economy, tax evasion, and transfer fraud – Definition, measurement, and data problems, *International Economic Journal*, 24 (4), 421–441.

Pertiwi, K. (2018). Contextualizing corruption: A cross-disciplinary approach to studying corruption in organizations, *Administrative Sciences*, 8 (12), 1–19.

Petrocelli, M., Piquero, A.R. and Smith, M.R. (2003). Conflict theory and racial profiling: An empirical analysis of police traffic stop data, *Journal of Criminal Justice*, 31 (1), 1–11.

Pettigrew, W.A. (2018). The changing place of fraud in seventeenth-century public debates about international trading corporations, *Business History*, 60 (3), 305–320.

Piazza, A. and Jourdan, J. (2018). When the dust settles: The consequences of scandals for organizational competition, *Academy of Management Journal*, 61 (1), 165–190.

Pillay, S. and Kluvers, R. (2014). An institutional theory perspective on corruption: The case of a developing democracy, *Financial Accountability & Management*, 30 (1), 95–119.

Pinto, J.K. (2014). Project management, governance, and the normalization of deviance, *International Journal of Project Management*, 32, 376–387.

Pinto, J., Leana, C.R. and Pil, F.K. (2008). Corrupt organizations or organizations of corrupt individuals? Two types of organization-level corruption, *Academy of Management Review*, 33 (3), 685–709.

Piquero, N.L. (2018). White-collar crime is crime: Victims hurt just the same, *Criminology & Public Policy*, 17 (3), 595–600.

Piquero N.L. and Schoepfer A. (2010). Theories of white-collar crime and public policy. In: Barlow H.D. and Decker S.H. (editors), *Criminology and Public Policy: Putting Theory to Work*. Philadelphia: Temple University Press.

Piquero, N.L. and Weisburd, D. (2009). Developmental trajectories of white-collar crime, in: *The Criminology of White-Collar Crime*, Simpson, S. and Weisburd, D. (editors), York, NY: Springer, 153–171.

Piquero, N.L., Piquero, A.R., Gies, S. and Green, B. (2021). Preventing identity theft: Perspectives on technological solutions from industry insiders, *Victims & Offenders*, 16 (2), 444–463.

Plesner (2020). *Response to DFSA-letter: Anmodning om redegørelse om Danske Bank A/S' gældsinddrivelsessystem (Response to DFSA letter: Request for account concerning Danske Bank Inc.'s debt collection system)*, investigation report by Danske Bank, law firm Plesner, Copenhagen, Denmark, 120 pages.

Podgor, E.S. (2007). The challenge of white collar sentencing, *Journal of Criminal Law and Criminology*, 97 (3), 1–10.

Pontell, H.N., Black, W.K. and Geis, G. (2014). Too big to fail, too powerful to jail? On the absence of criminal prosecutions after the 2008 financial meltdown, *Crime, Law and Social Change*, 61 (1), 1–13.

Pontell, H.N., Tillman, R. and Ghazi-Tehrani, A.K. (2021). In-your-face Watergate: Neutralizing government lawbreaking and the war against white-collar crime, *Crime, Law and Social Change*, published online doi 10.1007/s10611-021-09954-1, 19 pages.

Porretto, J. (2002). WorldCom profit falls but company says finances are solid, *Associated Press*, February 7, https://infoweb.newsbank.com/apps/news/document-view?p=AWNB&t=&sort=YMD_date%3AA&maxresults=20&f=advanced&val-base-0=world com&fld-base-0=alltext&bln-base-1=and&val-base-1=scandal&fld-base-1=alltext&bln-base-2= and&val-base-2=accounting%20scandal&fld-base-2=alltext&bln-base-3=and&val-base-3= 2002&fld-base-3=YMD_date&bln-base-4=and&val-base-4=ebbers&fld-base-4=alltext&doc ref=news/0F86C5B0DB8FBDD4.

Potipiroon, W. and Wongpreedee, A. (2020). Ethical climate and whistleblowing intentions: Testing the mediating roles of public service motivation and psychological safety among local government employees, *Public Personnel Management*, published online doi https://10.1177/ 0091026020944547.

Pratt, T.C. and Cullen, F.T. (2005). Assessing macro-level predictors and theories of crime: A meta-analysis, *Crime and Justice*, 32, 373–450.

Puente, M. (2020). Lori Loughlin released from prison after serving 2-month sentence in college bribery scheme, *USA Today*, www.eu.usatoday.com, published December 28.

PwC (2003). *Report of investigation by the special investigative committee of the Board of Directors of WorldCom Inc.*, Wilmer Cutler Pickering, https://www.concernedshareholders.com/CCS_WCSpecialReportExc.pdf.

PwC (2015). *Auditor-General for the Federation. Investigative Forensic Audit into the Allegations of Unremitted Funds into the Federation Accounts by the NNPC*, engagement leader Pedro Omontuemhen, PricewaterhouseCoopers, Lagos, Nigeria, https://www.premiumtimesng.com/docs_download/Full%20report–20billion%20dollars%20missing%20oil%20money.pdf?cf=1.

PwC. (2019). *Ekstern undersøgelse af tilskudsadministrationen 1977–2018 – Udarbeijdet for Socialstyrelsen (External examination of the benefits administration 1977–2018 – Prepared for the Social security administration)*, audit firm PwC, Copenhagen, Denmark, February, 80 pages.

Qiu, B. and Slezak, S.L. (2019). The equilibrium relationships between performance-based pay, performance, and the commission and detection of fraudulent misreporting, *The Accounting Review*, 94 (2), 325–356.

Ragothaman, S.C. (2014). The Madoff debacle: What are the lessons? *Issues in Accounting Education*, 29 (1), 271–285.

Ramoglou, S. and Tsang, E.W.K. (2016). A realist perspective of entrepreneurship: Opportunities as propensities, *Academy of Management Review*, 41, 410–434.

Randers, J. (2019). The great challenge for system dynamics on the path forward: implementation and real impact, *System Dynamics Review*, 35 (2), 19–24.

Rashbaum, W.K. and Kaplan, T. (2015). U.S. says assembly speaker took millions in payoffs, abusing office, *The New York Times*, Friday, January 23, pages A1 and A24.

Rehg, M.T., Miceli, M.P., Near, J.P. and Scotter, J.R.V (2009). Antecedents and outcomes of retaliation against whistleblowers: Gender differences and power relationships, *Organization Science*, 19 (2), 221–240.

Reporter (2013). Nigerians yawn over missing billions, *The Sun*, December 31, https://infoweb.newsbank.com/apps/news/document-view?p=AWNB&t=&sort=YMD_date%3AD&maxresults=20&f=advanced&val-base-0=NNPC&fld-base-0=alltext&bln-base-1=and&val-base-1=oil%20revenues&fld-base-1=alltext&bln-base-2=and&val-base-2=2013&fld-base-2=YMD_date&docref=news/14C0EF3456A37C88.

Resodihardjo, S.L., Carroll, B.J., Eijk, C.J.A. and Maris, S. (2015). Why traditional responses to blame games fail: The importance of context, rituals, and sub-blame games in the face of raves gone wrong, *Public Administration*, 94 (2), 350–363.

Reuters (2019). Norway's DNB investigates allegedly improper Samherji payments to Namibia, *Under Current News*, www.undercurrentnews.com, published November 15.

Reuters (2020). Danske Bank admits it knew of erroneous debt collection for years, *Financial Post*, www.financialpost.com, published September 11.

Rise, E. (2014). Alarmselskap skifter navn (Alarm company changes its name), Norwegian magazine *Aktuell Sikkerhet*, www.aktuellsikkerhet.no, published February 4.

Rodriguez, P., Uhlenbruck, K. and Eden, L. (2005). Government corruption and the entry strategies of multinationals, *Academy of Management Review*, 30 (2), 383–396.

Rooij, B. and Fine, A.D. (2020). Preventing corporate crime from within: Compliance management, whistleblowing, and internal monitoring, in: Rorie, M.L. (editor), *The Handbook of White-Collar Crime*, Hoboken, NJ: Wiley & Sons, chapter 15, pages 229–245.

Rosoff, S.M. (2009). The role of mass media in the Enron fraud, in: Pontell, H.N. and Geis, G. (editors), *International Handbook of White-Collar and Corporate Crime*, New York, NY: Springer.

Rothacker, R. (2016). Banking – Wells Fargo gives few details about firings, *Charlotte Observer*, published September 10, https://infoweb.newsbank.com/apps/news/document-

view?p=AWNB&t=&sort=YMD_date%3AD&maxresults=20&f=advanced&val-base-0=rothack
er&fld-base-0=Author&bln-base-1=and&val-base-1=wells%20fargo&fld-base-1=alltext&bln-
base-2=and&val-base-2=eshet&fld-base-2=alltext&docref=news/15F5B3B95E914970.

Rothe, D.L. (2020). Moving beyond abstract typologies? Overview of state and state-corporate crime, *Journal of White-Collar and Corporate Crime*, 1 (1), 7–15.

Rothe, D.L. and Medley, C. (2020). Beyond state and state-corporate crime typologies: The symbolic nature, harm, and victimization of crimes of the powerful and their continuation, in Rorie, M. (editor), *The Handbook of White-Collar Crime*, Hoboken, NJ: John Wiley & Sons, chapter 6, pages 81–94.

Rousseau, D.M., Sitkin, S.B., Burt, R.S. and Camerer, C. (1998). Not so different after all: A cross-discipline view of trust, *Academy of Management Review*, 23 (3), 393–404.

Samherji (2019a). *Statement from Samherji: Press release*, www.samherji.is, published November 11 by margret@samherji.is.

Samherji (2019b). *Samherji CEO steps aside while investigations are ongoing*, www.samherji.is, published November 14 by margret@samherji.is.

Samherji (2020a). *Samherji's Namibia investigation finalized*, Samherji ice fresh seafood, website https://www.samherji.is/en/moya/news/samherjis-namibia-investigation-finalized, Akureyri, Iceland, published by margret@samherji.is.

Samherji (2020b). *Fees for quotas were in line with market prices in Namibia*, Samherji seafood, http://www.samherji.is, published September 25 by Margrét Ólafsdóttir, margret@samherji.is.

Sampson, A. (2020). Art billionaire and collector Leon Black investigated over financial dealings with Epstein, *Tatler*, www.tatler.com, published August 25.

Sands. (2019). *Factual report: Oceanteam ASA Investigation of related party transactions*, law firm Sands, Oslo, Norway, November 4, 256 pages.

Sari, Y.K., Shaari, Z.H. and Amar, A.B. (2017). Measurement development of customer patronage of petrol station with convenience store, *Global Business and Management Research: An International Journal*, 9 (1), 52–62.

Samfunnsøkonomisk analyse (2017). *Analyse av former, omfang og utvikling av arbeidsmarkedskriminalitet (Analysis of the forms, scope and development of labor market crime)*, Samfunnsøkonomisk analyse, Oslo, Norway, www.samfunnsokonomisk-analyse.no.

Saunders, M., Lewis, P. and Thornhill, A. (2007). *Research Methods for Business Students*, 5th edition, London, UK: Pearson Education.

Sawchuk, B. (2017). Accusations fly over Pelham, *The Tribune*, https://infoweb.newsbank.com/apps/news/document-view?p=AWNB&t=&sort=YMD_date%3AD&maxresults=20&f=advan ced&val-base-0=east%20fonthill%20development%20project&fld-base-0=alltext&bln-base -1=and&val-base-1=%2417%20million&fld-base-1=alltext&docref=news/167A6E0AB4FE2D68, published October 20.

Scheaf, D.J. and Wood, M.S. (2021). Entrepreneurial fraud: A multidisciplinary review and synthesized framework, *Entrepreneurship: Theory and Practice*, published online doi 10.1177/0422587211001818, pages 1–36.

Schjelderup, G. (2020). Skatteparadis (Tax paradise), *Store Norske Leksikon (Large Norwegian Encyclopedia)*, www.snl.no/skatteparadis, published February 1.

Schmal, F., Sasse, K.S. and Watrin, C. (2021). Trouble in paradise? Disclosure after tax haven leaks, *Journal of Accounting, Auditing & Finance*, pages 1–22 published online 10.1177/0148558X20986348.

Schmidt, J.B. and Calantone, R.J. (2002). Escalation of commitment during new product development, *Journal of the Academy of Marketing Science*, 30 (2), 103–118.

Schnatterly, K., Gangloff, K.A. and Tuschke, A. (2018). CEO wrongdoing: A review of pressure, opportunity, and rationalization, *Journal of Management*, 44 (6), 2405–2432.

Schneider, S. (2006). Privatizing economic crime enforcement: Exploring the role of private sector investigative agencies in combating money laundering, *Policing & Society*, 16 (3), 285–312.

Schneider, F., Buehn, A. and Montenegro, C.E. (2010). *Shadow Economies All over the World: New Estimates for 162 Countries from 1999 to 2007*, The World Bank, Development Research Group, Poverty and Inequality Team, www.gfintegrity.org.

Schneider, F. and Williams, C.C. (2013). *The Shadow Economy*, The Institute of Economic Affairs, London, UK.

Schoultz, I. and Flyghed, J. (2016). Doing business for a 'higher loyalty' How Swedish transnational corporations neutralize allegations of crime, *Crime, Law and Social Change*, 66 (2), 183–198.

Schoultz, I. and Flyghed, J. (2020a). From "we didn't do it" to "we've learned our lesson": Development of a typology of neutralizations of corporate crime, *Critical Criminology*, 28, 739–757.

Schoultz, I. and Flyghed, J. (2020b). Denials and confessions: An analysis of the temporalization of neutralizations of corporate crime, *International Journal of Law, Crime and Justice*, 62, September, Article 100389.

Schoultz, I. and Flyghed, J. (2021). "We have been thrown under the bus": Corporate versus individual defense mechanisms against transnational corporate bribery charges, *Journal of White Collar and Corporate Crime*, 2 (1), 24–35.

Schoepfer, A. and Piquero, N.L. (2006). Exploring white-collar crime and the American dream: A partial test of institutional anomie theory, *Journal of Criminal Justice*, 34 (3), 227–235.

Schultz, J. (2019). Wikborg Rein-gransker om Samherji: -Planen er å være ute av Namibia innen få måneder (Wikborg Rein investigator about Samherji: -The plan is to be out of Namibia within a few months, daily Norwegian business newspaper *Dagens Næringsliv*, www.dn.no, published December 1.

Schultz, J. and Trumpy, J. (2019a). NRK: DNB brukte mer enn et år på å stenge Samherji-kontoer (NRK: DNB spent more than a year to close Samherji accounts), Norwegian daily business newspaper *Dagens Næringsliv*, www.dn.no, published August 26.

Schultz, J. and Trumpy, J. (2019b). Björgolfur Johannsson ble Samherji-sjef etter hvitvaskingsavsløring: -Jeg tror ikke det har vært noen bestikkelser, Norwegian daily business newspaper *Dagens Næringsliv*, http://www.samherji.is, published December 13.

Schweitzer, M.E., Ordóñez, L. and Douma, B. (2004). Goal setting as a motivator of unethical behavior, *Academy of Management Journal*, 47 (3), 422–432.

Scott, M.B. and Lyman, S.M. (1968). Accounts, *American Sociological Review*, 33 (1), 46–62.

Seiders, K., Voss, G.B., Godfrey, A.L. and Grewal, D. (2007). SERVCON: Development and validation of a multidimensional service convenience scale, *Journal of the Academy of Marketing Science*, 35, 144–156.

Seljan, H., Kjartansson, A. and Drengsson, S.A. (2019). What Samherji wanted hidden, Kveikur at *RUV*, public broadcasting on Iceland, www.ruv.is/kveikur/fishrot/fishrot.

Senge, P. (1990). *The Fifth Discipline*, New York, NY: Currency Doubleday.

Seron, C. and Munger, F. (1996). Law and inequality: Race, gender . . . and, of course, class, *Annual Review of Sociology*, 22, 187–212.

Shadnam, M. and Lawrence, T.B. (2011). Understanding widespread misconduct in organizations: An institutional theory of moral collapse, *Business Ethics Quarterly*, 21 (3), 379–407.

Shah, S. (2002). ABB demands Barnevik repay part of pension, *Independent*, http://www.independent.co.uk, published February 14.

Shapiro S.P. (1990). Collaring the crime, not the criminal: Reconsidering the concept of white-collar crime, *American Sociological Review* 55: 346–365.

Shawver, T. and Clements, L.H. (2019). The impact of value preferences on whistleblowing intentions of accounting professionals, *Journal of Forensic and Investigative Accounting*, 11 (2), 232–247.

Shearman Sterling (2017). *Independent Directors of the Board of Wells Fargo & Company: Sales Practices Investigation Report*, April 10, 113 pages, Sanger, S.W., Duke, E.A., James, D.M. and Hernandez, E. https://www08.wellsfargomedia.com/assets/pdf/about/investor-relations/pre sentations/2017/board-report.pdf.

Shepardson, D. and Burden, M. (2014). GM recalls 778K cars to replace ignition switches after fatal crashes, *Detroit News*, February 13, https://infoweb.newsbank.com/apps/news/document-view?p=AWNB&t=&sort=YMD_date%3AA&maxresults=20&f=advanced&val-base-0=ignition%20switch%20failure&fld-base-0=alltext&bln-base-1=and&val-base-1=GM&fld-base-1=all text&bln-base-2=and&val-base-2=cobalt&fld-base-2=alltext&bln-base-3=and&val-base-3=2014&fld-base-3=YMD_date&bln-base-4=and&val-base-4=learned&fld-base-4=alltext&doc ref=news/14BF79CC1AB3B180.

Shepherd, D. and Button, M. (2019). Organizational inhibitions to addressing occupational fraud: A theory of differential rationalization, *Deviant Behavior*, 40 (8), 971–991.

Shichor, D. and Heeren, J.W. (2021). Reflecting on corporate crime and control: The Wells Fargo banking saga, *Journal of White Collar and Corporate Crime*, 2 (2), 97–108.

Shover, N., Hochstetler, A. and Alalehto, T. (2012). Choosing white-collar crime, in: Cullen, F.T. and Wilcox, P. (editors), *The Oxford Handbook of Criminological Theory*, UK: Oxford, Oxford University Press.

Simester, D. and Zhang, J. (2010). Why are bad products so hard to kill? *Management Science*, 56 (7), 1161–1179.

Simmons, A. (2018). Why students cheat and what to do about it, *Edutopia*, www.edutopia.org.

Siponen, M. and Vance, A. (2010). Neutralization: New insights into the problem of employee information security policy violations, *MIS Quarterly*, 34 (3), 487–502.

Sivertsen, N.S: (2018). Danske Bank siktet for hvitvasking (Danske Bank charged with money laundering), daily Norwegian financial newspaper *Finansavisen*, November 28.

Skardhamar, T. and Telle, K. (2012). Post-release employment and recidivism in Norway, *Journal of Quantitative Criminology*, 28 (4), 629–649.

Skilton, P.F. and Robinson, J.L. (2009). Traceability and normal accident theory: How does supply network complexity influence the traceability of adverse events? *Journal of Supply Chain Management*, 45(3), 40–53.

Sleesman, D.J., Conlon, D.E., McNamara, G. and Miles, J.E. (2012). Cleaning up the big muddy: A meta-analysis review of the determinants of escalation of commitment, *Academy of Management Journal*, 55 (3), 541–562.

Slawotsky, J. (2015). Reining in recidivist financial institutions, *Delaware Journal of Corporate Law*, 40 (1), 280–352.

Sleesman, D.J., Lennard, A.C., McNamara, G. and Conlon, D.E. (2018). Putting escalation of commitment in context: A multilevel review and analysis, *Academy of Management Annals*, 12 (1), 178–207.

Slottje, P., Sluijs, J.P. and Knol, A.B. (2008). *Expert elicitation: Methodological suggestions for its use in environmental health impact assessments*, RIVM Letter report, National Institute for Public Health and the Environment, the Netherlands.

Smith. (2020). *Operational Review of Exposure to Corrupt Practices in Humanitarian Aid Implementation Mechanisms in the DRC*, Adam Smith International, http://www.reliefweb.int, written by N. Henze, F. Grünewald, and S. Parmar, published in July.

Sohoni, T. and Rorie, M. (2021). The whiteness of white-collar crime in the United States: Examining the role of race in a culture of elite white-collar offending, *Theoretical Criminology*, 25 (1), 66–87.

Solgård, J. (2020). «Bestemors favorittbank» ga milliardlån til tidligere Wirecard-sjef («Grandma's favorite bank» gave billions in loans to former Wirecard boss), daily Norwegian business newspaper *Dagens Næringsliv*, http://www.dn.no, published July 9.

Solgård, J. (2021). Danske Banks toppsjef Chris Vogelzang går på dagen (Danske Bank's top executive Chris Vogelzang leaves on the day), daily Norwegian business newspaper *Dagens Næringsliv*, http://www.dn.no, published April 19.

Spector, J. (2015). Lawmaker accused in graft scheme, USA Today, Friday, January 23, page 4A.

Spiekermann, U. (2018). Cleaning San Francisco, cleaning the United States: The graft prosecutions of 1906–1909 and their nationwide consequences, *Business History*, 60 (3), 361–380.

Srivastava, S.B. and Goldberg, A. (2017). Language as a window into culture, *California Management Review*, 60 (1), 56–69.

Stadler, W.A., Benson, M.L. and Cullen, E.T. (2013). Revisiting the special sensitivity hypothesis: The prison experience of white-collar inmates, *Justice Quarterly*, 30 (6), 1090–1114.

State Auditor (2020). *University of California*, California State Auditor, 621 Capitol Mall, Sacramento, Calfornia, USA, report of investigation 82 pages.

Staw, B.M. (1976). Knee-deep in the big muddy: A study of escalating commitment to a chosen course of action, *Organizational Behavior and Human Performance*, 16, 27–44.

Staw, B.M. and Ross, J. (1978). Commitment to a policy decision: A multitheoretical perspective, *Administrative Science Quarterly*, 23, 40–64.

Sterman, J.D. (2018). System dynamics at sixty: The path forward, System Dynamics Review, 34 (1), 5–47.

Sterman, J.D. (2000). *Business Dynamics: Systems Thinking and Modeling for a Complex World*, Boston: Irwin McGraw-Hill.

Stingl, V. and Geraldi, J. (2017). Errors, lies and misunderstandings: Systematic review on behavioral decision making in projects, *International Journal of Project Management*, 35, 121–135.

Stingl, V. and Geraldi, J. (2017). Errors, lies and misunderstandings: Systematic review on behavioral decision making in projects, *International Journal of Project Management*, 35, 121–135.

Storbeck, O. (2020). Wirecard: The frantic final months of a fraudulent operation, *Financial Times*, www.ft.com, published August 25.

Storbeck, O. (2021a). Prosecutors delayed arrest warrant for Wirecard's Jan Marsalek, *Financial Times*, www.ft.com, published January 29.

Storbeck, O. (2021b). German parliament expands probe into EY's audits of Wirecard, *Financial Times*, www.ft.com, published April 22.

Storbeck, O. and Morris, S. (2021). BaFin files insider trading complaint against Deutsche Bank board member, *Financial Times*, www.ft.com, published April 19.

Strandli, A. (2019). Oceanteam vil stanse granskningen av selskapet (Oceanteam wants to stop the investigation of the company), daily Norwegian financial newspaper *Finansavisen*, www.finansavisen.no, published May 5.

Sundström, M. and Radon, A. (2015). Utilizing the concept of convenience as a business opportunity in emerging markets, *Organizations and Markets in Emerging Economies*, 6 (2), 7–21.

Sutherland, E.H. (1939). White-collar criminality, *American Sociological Review*, 5 (1), 1–12.

Sutherland, E.H. (1983). *White Collar Crime – The Uncut Version*, New Haven, CT: Yale University Press.

Svendsen, M. and Solheimsnes, P.A. (2021). Massesøksmål mot alarmselskaper (Mass lawsuits against alarm companies), daily Norwegian newspaper *Aftenposten*, Wednesday, April 29, page 22.

Sykes, G. and Matza, D. (1957). Techniques of neutralization: A theory of delinquency, *American Sociological Review*, 22 (6), 664–670.

Szalma, J.L. and Hancock, P.A. (2013) A signal improvement to signal detection analysis: fuzzy SDT on the ROCs, *Journal of Experimental Psychology: Human Perception and Performance*, 39 (6), 1741–1762.

Tankebe, J. (2019). Cooperation with the police against corruption: Exploring the roles of legitimacy, deterrence and collective action theories, *British Journal of Criminology*, 59, 1390–1410.

Taylor, J. (2018). White-collar crime and the law in nineteenth-century Britain, *Business History*, 60 (3), 343–360.

Taylor, K. (2020). Lori Loughlin released from federal prison, New York Times, www.nytimes.com, published December 28.

Thaxton, S. and Agnew, R. (2018). When criminal coping is likely: An examination of conditioning effects in general strain theory, *Journal of Quantitative Criminology*, 34, 887–920.

Thompson, R. (2017). With BP settlement claims winding down, Lafayette lawyer Parick Juneau turns attention to Takata air bag recall, *The Advocate*, www.theadvocate.com, published October 29.

Tillman, R. and Pontell, H.N. (1992). Is justice "collar-blind"? Punishing Medicaid provider fraud, *Criminology*, 30, 547–574.

Tombs, S. and Whyte, D. (2003). Scrutinizing the powerful: Crime, contemporary political economy, and critical social research. In S. Tombs and D. Whyte (editors), *Unmasking the crimes of the powerful* (pages 3–48), New York: Lang.

Tombs, S. and Whyte, D. (2020). The shifting imaginaries of corporate crime, *Journal of White Collar and Corporate Crime*, 1 (1), 16–23.

Toolami, B.N., Roodposhti, F.R., Nikoomaram, H., Banimahd, B. and Vakilifard, H. (2019). The survey of whistleblowing intentions for accounting frauds based on demographic individual differences among accounting staff, *International Journal of Finance and Managerial Accounting*, 4 (14), 1–13.

Transparency (2018). Corruption perceptions index 2018, *Transparency International*, www.transparency.org/cpi2018.

Trullen, J., Bos-Nehles, A. and Valverde, M. (2020). From intended to actual and beyond: A cross-disciplinary view of (human resource management) implementation, *International Journal of Management Reviews*, British Academy of Management, pages 1–27, doi 10.1111/ijmr.12220.

Trumpy, J. (2016). Avgått Telenor-direktør i ny havn (Resigned Telenor executive in new harbor), daily Norwegian business newspaper *Dagens Næringsliv*, Thursday, July 14, page 16.

Unnever, J.D., Benson, M.L. and Cullen, F.T. (2009). Public support for getting tough on corporate crime: Racial and political divides, *Journal of Research in Crime and Delinquency*, 45 (2), 163–190.

Vasiu, V.I. and Podgor, E.S. (2019). Organizational opportunity and deviant behavior: Convenience in white-collar crime, Criminal Law and Criminal Justice Books, Rutgers, the State University of New Jersey, July, www.clcjbooks.rutgers.edu.

Valkenhoef, G. and Tervonen, T. (2016). Entropy-optimal weight constraint elicitation with additive multi-attribute utility models, *Omega*, 64, 1–12.

Van de Ven, A.H. and Poole, M.S. (1990). Methods for studying innovation development in the Minnesota Innovation Research Program, *Organization Science*, 1 (3), 313–335.

Van de Ven, A.H., Polley, D., Garud, R. and Venkataraman, S. (2008). *The Innovation Journey*, New York, NY: Oxford University Press.

Van Erp, J. (2018). The organization of corporate crime: Introduction to special issue of administrative sciences, *Administrative Sciences*, 8 (36), 1–12.

Van Erp, J. (2020). The role of private actors in the regulation and enforcement of corporate environmental harm, in: Madeleine De Cock Buningh and Linda Senden (editors), *Private Regulation and Enforcement in the EU – Finding the Right Balance from a Citizen's Perspective*, chapter 12, 353–374.

Van Erp, J. and Lord, N. (2020). Is there a 'European corporate criminology? Introduction to the Special Issue on European corporate crime, *European Journal of Criminology*, 17 (1), 3–8.

Van Erp, J., Faure, M.G., Liu, Y., Karavias, M., Nollkaemper, A. and Philipsen, N. (2019a). Introduction: The concept of smart mixes for transboundary environmental harm, in Van Erp, J., Faure, M., Nollkaemper, A. and Philipsen, N. (editors), *Smart Mixes for Transboundary Environmental Harm*, UK, Cambridge: Cambridge University Press, 3–24.

Van Erp, J., Nollkaemper, A., Fuare, M. and Philipsen, N. (2019b). Conclusion: Smart mixes in relation to transboundary environmental harm, in Van Erp, J., Faure, M., Nollkaemper, A. and Philipsen, N. (editors), *Smart Mixes for Transboundary Environmental Harm*, UK, Cambridge: Cambridge University Press, 329–344.

Veblen, T. (1899). *The Theory of the Leisure Class: An Economic Study of Institutions*, Macmillan, NY: New York.

Vega, T. (2015). Ex-State Senate Chief Is Guilty of Bribery, *The New York Times*, Friday, February 6, page A20.

Vaughan, D. (1996). *The Challenger Launch Decision: Risky Technology, Culture, and Deviance at NASA*, Illinois, Chicago: University of Chicago Press.

Vries, K. (1998). Charisma in action: The transformational abilities of Virgin's Richard Branson and ABB's Percy Barnevik, *Organizational Dynamics*, 26 (3), 7–21.

Walburg, C. (2020). White-collar and corporate crime: European perspectives, in: Rorie, M.L. (editor), *The Handbook of White-Collar Crime*, Hoboken, NJ: Wiley & Sons, chapter 21, pages 337–346.

Walker, W. (2000). Entrapment in large technology systems: Institutional commitment and power relations, *Research Policy*, 29 (7), 833–846.

Wall-Parker, A. (2020). Measuring white collar crime, in: Rorie, M.L. (editor), *The Handbook of White-Collar Crime*, Hoboken, NJ: John Wiley & Sons, chapter 3, pages 32–44.

Wang, P. (2020). How to engage in illegal transactions: Resolving risk and uncertainty in corrupt dealings, *British Journal of Criminology*, 60, 1282–1301.

Waters, M. (2020). *The Real Wells Fargo: Board & Management Failures, Consumer Abuses, and Ineffective Regulatory Oversight*, U.S. House of Representatives, Washington, 113 pages.

Weick, K.E. (1995). What theory is not, theorizing Is, *Administrative Science Quarterly*, 40, 385–390.

Weick, K. E. and Sutcliffe, K.M. (2003). Hospitals as cultures of entrapment: A re-analysis of the Bristol Royal Infirmary, *California Management Review*, 45 (2), 73–84.

Welch, M., Fenwick, M. and Roberts, M. (1998). State managers, intellectuals, and the media: A content analysis of ideology in experts' quotes in feature newspaper articles on crime, *Justice Quarterly*, 15 (2), 219–241.

Weick, K.E., Sutcliffe, K.M. and Obstfeld, D. (2005). Organizing and the process of sensemaking, *Organization Science*, 16 (4), 409–421.

Welsh, D.T. and Ordonez, L.D. (2014). The dark side of consecutive high performance goals: Linking goal setting, depletion, and unethical behavior, *Organizational Behavior and Human Decision Processes*, 123, 79–89.

Welsh, D.T., Ordonez, L.D., Snyder, D.G. and Christian, M.S. (2014). The slippery slope: How small ethical transgressions pave the way for larger future transgressions, *Journal of Applied Psychology*, 100 (1), 114–127.

Welsh, D.T., Bush, J., Thiel, C. and Bonner, J. (2019). Reconceptualizing goal setting's dark side: The ethical consequences of learning versus outcome goals, *Organizational Behavior and Human Decision Processes*, 150, 14–27.

Welsh, D.T., Baer, M.D., Session, H. and Garud, N. (2020). Motivated to disengage: The ethical consequences of goal commitment and moral disengagement in goal setting, *Journal of Organizational Behavior*, 1–15, published online doi 10.1002/job.2467.

Wheelock, D., Semukhina, O. and Demidov, N.N. (2011). Perceived group threat and punitive attitudes in Russia and the United States, *British Journal of Criminology*, 51, 937–959.

Whyte, D. (2014). Regimes of permission and state-corporate crime, *State Crime Journal*, 3 (2), 237–246.

Whyte, D. (2016). It's common sense, stupid! Corporate crime and techniques of neutralization in the automobile industry, *Crime, Law and Social Change*, 66 (2), 165–181.

Wieczner, J. (2017). How Wells Fargo's Carrie Tolstedt went from Fortune most powerful woman to villain, *Fortune*, http://fortune.com/2017/04/10/wells-fargo-carrie-tolstedt-clawback-net-worth-fortune-mpw/, published April 10, 2017.

Williams, J.W. (2005). Reflections on the private versus public policing of economic crime, *British Journal of Criminology*, 45, 316–339.

Williams, J.W. (2008). The lessons of 'Enron' – Media accounts, corporate crimes, and financial markets, *Theoretical Criminology*, 12 (4), 471–499.

Williams, J.W. (2014). The private eyes of corporate culture: The forensic accounting and corporate investigation industry and the production of corporate financial security, in: Walby, K. and Lippert, R.K. (editors), *Corporate Security in the 21st Century – Theory and Practice in International Perspective*, Palgrave Macmillan, UK: Hampshire, Houndmills, 56–77.

Williams, M.L., Levi, M., Burnap, P. and Gundur, R.V. (2019). Under the corporate radar: Examining insider business cybercrime victimization through an application of routine activities theory, *Deviant Behavior*, 40 (9), 1119–1131.

Wilmer Cutler Pickering (2003). *Report of Investigation by the Special Investigative Committee of the Board of Directors of Enron Corp.*, William C. Powers, Raymond S. Troubh, Herbert S. Winokur, law firm Wilmer, Cutler & Pickering, http://i.cnn.net/cnn/2002/LAW/02/02/enron.report/powers.report.pdf.

Wingerde, K. and Lord, N. (2020). The elusiveness of white-collar and corporate crime in a globalized economy, in: Rorie, M.L. (editor), *The Handbook of White-Collar Crime*, Hoboken, NJ: Wiley & Sons, chapter 29, pages 469–483.

Xie, Y. and Keh, H.T. (2016). Taming the blame game: Using promotion programs to counter product-harm crises, *Journal of Advertising*, 45 (2), 211–226.

Zavyalova, A., Pfarrer, M.D., Reger, R.K. and Shapiro, D.L. (2012). Managing the message: The effects of firm actions and industry spillovers on media coverage following wrongdoing, *Academy of Management Journal*, 55 (5), 1079–1101.

Zimring, F.E. and Hawkins, G. (1978). Ideology and euphoria in crime control, *University of Toledo Law Review*, 10, 370–388.

Zvi, L. and Elaad, E. (2018). Correlates of narcissism, self-reported lies, and self-assessed abilities to tell and detect lies, tell truths, and believe others, *Journal of Investigative Psychology and Offender Profiling*, 15, 271–286.

Zysman-Quirós, D. (2020). White-collar crime in South and Central America: Corporate-state crime, governance, and the high impact of the Odebrecht corruption case, in: Rorie, M.L. (editor), *The Handbook of White-Collar Crime*, Hoboken, NJ: Wiley & Sons, chapter 23, pages 363–380.

Økokrim (2021). *Temarapport: Profesjonelle aktører (Theme Report: Professional Actors)*, Økokrim, Norwegian National Authority for Investigatoin and Prosecution of Economic and Environmental Crime, Oslo, Norway.

Index

https://doi.org/10.1515/9783110766950-017